WORKBOOK

S N A P

Student Notes and Problems

MATHEMATICS 9

Alberta Edition

Castle Rock
Research Corp

Publisher
Gautam Rao

Contributors
Rob Shkrobot
Krista Zirk

Canadian Cataloguing in Publication Data

Rao, Gautam, 1961 –
STUDENT NOTES AND PROBLEMS **–** Math 9

1. Mathematics – Juvenile Literature. I. Title

Published by
Castle Rock Research Corp.
2340 Manulife Place
10180 – 101 Street
Edmonton, AB T5J 3S4

6 7 8 FP 08 07 06

Printed in Canada

Dedicated to the memory of Dr. V. S. Rao

STUDENT NOTES AND PROBLEMS WORKBOOKS

Student Notes and Problems (SNAP) workbooks are a series of support resources in mathematics for students in grades 3 to 12 and in science for students in grades 9 to 12. SNAP workbooks are 100% aligned with curriculum. The resources are designed to support classroom instructions and provide students with additional examples, practice exercises, and tests. SNAP workbooks are ideal for use all year long at school and at home.

The following is a summary of the key features of all SNAP workbooks.

UNIT OPENER PAGES

- summarize the curriculum outcomes addressed in the unit in age-appropriate language
- identify the lessons by title
- list the prerequisite knowledge and skills the student should know prior to beginning the unit

LESSONS

- provide essential teaching pieces and explanations of the concepts
- include example problems and questions with complete, detailed solutions that demonstrate the problem-solving process

NOTES BARS

- contain key definitions, formulas, reminders, and important steps or procedures
- provide space for students to add their own notes and helpful reminders

PRACTICE EXERCISES

- include questions that relate to each of the curriculum outcomes for the unit
- provide practice in applying the lesson concepts

REVIEW SUMMARIES

- provide a succinct review of the key concepts in the unit

PRACTICE TESTS

- assess student learning of the unit concepts

ANSWERS AND SOLUTIONS

- demonstrate the step-by-step process or problem-solving method used to arrive at the correct answer

Answers and solutions are provided in each workbook for the odd-numbered questions. A *SNAP Solutions Manual* that contains answers and complete solutions for all questions is also available.

NOTES

CONTENTS

Number Concepts and Operations

Patterns and Relations

Shape and Space

Data Analysis

Answers and Solutions

NUMBER CONCEPTS AND OPERATIONS

When you are finished this unit, you should be able to . . .

- give examples of numbers that belong to the natural number system, whole number system, integral number system, and rational number system (SO 1)
- show that the rational number system contains the natural number system, whole number system, and integral number system all together (SO 1)
- determine if a given number belongs to the rational number system or not (SO 2)
- give examples of situations involving positive and negative square roots (SO 3)
- determine the square root of a number (SO 3)
- identify the principal square root of a number (SO 3)
- determine when only the principal square root of a number can be used to answer a problem (SO 3)
- write a number using exponents and identify the various parts of the number as being the base, exponent, and power (SO 4)
- write a number using exponents and variables, and identify the parts as being variable, base, or coefficient (SO 4)
- use the Laws of Exponents to simplify or solve questions of the following types (SO 5)
  - $x^2 \times x^5$
  - $\frac{n^5}{n^3}$
  - $\left(n^3\right)^4$
  - $(mn)^3$
  - $\left(\frac{x}{y}\right)^4$
  - $2^0 = 1$
  - $a^0 = 1$, when $a \neq 0$
  - $3^{-1} = \frac{1}{3}$
  - $b^{-x} = \frac{1}{b^x}$, when $x \neq 0$
- use the above exponent laws or a combination of the above exponent laws to find the answer to questions that involve exponents (SO 6)
- use the order of operations rules to properly enter a question into a calculator to get the solution (SO 7)
- write out and explain the solution acquired by using the order of operations rule (SO 7)
- solve real-life problems using rational numbers (SO 8)
- use exponent laws to simplify questions that have both variables and numbers, such as $\frac{25XY^4}{5XY^2}$ (SO 9)
- use exponent laws to solve questions involving only numbers, such as $\frac{5^2}{5^{-4}} \times \frac{5^6}{5^3}$ (SO 9)
- use your calculator to solve problems in which a combination of scientific notation and exponent laws have been used (SO 10)

PREREQUISITE SKILLS AND KNOWLEDGE

Prior to beginning this unit, you should be able to. . .

- identify natural numbers, whole numbers, and integers
- recognize the square root sign
- identify an exponent
- use a calculator to do simple computations
- calculate a solution using the order of operations

Lesson 1 NUMBER SYSTEMS

NOTES

Numbers can be classified into various number systems, some of which may be familiar to you.

Natural Numbers (N) are all numbers from one to infinity.
{1, 2, 3, ...}

Whole Numbers (W) are all numbers from zero to infinity. {0, 1, 2, 3, ...}

Integral Numbers or Integers (I) are all positive and negative whole numbers, including zero. {...,–2, –1, 0, 1, 2, ...}

Rational Numbers (Q) are any numbers that can be written as fractions.

$$\left\{\frac{a}{b} \text{ where } a, b \in \text{I}, b \neq 0\right\}$$

This notation is read as "*a* divided by *b* where *a* and *b* can be any integer, with the exception that *b* cannot be equal to zero."

Rational numbers can also be expressed in decimal form. Any number that is a terminating decimal or any number that is non-terminating and has a set pattern is a rational number. A set pattern is one in which the same sequence of digits repeats, e.g., $4.\overline{23}$

The following numbers are rational numbers.

$$\frac{1}{3} = 0.\overline{333},\ 14.71 = 14\frac{71}{100},\ \frac{1}{6} = 0.1\overline{6},\ \frac{1}{7} = 0.\overline{142\ 857}$$

Example 1

Is 0.371 59 a rational number?

Solution

Yes. It is rational because it can be written as the fraction $\frac{37\,159}{100\,000}$.

Remember that the ∞ symbol represents infinity.

The letters in brackets —N, W, I, and Q—are the symbols used for the number system.

Fractions and decimal values between whole number values are not included in the natural, whole, or integer number systems.

(e.g., $\frac{1}{4}$ and 2.5 are not included.)

Terminating means "ending." A terminating number is one that ends. (E.g., 4.769)

A bar over one or more numbers indicates that these digits repeat.

When the denominator of a particular fraction is a 7, the corresponding decimal number is a six-digit non-terminating number with a set pattern.

NOTES

The fraction $\frac{1}{3}$ is an example of a rational number. The number 2, or $\frac{2}{1}$, is also an example of a rational number, as is the number –4, or $\frac{-4}{1}$. Since the natural, whole, and integral numbers can all be written as fractions, they are also rational numbers.

The number 5 is a natural number and a whole number. The only number that is not in both the natural and whole number systems is 0, which is a whole number but not a natural number.

The diagram below illustrates the numbers that are included in each number system.

N: Natural numbers

W: Whole numbers

I: Integral numbers or integers

Q: Rational numbers

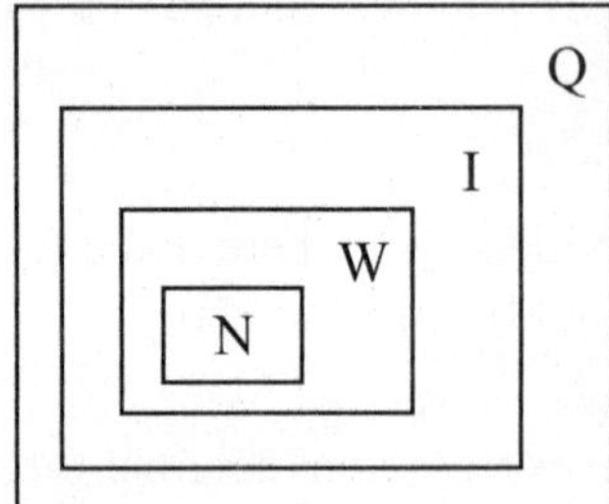

The set of integers includes the whole numbers and the natural numbers. The set of rational numbers includes the natural numbers, whole numbers, and integers.

Example 2

Give an example of a number that is an integer but is not a whole number.

Solution

A possible solution is –1. The answer could be any negative number because there are no negative numbers in the set of whole numbers.

NOTES

A number is **not** a rational number if it can be expressed as a non-terminating decimal with no set pattern. Such a number is called an Irrational Number (Q).

A commonly used number that is not a rational number is π. Type the value of π, $\frac{22}{7}$, into your calculator, and you will see 3.141 592 654 . . .
The ellipsis points at the end of the display (. . .) means that the number is non-terminating and that there is no set pattern to this number.

Example 3

Are the following numbers rational numbers?

a) $\sqrt{5}$ **b)** $0.0\overline{3}$

Solutions

a) No.
$\sqrt{5} = 2.236\ 067\ 977...$
It is a non-terminating number with no set pattern.

b) Yes.
The number $0.0\overline{3}$ repeats with a set pattern, and it can be written as the fraction $\frac{1}{30}$.

PRACTICE EXERCISES

1. To which sets of numbers does each of the following numbers belong?

a) $\frac{2}{3}$ **b)** –3 **c)** 3.74

d) 8 **e)** –7 **f)** $\sqrt{3}$

g) $1.\overline{3}$ **h)** 2.435 176 53… **i)** –7.298 67

2. Draw four boxes that nest inside one another. Let these boxes represent different sets of numbers and their relationship to each other. Correctly label each box as either N, W, I, or Q, where N = natural numbers, W = whole numbers, I = integers, and Q = rational numbers.

3. Explain why –8 is a rational number but not a whole number?

4. Which of the following numbers are rational numbers?

a) $0.\overline{8}$ **b)** 2.34 **c)** 2.151 515…

d) 3.14 **e)** 8.359 087… **f)** –15.679 54

5. The formula $V = \frac{1}{3}\pi r^2 h$ is used to determine the volume of a cone-shaped paper cup. To which set of numbers does $\frac{1}{3}$ belong?

Lesson 2 SQUARE ROOTS

NOTES

When an integer is squared, it produces an answer that is a **perfect square**, for example, $3\times3=9$. Thus, 9 is a perfect square. Examples of other perfect squares include $5\times5=25$, $6\times6=36$, $8\times8=64$, $-8\times-8=64$, and $-2\times-2=4$. Thus, 25, 36, 64, and 4 are all perfect squares.

Taking the square root of a number is the inverse operation to squaring a number. The square root of 9 can be 3 or –3 because $3\times3=9$ and $-3\times-3=9$.

Taking the square root of a number is the inverse operation of squaring a number.

The positive, or principal, square root of 9 is +3. A radical with no sign in front of it means that it is the principal square root of that value.
$\sqrt{9}=+\sqrt{9}=+3$

The square root of a number can be positive or negative.

The principal square root of 9 is +3, since (+3)(+3) = 9. A radical with a negative sign in front of it means that it is the negative square root of that value.
$-\sqrt{9}=-3$

The negative square root of 9 is –3, since (–3)(–3) = 9.
However, the square root of a negative number does not exist since the product of two identical numbers cannot be negative.
Therefore, $\sqrt{-9}$ does not exist.

The positive square root is called the **principal square root**.

There is no real square root of a negative number.

Example 1

Calculate $\sqrt{81}$.

Solution

$\sqrt{81}=+\sqrt{81}=+9$

In practical situations, you sometimes give only the positive square root of a number. (Remember, the positive square root is called the **principle square root**.)

For example, if a square-shaped garden has an area of 36 m^2, how long is each side? The formula for area of a square is $A=s^2$, where A is area and s is the length of a side. Solve the equation by performing the opposite operation to squaring, which is finding the square root.

$A=s^2$

$36=s^2$

$\pm\sqrt{36}=\sqrt{s^2}$

6 and $-6=s$

NOTES

The solution –6 is disregarded because a side measurement of the garden cannot have a negative value. Thus, the only practical solution is 6 m.

Example 2

If the area of a square is 400 cm^2, what is the length of each side?

Solution

$400 = s^2$ or $\sqrt{400} = \sqrt{100} \times \sqrt{4}$

$\pm\sqrt{400} = \sqrt{s^2}$ $= \sqrt{100} \times \sqrt{4}$

$20 \text{ and } -20 = s$ $= 10 \times 2$

$= 20 \text{ cm}$

The only practical solution is 20 cm because you cannot have a negative length.

If you are asked to solve an equation where a square root is involved, both the positive and negative solution should be identified.

Example 3

Solve the equation $n^2 = 0.25$.

Solution

$\pm\sqrt{n^2} = \sqrt{0.25}$

$n = 0.5 \text{ and } -0.5$

Both solutions are acceptable since the problem did not specify the sign of n.

The square root of a number that is not a perfect square should be rounded to the required number of decimal places.

Sometimes, the number you are taking the square root of is not a perfect square, so you may have to round your solution to a certain number of decimal places.

When finding the square root of a number that is not a perfect square, you can use either a calculator or a method of estimation.
When estimating, find the perfect squares that are immediately smaller and immediately larger than the number in question. Imagine the square root of your number to be between the square roots of the other two in direct proportion to the difference between them.

For example, to find the perfect square root of 52:
- find the perfect square with the closest *lower* value ($7 \times 7 = 49$)
- find the perfect square with the closest *higher* value ($8 \times 8 = 64$)
- find the difference between the two numbers ($64 - 49 = 15$)

NOTES

– find how close the original number is to the *lower* square
$(52 - 49 = 3)$
– express that amount as a fraction, and then convert it to a decimal
$\left(\frac{3}{15}\right) = \frac{1}{5} = 0.2$
– add that decimal to the *lower* perfect square root $(0.2 + 7 = 7.2)$
– that number is your approximate square root
$(7.2 \times 7.2 \approx 52)$ or $\left(7.2^2 \approx 52\right)$

Example 4

Determine the principal square root of 7 $\left(\text{in other words, find } \sqrt{7}\right)$, and round your answer to the nearest tenth.

Solution

Method 1

$\sqrt{7} = +\sqrt{7} = 2.645\,7$, or 2.6 when rounded to the nearest tenth

Method 2

You know that $\sqrt{4} = 2$ and that $\sqrt{9} = 3$.
So, the answer will be between 2 and 3.
The difference between 4 and 9 is 5. $(9 - 4 = 5)$
The number 7 is three more than 4. $(7 - 4 = 3)$

The square root of 7 is approximately $\frac{3}{5}$ more than the square root of 4.

$\left(\frac{3}{5}\right) = 0.6$

Therefore, the approximate square root of 7 is $\sqrt{4} + 0.6 = 2.6$

Example 5

Find both square roots of $\frac{1}{25}$.

Solution

$\pm\sqrt{\frac{1}{25}} = \pm\frac{\sqrt{1}}{\sqrt{25}} = \pm\frac{1}{5}$

The symbol ± means "plus or minus."

You could also convert the fraction to a decimal to get the equivalent solutions.

$\frac{1}{25} = 0.04$

Therefore, $\pm\sqrt{0.04} = 0.2$ and -0.2

PRACTICE EXERCISES

1. Solve each of the following problems.

a) $\sqrt{144}$ **b)** $\sqrt{12\ 100}$ **c)** $\sqrt{0.000\ 121}$

d) $\sqrt{\frac{1}{16}}$ **e)** $\sqrt{\frac{25}{49}}$

2. Solve each of the following square root problems. Round your answers to the nearest tenth.

a) $\sqrt{30}$ **b)** $\sqrt{125}$ **c)** $\sqrt{45}$

d) $\sqrt{1.57}$ **e)** $\sqrt{\frac{13}{27}}$ **f)** $\sqrt{9}$

3. Each of the following numbers represents the area of a square. Calculate the side length of each square to the nearest tenth.

a) 90 cm^2 **b)** 165 cm^2 **c)** 0.36 cm^2

d) 8 000 cm^2

4. Solve each of the following equations. Round your answers to the nearest tenth.

a) $x^2 = 169$ **b)** $n^2 = 4.9$ **c)** $n^2 = 113$

d) $y^2 = \frac{9}{25}$ **e)** $k^2 = 45$

5. Ben has a square garden with an area of 200 m^2.

a) How long is each side of Ben's garden, to the nearest tenth?

b) How much fence would Ben need to enclose his garden?

Lesson 3 EXPONENT TERMINOLOGY

In previous grades, you learned to express numbers in exponential form and to identify the various parts of an exponential expression. Let's review those terms and introduce some new ones.

NOTES

In the expression 2^3, the number 2 represents the **base** and the number 3 represents the **exponent**. Together, they represent a **power**.

A **power** is represented through a combination of a base and an exponent.

A variable may be used in an exponential expression. A variable is a letter that is used to represent a number. In the expression $3x^2$, the base is x, the exponent is 2, and the 3 is the **coefficient**.

A **variable** is a letter used to represent a number.

A **coefficient** is the number being multiplied by the variable.

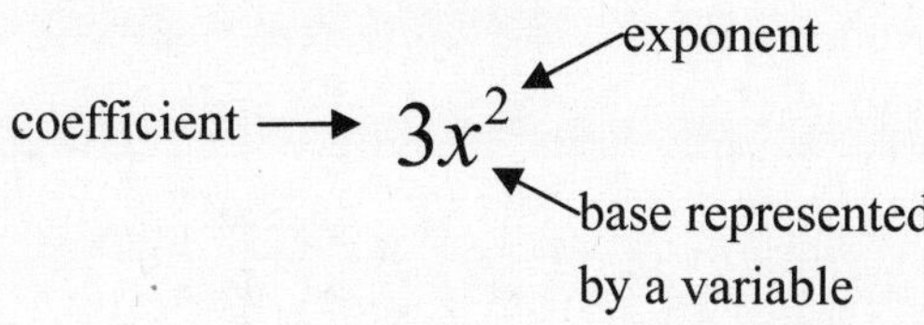

A coefficient is the number that is being multiplied by the variable.

Example 1

Identify the base, exponent, power, and coefficient in the expression $\frac{2}{3}n^5$.

Solution

The base is n, the exponent is 5, the power is n^5, and the coefficient is $\frac{2}{3}$.

Example 2

Identify the base, exponent, power, and coefficient in the expression $-3x^{(2x+5)}$

Solution

The base is x, the exponent is $2x + 5$, the power is $x^{(2x+5)}$, and the coefficient is -3.

PRACTICE EXERCISES

1. Identify the coefficients in each of the following expressions.

a) $2y^5$

b) $-4y^2$

c) $\frac{7}{8}m^3$

d) $-0.4y^9$

e) $336h^4$

f) $\left(\frac{\sqrt{5}}{2}\right)x^3$

Lesson 4 MULTIPLYING AND DIVIDING EXPONENTS

NOTES

Multiplying Powers

To **multiply** powers such as $2^3 \times 2^2$, you can expand each term and simplify.

In doing so, you get

$2 \times 2 \times 2 \times 2 \times 2 = 2^5$ or 32

Rather than expanding each term, you could simply add the exponents.

To multiply powers, add the exponents together if bases are the same.

If the terms being multiplied have the same bases, you can simplify the question by simply adding the exponents. The same rule is applied when the bases are variables.

Example 1

Simplify the expression $3^2 \times 3^5 \times 3^4$.

Solution

Since all the bases are the same, you can add the exponents:

$3^{2+5+4} = 3^{11}$

Example 2

Simplify the expression $n^{-3} \times n^6$.

Solution

$n^{-3+6} = n^3$

Example 3

Simplify the expression $x^2y^4 \times x^3y^2$.

Solution

Add the exponents of the common bases only: $x^{2+3}y^{4+2} = x^5y^6$

Thus, it can be said that $x^n \times x^m = x^{n+m}$.

$x^n \times x^m = x^{n+m}$

NOTES

To divide powers, the same idea of expanding the terms to determine the exponent law can be applied.

To divide $\frac{3^5}{3^3}$, you can expand and simplify to get

$$\frac{3\times3\times3\times3\times3}{3\times3\times3}.$$

If you can cancel out the common 3s, you get

$$\frac{\cancel{3}\times\cancel{3}\times\cancel{3}\times3\times3}{\cancel{3}\times\cancel{3}\times\cancel{3}} \text{ or } 3\times3=3^2.$$

Thus, the rule for division of terms with common bases is to subtract the exponents: $5-3=2$.

Example 4

Simplify the expression $4^8 \div 4^2$.

Solution

$4^{8-2}=4^6$

Example 5

To divide powers, subtract the exponents if the bases are the same. Thus, it can be said that $x^m \div x^n = x^{m-n}$.

Simplify the expression $\frac{x^7}{x^4}$.

Solution

$x^{7-4}=x^3$

Example 6

Simplify the expression $\frac{n^4\times n^8}{n^3}$.

Solution

First, simplify the top using the multiplication law, and then follow the division law.

Thus, you get $\frac{n^{12}}{n^3}=n^9$.

Thus, it can be said that $x^m \div x^n = x^{m-n}$, with the restriction that the variable x cannot equal zero, because division by zero is undefined.

PRACTICE EXERCISES

1. Simplify each of the following expressions by writing as a single power.

a) $4^4 \times 4^3$ **b)** $5^3 \times 5^6 \times 5^4$ **c)** $7^5 \times 7^{-3}$

d) $x^4 \times x^8$ **e)** $f^3 \times f^{-5} \times f^{-4}$ **f)** $(-8)(-8)^3(-8)^4$

2. Simplify each of the following expressions by writing as a single power.

a) $x^4 \div x^3$ **b)** $\dfrac{10^5}{10^3}$ **c)** $n^8 \div n^{10}$

d) $(-4)^3 \div (-4)$ **e)** $\left(\dfrac{3}{7}\right)^{12}\left(\dfrac{3}{7}\right)^{9}$

3. Simplify each of the following expressions by applying the multiplication and division laws as necessary.

a) $\dfrac{6^8 \times 6^4}{6^3}$ **b)** $\dfrac{a^4}{a^3 \times a^5}$ **c)** $\dfrac{1.2^5 \times 1.2^3}{1.2^1}$

d) $\dfrac{n^4 \times n^3}{n^6 \times n^2}$ **e)** $\dfrac{y^4}{y^2} \times \dfrac{y^8}{y^3}$

4. An astronomer estimated that there are about 10^{13} galaxies in the universe and that each galaxy has about 10^{11} stars in it. Approximately how many stars are there in the universe?

Lesson 5 POWER OF PRODUCTS, QUOTIENTS, AND POWERS

NOTES

The exponent law for the **power of a product** can be expressed as

$$\left(x^1y^1\right)^n = x^{1\times n}y^{1\times n}$$

$$(xy)^n = x^ny^n$$

The exponent of each variable inside the brackets is multiplied by the exponent outside the brackets. Remember that when no number is written for the exponent, the exponent is 1.

Example 1

Simplify the expression $\left(m^3n^5\right)^2$.

Solution

$$\left(m^3n^5\right)^2 = m^{3\times2}n^{5\times2}$$

$$\left(m^3n^5\right)^2 = m^6n^{10}$$

Example 2

Simplify the expression $\left(nt^4\right)^3$.

Solution

$$\left(nt^4\right)^3 = n^{1\times3}t^{4\times3}$$

$$\left(nt^4\right)^3 = n^3t^{12}$$

The exponent law for the **power of a quotient** can be expressed as

$$\left(\frac{x}{y}\right)^n = \left(\frac{x^{1\times n}}{y^{1\times n}}\right)$$

$$\left(\frac{x}{y}\right)^n = \frac{x^n}{y^n}$$

The variable y cannot equal zero because division by zero is undefined.

Example 3

NOTES

Simplify the expression $\left(\frac{m^4}{n^6}\right)^3$.

Solution

$$\begin{aligned}\left(\frac{m^4}{n^6}\right)^3 &= \frac{m^{4\times3}}{n^{6\times3}}\\ &= \frac{m^{12}}{n^{18}}\end{aligned}$$

The exponent law for the **power of a power** can be expressed as

$$\left(x^m\right)^n = x^{m\times n}$$

$$\left(x^m\right)^n = x^{mn}$$

Example 4

Simplify the expression $\left(5^2\right)^3$.

Solution

$$\begin{aligned}\left(5^2\right)^3 &= 5^{2\times3}\\ &= 5^6\end{aligned}$$

Example 5

Simplify the expression $\left(n^2\right)^3\times\left(n^{-1}\right)^2$.

Solution

$$\begin{aligned}\left(n^2\right)^3\times\left(n^{-1}\right)^2 &= n^{2\times3}\times n^{-1\times2}\\ &= n^6\times n^{-2}\\ &= n^4\end{aligned}$$

NOTES

Example 6

Simplify the expression $\left(2^4 \div 2^8\right)^3$.

Solution

$$\begin{aligned}\left(2^4 \div 2^8\right)^3 &= \left(2^{4-8}\right)^3\\ &= \left(2^{-4}\right)^3\\ &= 2^{-4\times 3}\\ &= 2^{-12}\end{aligned}$$

Alternatively, you could simplify inside the brackets first.

$$\begin{aligned}\left(\frac{2^4}{2^8}\right)^3 &= \left(\frac{2^{4\times 3}}{2^{8\times 3}}\right)\\ &= \frac{2^{12}}{2^{24}}\\ &= 2^{12-24}\\ &= 2^{-12}\end{aligned}$$

PRACTICE EXERCISES

1. Simplify each of the following expressions.

a) $\left(x^2y^3\right)^4$

b) $\left(\dfrac{r^3}{p^{-2}}\right)^5$

c) $\left(\dfrac{5}{8^2}\right)^3$

d) $\left(\dfrac{3}{7}\right)^2$

e) $\left(3^4\right)^6$

2. Simplify each of the following expressions.

a) $\left(2^{-3}\right)^4$

b) $\left(v^4\right)^6$

c) $\left(v^{-4}\right)^{-6}$

d) $\left[(-2)^3\right]^4$

e) $\left[(-5)^3\right]^4$

3. Simplify each of the following expressions.

a) $\left(7^5\times 7^2\right)^8$

b) $\left(3^5\times 3^{-2}\right)^{-3}$

c) $\left(5^{11}\div 5^6\right)^4$

d) $\left[(-2)^4\div(-2)^8\right]^2$

e) $\left(\frac{1.3^4}{1.3^{-2}}\right)^3$

f) $\left(g^4\div g\right)^6$

g) $\left(mn^4\right)^6$

h) $\left(m^5\times m^{-3}\right)^4$

i) $\left(t^4\right)^3\div\left(t^7\right)^2$

j) $\left(3^{-2}\right)^{-1}\times\left(3^4\right)^{-2}$

Lesson 6 ZERO AND NEGATIVE EXPONENTS

Any number with a **zero exponent** is equal to 1, except 0^0, which is undefined. Let's look at evidence that would support this exponent law.

NOTES

Any number with a zero exponent is equal to 1, except 0^0, which is undefined.

To simplify $\frac{2^3}{2^3}$, use the division law of exponents.

$$\frac{2^3}{2^3} = 2^{3-3} = 2^0 \text{ or}$$

$$\frac{2^3}{2^3} = \frac{2\times2\times2}{2\times2\times2}$$

$$= \frac{8}{8}$$

$$= 1$$

This answer can be derived using any base number other than zero.

Example 1

Evaluate 4×5^0.

Solution

$5^0 = 1$

Therefore,

$4\times1 = 4$

Thus, it can be said that $x^0 = 1$, where $x \neq 0$.

$x^0 = 1$, where $x \neq 0$

You cannot expand a **negative exponent**. Thus something must be done to simplify the negative exponents so they can be evaluated.

Consider…

$$\frac{3^2}{3^5} = 3^{2-5}$$

$$= 3^{-3}$$

However, you cannot expand the negative exponent here.
Instead, you can try expanding the original terms.

$$\frac{3^2}{3^5} = \frac{\cancel{3}\times\cancel{3}}{\cancel{3}\times\cancel{3}\times3\times3\times3}$$

$$\frac{3^2}{3^5} = \frac{1}{3\times3\times3}$$

$$\frac{3^2}{3^5} = \frac{1}{3^3}$$

$$\frac{3^2}{3^5} = \frac{1}{27}$$

NOTES

A negative sign in an exponent means that when the base is inverted, it turns into a positive number. **Invert** means "to flip upside-down."

Notice that the initial answer was 3^{-3}, and the answer here is $\frac{1}{3^3}$. These answers are equal. So, $3^{-3} = \frac{1}{3^3}$, which is the reciprocal of 3^3.

Therefore 3^{-3} is the reciprocal of 3^3.

In general, x^{-n} is the reciprocal of x^n, $x^{-n} = \frac{1}{x^n}$, and $x \neq 0$.

In this case, now that the exponent has been made positive, you can evaluate $\frac{1}{3^3}$ to get $\frac{1}{27}$.

So, when dealing with negative exponents, use the reciprocal of the base.

Making the exponent positive should be your last step in the simplification of a question involving negative exponents. The previously discussed exponent laws should be applied first.

Example 2

Evaluate each of the following expressions using exponent laws.

a) 4^{-2}

Solution

$$4^{-2} = \frac{1}{4^2} = \frac{1}{16}$$

b) $(-2)^{-3}$

Solution

$$(-2)^{-3} = \frac{1}{(-2)^3} = \frac{1}{-8}$$

c) $\left(\frac{2}{3}\right)^{-2}$

Solution

$$\left(\frac{2}{3}\right)^{-2} = \left(\frac{3}{2}\right)^{2} = \frac{9}{4}$$

NOTES

d) $\left(\frac{4}{5}\right)^{-2}$

Solution

$$\left(\frac{4}{5}\right)^{-2} = \left(\frac{1}{\left(\frac{4}{5}\right)}\right)^{2}$$

$$= \left(\frac{5}{4}\right)^{-2}$$

$$= \frac{25}{16}$$

Example 3

Simplify and evaluate each of the following expressions. Use exponent laws before making any negative exponents positive.

a) $\left(\frac{1}{2}\right)^{-3}$

Solution

$$\frac{1}{2^{-3}} = \frac{2^3}{1} = 8$$

b) $3^{-5} \times 3^3$

Solution

$$3^{-5} \times 3^3 = 3^{-5+3}$$

$$= 3^{-2}$$

$$= \frac{1}{3^2}$$

$$= \frac{1}{9}$$

c) $\frac{4^3 \times 4^{-2}}{4^{-4}}$

Solution

$$\frac{4^3 \times 4^{-2}}{4^{-4}} = \frac{4^{3+(-2)}}{4^{-4}}$$

$$= \frac{4^1}{4^{-4}}$$

$$= 4^{1-(-4)}$$

$$= 4^5 = 1\ 024$$

NOTES

Example 4

Simplify each of the following expressions.

a) $x^{-2} \times x^{-3}$

Solution

$$\begin{aligned} x^{-2} \times x^{-3} &= x^{-2+-3} \\ &= x^{-2-3} \\ &= x^{-5} \end{aligned}$$

b) $(n^2)^0$

Solution

$$\begin{aligned} \left(n^2\right)^0 &= n^{2\times 0} \\ &= n^0 \\ &= 1\text{, where } n \neq 0 \end{aligned}$$

c) $\dfrac{y^4 \times y^{-2}}{y^{-3}}$

Solution

$$\begin{aligned} \frac{y^4 \times y^{-2}}{y^{-3}} &= \frac{y^2}{y^{-3}} \\ &= y^{2-(-3)} \\ &= y^{2+3} \\ &= y^5 \end{aligned}$$

PRACTICE EXERCISES

1. Calculate each of the following expressions.

a) $(-3)^0$

b) 4^{-1}

c) $-(6)^0$

d) -7^{-3}

e) -5^0

f) $-(-8)^0$

g) $-(-4)^2$

h) $-(-4)^{-2}$

i) 3^{-4}

j) $\left(\frac{3}{4}\right)^{-3}$

k) 6^{-2}

l) $\frac{1}{10^3}$

m) $\left(\frac{-2}{3}\right)^{-3}$

n) $\left(\frac{4}{-5}\right)^{-2}$

o) $-\left(\frac{7}{3}\right)^{-2}$

2. Simplify and evaluate each of the following expressions using applicable exponent laws.

a) $3^3 \times 3^{-1}$

b) $4^2 \times 4^{-3} \times 4^4$

c) $\frac{8^{-2}}{8^1}$

d) $\frac{2^5}{2^{-1}} \times \frac{2^{-2}}{2}$

e) $\frac{5^{-3}}{5^{-5} \times 5^2}$

3. Simplify each of the following expressions using the laws of exponents.

a) $n^6 \times n^{-2}$

b) $\left(a^{-3}\right)^{-3}$

c) $\left(\dfrac{m^3}{n^2}\right)^{-4}$

d) $\dfrac{r^{-2}}{r^{-2}}$

e) $\dfrac{a^5 \times a^{-3}}{a^6}$

PRACTICE QUIZ

1. Which of the following numbers belong to the integral number system?

A. -7 **B.** $\frac{1}{4}$ **C.** 0.75 **D.** π

2. Which of the following numbers is **not** a rational number?

A. $\frac{-1}{6}$ **B.** $0.\overline{35}$ **C.** $\sqrt{8}$ **D.** $\frac{22}{7}$

3. In the equation $x^2 = 81$, $x =$

A. 9 **B.** 8.1 **C.** 9 and -9 **D.** -9

4. If a square lid of a box has an area of $150\ \text{cm}^2$, what is the approximate length of the box?

A. 75 cm **B.** 49 cm **C.** 37.5 cm **D.** 12.2 cm

5. The coefficient in the term $-2xy^2$ is

A. 2 **B.** 1 **C.** -1 **D.** -2

6. Written as a single power, the expression $2^{-6} \times 2^{-3} \times 2^{7}$ is

A. 2^{-2} **B.** 2^3 **C.** 8^2 **D.** 2^{126}

7. Which of the following powers is a simplification of $\frac{7^{-1}}{7^3}$?

A. 7^{-4} **B.** $7^{\frac{1}{3}}$ **C.** 7^2 **D.** 7^3

8. Simplified, the expression $\left(x^2y^4\right)^3$ is

A. x^5y^7 **B.** x^6y^4 **C.** x^6y^{12} **D.** $x^{24}y^{24}$

9. When evaluated, the expression $5x^0 =$

A. 5 **B.** 0 **C.** $\frac{1}{5}$ **D.** –5

10. An equivalent form of 6^{-1} is

A. $\frac{1}{6^{-1}}$ **B.** $\frac{6}{1}$ **C.** $\frac{1}{6}$ **D.** –6

11. The simplified product of $\frac{3^2}{3^{-1}} \times \frac{3^{-4}}{3^{-1}}$ is

A. 81 **B.** 1 **C.** $\frac{1}{4}$ **D.** 0

12. When simplified, the expression $\left(\frac{x}{y^3}\right)^4$ is

A. $\frac{x^4}{y^7}$ **B.** $\frac{x^5}{y^7}$ **C.** $\frac{x}{y^{12}}$ **D.** $\frac{x^4}{y^{12}}$

Lesson 7 USING EXPONENT LAWS TO SIMPLIFY, EVALUATE, AND IDENTIFY PATTERNS

NOTES

You can use the exponent laws learned in the previous lessons to simplify, evaluate, and identify patterns. The exponent laws reduce the number of calculations needed to solve problems and assist in identifying patterns in problems.

For example, to find the product $3^3 \times 3^5$ without using exponent laws, you would expand and multiply.

$3^3 \times 3^5 = 3 \times 3 \times 3 \times 3 \times 3 \times 3 \times 3 \times 3 = 6\,561$

However, using the exponent laws, you can shorten the process.

$3^3 \times 3^5 = 3^{3+5} = 3^8$

Example 1

What is the next term in the sequence $2^3, 2^2, 2^1, 2^0, 2^{-1}, 2^{-2}, 2^{-3} \ldots$?

Solution

2^{-4}

Example 2

What is the relationship between 2^3 and 2^{-3}?

Solution

The value 2^{-3} is the reciprocal of 2^3.

$2^{-3} = \frac{1}{2^3} = \frac{1}{8}$ and $2^3 = 8$

This relationship illustrates the negative exponent law, which states that a base to a negative exponent is the reciprocal of the base to a positive exponent.

Example 3

How are the expressions $(-2)^4$ and -2^4 different?

Solution

The expression $(-2)^4$ means $-2 \times -2 \times -2 \times -2 = 16$, while the expression -2^4 means $-2 \times 2 \times 2 \times 2 = -16$. Since the negative symbol is not contained within brackets, it represents a coefficient of (–1). Following the order of operations (BEDMAS), the power is always dealt with first and the coefficient is multiplied later.

NOTES

Example 4

If the price of a hamburger doubles every two years, what will it cost in 50 years?

Solution

Start by identifying the pattern. Pick a starting price for the hamburger, for example, \$1.

Year	Year 0	Year 2	Year 4	Year 6	Year 8
Price	\$1	\$2	\$4	\$8	\$16

Since the price of the hamburger is doubling, the base number will be 2.

Since the price doubles every two years, take the total number years and divide by 2 to get the exponent.

Using $2^{\left(\frac{50}{2}\right)}$ × the original value of the hamburger, you get

$2^{\left(\frac{50}{2}\right)} \times \$1 = \$33\ 554\ 432$.

So, the price of the hamburger in 50 years would be \$33 554 432.

Example 5

Simplify the expression $n^{-2} \times n^5$ and then evaluate for $n = 2$.

Solution

$$\begin{aligned} n^{-2} \times n^5 &= n^{-2+5} \\ &= n^3 \\ &= (2)^3 \\ &= 8 \end{aligned}$$

Always put the value being substituted into the question in brackets.

NOTES

Example 6

Use exponent laws to help you solve the following equations.

a) $n^4 \times n^2 = 64$

Solution

$n^6 = 64$

You can use a calculator and the "guess-and-test" method to find a number to the 6th power that gives an answer of 64. The correct solution is $n = 2$.

Since squaring and taking the square root are opposite operations, n^6 and $\sqrt[6]{n}$ are opposite operations.

b) $n^{-5} = \frac{1}{32}$

Solution

$\frac{1}{n^5} = \frac{1}{32}$ is an equivalent form to the above equation.

Now use the "guess-and-test" method to find a number to the 5th power that equals 32. The solution is $n = 2$.

Example 7

When expanded, what are the last two digits of 11^{100}?

Solution

Use your calculator to find the last two digits for the first nine values with a base of 11.

Power	11^0	11^1	11^2	11^3	11^4	11^5	11^6	11^7	11^8	11^9
Last two digits	01	11	21	31	41	51	61	71	81	91

When 11 is the base, the value of the exponent will always be the same as the value of the second-last digit of the expanded number. The last digit is always 1.

Notice that the tens digit matches the exponent in each case. When we get to 11^{10}, the pattern will repeat, giving 101. Thus, 11^{100} would go through the above pattern 10 times, and the last two digits of 11^{100} would be 01.

PRACTICE EXERCISES

1. **a)** Describe the pattern 4^2, 4^1, 4^0, 4^{-1}, 4^{-2}....

b) Express the next number in the pattern as a positive number, and then express it in its expanded form.

2. Evaluate each of the following expressions.

a) $(-1)^4$ **b)** -1^4 **c)** $-(-3)^3$

d) $-(3)^3$ **e)** $(-4)^{-3}$ **f)** -6^{-2}

3. The price of a hot dog triples every 6 years. If the hot dog costs \$1.50 today, how much will it cost in 60 years?

4. Simplify each of the following expressions and then evaluate for $n = -3$.

a) $\dfrac{n^{-1}}{n^{-2}}$

b) $\left(n^{2}\right)^{2}$

c) $\dfrac{\left(n^{-2}\right)^{3}}{n^{-8}}$

d) $n^{5} \times n^{-6}$

5. Simplify each of the following equations using exponent laws. Use “guess-and-test” to solve.

a) $n^{5} \div n^{3} = 25$

b) $\left(n^{3}\right)^{2} = 729$

c) $n^{8} \times n^{-12} = \dfrac{1}{256}$

6. Using a calculator, find the first nine values with a base of 6. Then, by examining the last two digits of these numbers, determine the last two digits of 6^{20}.

Lesson 8 USING EXPONENT LAWS TO SIMPLIFY QUESTIONS INVOLVING COEFFICIENTS AND VARIABLES AND TO EVALUATE COMPLEX NUMERICAL QUESTIONS

NOTES

Exponent laws apply to variables in the same way as they do to numbers.

A **coefficient** is a number that is being multiplied by a variable.

In the previous lessons, you simplified questions that had coefficients of one. In this lesson, you will be performing the indicated operation on the coefficients as well as following the appropriate exponent laws when simplifying the variables.

If you are multiplying two terms made up of coefficients and variables, multiply the coefficients and add the exponents of the variables that have common bases.

If you are dividing two terms made up of coefficients and variables, divide the coefficients and subtract the exponents of the variables that have common bases.

Example 1

Simplify the expression $(5x^2y^3)(6x^4y^2)$.

Solution

You should simplify in parts, remembering to carry out the indicated operation on the coefficients.

$$5\times6\times x^2\times x^4\times y^3\times y^2=30\times x^{2+4}\times y^{3+2}$$

$$5\times6\times x^2\times x^4\times y^3\times y^2=30x^6y^5$$

Example 2

Simplify the expression $\dfrac{12x^5y^{-3}}{4x^4y^{-4}}$.

Solution

$$\frac{12x^5y^{-3}}{4x^4y^{-4}}=\frac{12}{4}\times x^{5-4}\times y^{-3-(-4)}=3xy$$

NOTES

Example 3

Simplify the expression $\left(\frac{m^3}{n^4}\right)^5$.

Solution

$$\begin{aligned}\left(\frac{m^3}{n^4}\right)^5 &= \frac{m^{3\times5}}{n^{4\times5}}\\ &= \frac{m^{15}}{n^{20}}\end{aligned}$$

Example 4

Simplify the expression $\frac{42x^{-2}y^5}{6x^4y}$.

Solution

$$\begin{aligned}\frac{42x^{-2}y^5}{6x^4y} &= 7x^{-2-4}y^{5-1}\\ &= 7x^{-6}y^4\end{aligned}$$

Example 5

Simplify and evaluate the expression $\frac{5^3}{5^2}\times\frac{4^6\times4^{-2}}{\left(4^2\right)^2}$.

Solution

$$\begin{aligned}\frac{5^3}{5^2}\times\frac{4^6\times4^{-2}}{\left(4^2\right)^2} &= 5\times\frac{4^4}{4^4}\\ &= 5\times4^0\\ &= 5\times1\\ &= 5\end{aligned}$$

PRACTICE EXERCISES

1. Simplify each of the following expressions.

a) $\left(x^{-3}\right)^{2}$

b) $\dfrac{m^{2}n^{3}}{mn^{-2}}$

c) $\dfrac{x^{4}y^{7}z^{-3}}{x^{2}y^{-5}z^{2}}$

d) $\left(4g^{3}h^{5}\right)\left(-5g^{-4}h^{3}\right)$

e) $\left(3g^{-5}h^{5}\right)\left(5g^{-4}h^{3}\right)$

f) $\left(ab^{-3}\right)^{-5}$

g) $\dfrac{-36a^{5}b^{-3}}{-12a^{6}b^{-5}}$

h) $\left(\dfrac{m^{2}n^{-3}}{m^{4}n}\right)^{2}$

i) $\left(6x^{2}y^{-4}\right)\left(-12y^{5}\right)$

j) $\dfrac{12a^{3}b^{-3}}{-18a^{5}b^{2}}$

2. Simplify and evaluate each of the following expressions.

a) $\dfrac{2^{5}}{2^{-2}}\times\dfrac{2^{-4}}{2^{2}}$

b) $\dfrac{(-3)^{9}\times(-3)^{-6}}{(-3)^{2}}$

c) $\dfrac{3^{7}}{3^{3}}\times\dfrac{9^{2}\times9^{0}}{9^{2}\times9^{-3}}$

Lesson 9 USING THE CALCULATOR TO KEY IN AND SOLVE BEDMAS QUESTIONS

The calculator is a tool that you should be skilled in using to solve mathematical problems. It is important to be able to use different calculator methods to obtain the same answer.

NOTES

BEDMAS stands for the order of operations for solving expressions, working from left to right.

B is for brackets; operations within them are always performed first.

E is for exponents; operations with exponents are performed next.

D and **M** are for division and multiplication, which are performed next, from left to right, whichever operation comes first.

A and **S** are for addition and subtraction, which are performed next, from left to right, whichever operation comes first.

Example 1

Identify the keystrokes required to solve $(21.3-14.7)\times(14.7+3.6)$ and then give the solution.

Solution

$(21.3-14.7)\times(14.7+3.6) = (6.6)\times(18.3) = 120.78$

[( ] [2] [1] [.] [3] [−] [1] [4] [.] [7] [ )] [×]
[( ] [1] [4] [.] [7] [+] [3] [.] [6] [ )] [=] [×]

The solution is 120.78.

You may also use your memory key to help you solve a question. Applying this method, you get

[2] [1] [.] [3] [−] [1] [4] [.] [7] [=] [M+] [1] [4] [.] [7]
[+] [3] [.] [6] [=] [×] [MR] [=]

The solution is 120.78.

You must remember to follow the BEDMAS order of operations when entering the keystrokes. Always begin by completing the operations within the brackets.

Example 2

Identify the keystrokes necessary to solve $\frac{31.6\times7.3}{(5.2\times8.2)-5.4}$ on a calculator, and then give the solution.

Solution

$(31.6 \times 7.3) \div ((5.2 \times 8.2) - 5.4)$

[( ] [3] [1] [.] [6] [×] [7] [.] [3] [ )] [÷] [( ] [( ] [5] [.]
[2] [×] [8] [.] [2] [ )] [−] [5] [.] [4]

$\frac{31.6\times7.3}{(5.2\times8.2)-5.4} = 6.1944\ldots$

Rounded to two decimal places, the solution is 6.19.

PRACTICE EXERCISES

1. Use your calculator to solve each of the following expressions using as few keystrokes as possible. Record the keying sequence and the answer, rounding your answer to the nearest tenth.

a) $21.4 \times (64.1 - 37.8)$

b) $\dfrac{20.3 \times 14.5}{15.5}$

c) $(-35.5 - 13) \div (15.7 - 21.3)$

d) $\dfrac{311.4}{6.5 \times 22.4} - 101$

e) $\dfrac{14.9 - 8.3}{15.4 - (8.2 \times 4.7)}$

Lesson 10 SCIENTIFIC NOTATION CALCULATIONS

Scientific notation is used to write large numbers in a shorter way. Remember that when a number is written in scientific notation, the first number is always between 1 and 10 and the second number is a power of 10. An example, 4.2×10^3 is scientific notation for the number 4 200.

NOTES

In scientific notation, the first number is always between 1 and 10; the second number is a power of 10.

When going from scientific notation to standard form, move the decimal to the right as many places as the value of the exponent if the exponent is positive.

If the exponent is negative, move the decimal to the left as many places as the value of the exponent. For example, $3.46\times10^{-4}=0.000\ 346$.
The exponent is negative, so the decimal was moved 4 places to the left.

When going from standard form to exponential form, the reverse process takes place. For example, $0.487=4.87\times10^{-1}$.
The decimal has been moved one place to the right, so the exponent is a negative number.

Now you will use the calculator to help solve questions involving scientific notation. Your calculator should have a button labelled "ee" or "EXP. "
To enter a number like 2.57×10^3, enter 2.57 "EXP" 3 = to get the solution 2 570.

Example 1

Identify the keystrokes needed and then give the solution for $(5.1\times10^6)\times(2.34\times10^{-2})$.

Solution

119 340

Example 2

Identify the keystrokes needed and then give the solution for $\dfrac{2.55\times10^{-9}}{3.0\times10^{-14}}$.

Solution

85 000

NOTES

Example 3

Earth's diameter is about 1.3×10^4 km. The sun's diameter is about 1.4×10^6 km. How many times greater is the diameter of the sun than the diameter of Earth?

Solution

Divide the diameter of the sun by the diameter of Earth to find how many times greater the diameter of the sun is.

$$\frac{1.4\times10^6}{1.3\times10^4}$$

Using your calculator, you should get approximately 107.7.

The sun's diameter is about 107.7 times greater than Earth's diameter.

PRACTICE EXERCISES

1. Simplify each of the following expressions. Write the final answer in scientific notation.

   a) $(4.3\times10^{4})(3.8\times10^{-2})$

   b) $(-7.8\times10^{-4})(3.1\times10^{-5})$

   c) $(5.98\times10^{4})(6.1\times10^{5})$

2. Simplify each of the following expressions. Write the final answer in standard form to the nearest hundredth.

   a) $\dfrac{7.89\times10^{5}}{-2.6\times10^{2}}$

   b) $\dfrac{8.43\times10^{5}}{3.3\times10^{7}}$

   c) $\dfrac{2.55\times10^{-8}}{3.1\times10^{-14}}$

3. A spacecraft is travelling at 60 000 km/h. At this rate, it will take 296 000 years to reach one of the brightest stars in the sky. How far is the star from the spacecraft's takeoff point on Earth?

REVIEW SUMMARY

- A rational number is any number that can be written as a fraction, as long as the decimal equivalent terminates or repeats with a set pattern. A non-terminating, non-repeating decimal is an irrational number.
- An irrational number is a decimal number that is non-terminating and does not have a set pattern.
- The rational number system includes the natural, whole, and integral number systems.
- The principal square root of a number is the positive square root.
- When taking the square root to solve an equation, give both the positive and negative solutions.
- The coefficient is the number that is being multiplied by the variable.
- When multiplying identical bases, add the exponents.
- When dividing identical bases, subtract the exponents.
- When simplifying a power of a power, multiply the exponents.
- Any number to the exponent zero, except zero, is equal to one.
- To simplify a question with a negative exponent, take the reciprocal of the base and make the exponent positive.
- Apply the order of operations when calculating solutions to complex questions using your calculator.
- Remember to look for patterns when solving problems involving rational numbers.
- When simplifying questions that involve variables as well as coefficients, perform the indicated operations on the coefficients and follow the exponent laws for the variables.
- Before evaluating questions, first simplify using exponent laws and then make any negative exponents positive.
- When calculating scientific notation questions, remember that the button labelled “Exp” or “ee” on your calculator is used to represent base 10.

PRACTICE TEST

1. The radical $\sqrt{2}$ belongs to which of the following number systems?

A. Rational **B.** Integral **C.** Whole **D.** Irrational

2. Which of the following numbers is a rational number?

A. 0.536872 **B.** $\sqrt{5}$ **C.** 2.79865… **D.** π

3. The diagram below represents a target. The small square in the middle of the target has an area of 25 cm^2. If the large square has an area of 441 cm^2, how far is the side of the small square from the edge of the target?

A. 16 cm **B.** 11 cm **C.** 8 cm **D.** 5.5 cm

4. If $n^2 = 289$, then n equals

A. 18 **B.** 17 **C.** 17 and –17 **D.** –17

5. The coefficient in $\frac{2}{3}x^2y^5$ is

A. 7 **B.** 5 **C.** 2 **D.** $\frac{2}{3}$

6. An expression that is the equivalent of $\left[(-2)^3\right]^6$ is

A. $(-2)^{18}$ **B.** $(-2)^9$ **C.** 2^2 **D.** 2^9

7. Which of the following expressions is the equivalent of $\frac{2^3 \times 2^8}{2^4}$?

A. 2^7 **B.** 4^7 **C.** 2^{15} **D.** $\frac{4^{11}}{2^4}$

8. Which of the following expressions is equal to 256?

A. $(-2)^2 \times (-2)^2$ **B.** $(-2^4)^4$ **C.** $(-2^7)^1$ **D.** $(2^2)^3 \times (-2)^2$

9. Which of the following expressions is the equivalent of $(5y^2)(6y^6)$?

A. y^8 **B.** $11y^8$ **C.** $30y^8$ **D.** $30y^{12}$

10. Which of the following statements is correct?

A. $(-2)^{-4} = 16$ **B.** $(-2)^{-4} = \frac{1}{8}$ **C.** $(-2)^{-4} = \frac{1}{16}$ **D.** $(-2)^{-4} = -8$

11. When simplified, the expression $\frac{\left(4x^3y^2\right)\left(4x^5y^6\right)}{2x^3y^4}$ is

A. $8x^8y^3$ **B.** $8x^5y^4$ **C.** $8x^2y^4$ **D.** $6x^5y^8$

12. Which of the following expressions is equal to 1?

A. $2^4 \times 2^0 \times 2$ **B.** $2^{-4} \div 2^4$ **C.** $2^7 \times 2^{-3} \div 2^4$ **D.** $2^0 \times 2$

13. What is the length, to one decimal place, of one side of a square that has an area of 44.5 cm^2?

A. 26.7 cm **B.** 22.3 cm **C.** 13.4 cm **D.** 6.7 cm

14. Given $x = -2$, the expression $\frac{\left(x^3\right)^2}{x^4}$ is equal to

A. 16 **B.** 4 **C.** –4 **D.** –8

15. Which of the following expressions is the equivalent to $\dfrac{3.6\times10^{6}}{1.5\times10^{-3}}$?

A. 2.4×10^{-2} **B.** 2.4×10^{3} **C.** 2.4×10^{6} **D.** 2.4×10^{9}

16. What is the last digit in the expansion of 3^{30}?

A. 9 **B.** 7 **C.** 3 **D.** 1

17. The diameter of an atom is typically 1×10^{-10} m. The diameter of its nucleus is typically about 1×10^{-14} m. How many times larger is the diameter of the atom than the diameter of its nucleus?

A. $10^{1.4}$ **B.** 10^{4} **C.** 10^{24} **D.** 10^{140}

18. Which of the following expressions is the equivalent of $(2.1\times10^{7})\times(5.9\times10^{-4})$?

A. 1.239×10^{4} **B.** 1.239×10^{3} **C.** 1.239×10^{3} **D.** 1.239×10^{-28}

19. Use a calculator to determine the solution to the expression $\dfrac{0.095\times2\,550+0.125\times4\,229}{5}$.

A. 374.975 **B.** 374.957 **C.** 347.957 **D.** 154.175

20. Which of the following expressions is the equivalent of $9x^3y^2 \div 3xy^2$?

A. $6x^2$ **B.** $3x^4y^4$ **C.** $3x^2y$ **D.** $3x^2$

PATTERNS AND RELATIONS

When you are finished this unit, you should be able to . . .

- create patterns and use logical thinking to help solve problems (SO 1)
- write an equation that represents a given word problem (SO 2)
- manipulate equations and expressions so they can be written in different ways (SO 3)
- use algebra tiles or diagrams to show how to solve an equation (SO 4)
- solve and verify equations of the types below (SO 5)
  - $2x = 4 + 3x$
  - $3(x + 4) = 5$
  - $6x + 5 = 3x - 7$
  - $2(4x + 5) = -3(2x - 6)$
  - $\frac{4}{x} = 8$
- solve inequalities (SO 6)
- graph solutions to inequalities on a number line (SO 6)
- verify solutions to an inequality (SO 6)
- identify the constant, coefficients, and variables in polynomials (SO 7)
- substitute numbers for variables and evaluate polynomial expressions (SO 8)
- use algebra tiles or diagrams to show how to add and subtract polynomials (SO 9)
- add and subtract polynomials (SO 10)
- use diagrams or algebra tiles to show how to multiply, divide, and factor polynomials (monomials, binomials, and trinomials where the coefficient of x^2 is only 1) (SO 11)
- multiply a monomial by a monomial (SO 12)
- multiply a monomial by a polynomial (SO 12)
- multiply two binomials in the order of First terms, Outer terms, Inner terms, and Last terms (FOIL) (SO 12)
- simplify polynomials by adding like terms (SO 13)
- factor trinomials of the form $x^2 + bx + c$, where the x^2 term has a coefficient of 1 (SO 13)
- divide a polynomial by a monomial (SO 14)

PREREQUISITE SKILLS AND KNOWLEDGE

Prior to beginning this unit, you should be able to. . .

- identify patterns from simple problems
- create a table of values from a given equation
- create simple equations from given word problem
- solve and verify one- and two-step equations
- solve problems using equations
- multiply, divide, add, and subtract integers

Lesson 1 WORD PROBLEMS TO EQUATIONS

NOTES

When converting from a problem to an equation, remember to look for key words and what they represent mathematically.

Words that represent **addition** include *increase*, *more than*, *sum*, and *greater than*.

Words for **subtraction** include *minus*, *reduced*, *decreased*, and *difference*.

Words for **multiplication** include *times* and *product*.

Words for **division** include *into*, *quotient*, and *divided by*.

Use a **variable** to represent an unknown that you are trying to find.

When creating an equation, some words that you can use to represent **equal to** (=) are *result* and *total*.

Example 1

Write an equation for a situation in which a number is increased by 3 and the result is 21.

Solution
Let $x =$ number
$x+3=21$

Example 2

Write an equation for a situation where half of a number reduced by 5 results in an answer of 12.

Solution
Let $x =$ number
$\frac{1}{2}x-5=12$

Example 3

The cost to rent a DVD player is $5 per day, plus a $15 deposit. Bill paid $30 for his DVD rental. Write an equation to find the number of days he rented the DVD player.

Solution
Let $x =$ the number of days Bill rented the DVD player
$15+5x=30$

NOTES

$15+5x=30$
$15-15+5x=30-15$
$5x=15$
$x=3$
Bill rented the DVD player for three days.

Example 4

The area of Lake Superior is 5 times the area of Lake Ontario. The sum of the areas of the two lakes is 105 000 km^2. Write an equation to find the area of each lake.

Solution
Let x = area of Lake Ontario
$5x$ = area of Lake Superior
$1x+5x=105\ 000\ \text{km}^2$
Collect like terms.
$6x = 105\ 000\ \text{km}^2$
$x = 17\ 500$
So, the area of Lake Ontario is 17 500 km^2.
Now, the area of Lake Superior is $5x$.
Therefore, it is
$5 \times 17\ 500\ \text{km}^2 = 87\ 500\ \text{km}^2$.

PRACTICE EXERCISES

1. Write an equation to represent each of the following word problems.

a) Ten times a number increased by 5 is 65.

b) The difference between 34 and a larger number is 6.

c) A number tripled and then reduced by 7 results in 29.

d) The square of a number is 36.

e) Bill has $45 more in his bank account than in his pocket. Bill has a total of $105. How much is in his pocket?

f) The sum of two consecutive integers is 37. Find the integers.

g) The flying distance from Edmonton to Winnipeg is 4 times the flying distance from Edmonton to Calgary. The sum of these two distances is 1550 km.

h) After 3 computers are removed from a classroom, 18 computers remain. How many computers were there before the 3 were removed?

Lesson 2 MANIPULATING EQUATIONS

NOTES

Equations are manipulated to isolate the variable.

It is often necessary to manipulate the form of an equation in order to solve for a variable. For example, in the formula Area = length × width $(A = l \times w)$, you can manipulate the equation to find the length if you are given the area and the width. The equation would be rewritten as $l = \frac{A}{w}$.

You can find the circumference of a circle by using the formula $C = 2\pi r$. However, you can also manipulate this formula when you need to find the radius of various circles.

$C = 2\pi r$

To isolate *r*, use the inverse operation of multiplication.

Divide both sides of the equation by 2π.

$$\frac{C}{2\pi} = \frac{\cancel{2\pi} r}{\cancel{2\pi}}$$

Reducing the right side, you are left with $\frac{C}{2\pi} = r$.

Example 1

Given $P = 2l + 2w$, solve the equation for w.

Solution

Subtract $2l$ from both sides of the equation.

$P - 2l = \cancel{2l} - \cancel{2l} + 2w$

$P - 2l = 2w$

Now, divide both sides of the equation by 2.

$$\frac{P-2l}{2} = \frac{\cancel{2}w}{\cancel{2}}$$

$$\frac{P-2l}{2} = w$$

Use opposite, or **inverse**, operations to isolate the specified variable.

Now substitute values in for P and l to solve for w.

PRACTICE EXERCISES

1. **Rewrite each of the following equations to isolate the identified variable.**

a) $A = lw$ to solve for l

b) $3a - 2b = -8$ to solve for b

c) $I = prt$ to solve for r

d) $A = \pi r^2$ to solve for r

e) $y = mx + b$ to solve for m

f) $A = \frac{bh}{2}$ to solve for h

Lesson 3 USING ALGEBRA TILES TO SOLVE EQUATIONS

NOTES

Algebra tiles can be used as a manipulatives to assist in solving equations. If you have a set of algebra tiles, you can use them to help you solve the following questions. If you do not have a set of tiles, you can draw a diagram of how the tiles are used to solve the equations. By actually manipulating the tiles or drawing a diagram of how they are used, you can see the steps that take place in solving an equation.

Shaded symbols represent positive numbers and variables. Unshaded symbols represent negative numbers and variables.

The following symbols can be used to assist in solving equations.

[shaded tall tile] $= +x$ [unshaded tall tile] $= -x$ [shaded small tile] $= +1$ [unshaded small tile] $= -1$

Remember to use the equation-solving skills that you have already learned. Manipulate the equation by performing the opposite, or inverse, operations as you work toward isolating the variables on one side of the equation and the numbers on the other side of the equation.

When you have the same number of positive tiles and negative tiles of the same type on one side of the equation, they will cancel each other out. This cancelling out is known as the **zero principle**. The **zero principle** states that an equal number of positives and an equal number of negatives will add up to zero.

The **zero principle** is applied when a negative and positive tile are put together, thereby cancelling each other out.

The last step should be to share the number on one side of the equation with the number of variables on the other side of the equation. This represents dividing both sides of the equation by the coefficient. For example, if you are left with $3x = 6$, then each x value would represent (or share) 2.

When solving equations, remember to perform the opposite operation as you work toward isolating the variable on one side of the equation.

Example 1

Use algebra tiles to solve $3x - 2 = 6 - x$.

When using tiles to represent an equation, the variable x is represented by a shaded symbol.

Solution

First draw or lay out the tiles to represent the equation.

$3x \quad - \quad 2 \quad = \quad 6 \quad - \quad x$

[3 shaded tall tiles] [2 unshaded small tiles] = [6 shaded small tiles] [1 unshaded tall tile]

NOTES

Add 2 number tiles to both sides of the equation to get all the numbers on the right side.

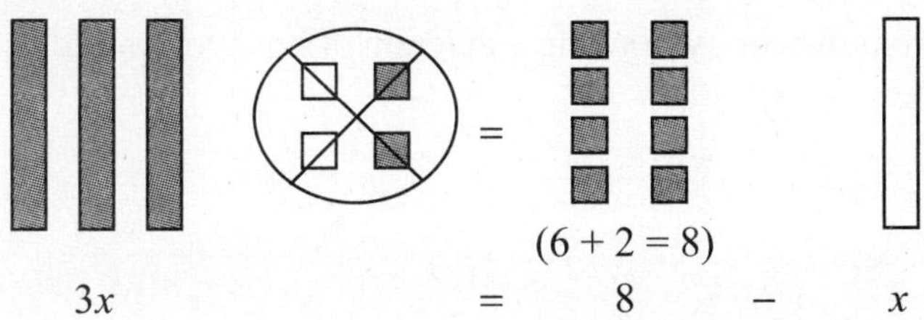

In this case, the 2s are eliminated on the left side.

The positive tiles cancel out the neative tiles on the left side of the equation.

Next, add a positive x tile to both sides to get all the variables on one side.

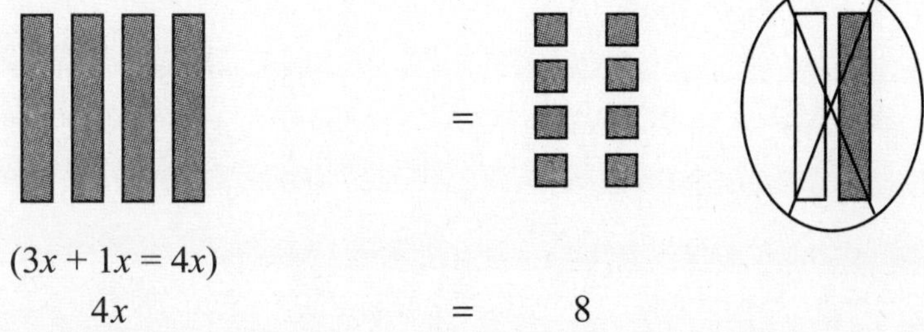

The positive tile cancels out the negative tile on the right side.

Now, share each variable tile with an equal number of number tiles. This represents dividing both sides of the equation by 4. The tiles below have been turned sideways to make it easier to see how many number tiles go with each variable tile.

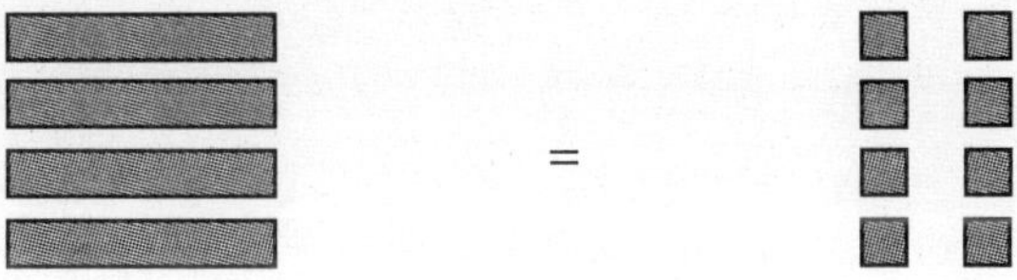

You can see that each variable tile(x) = 2 number tiles.

Therefore, the solution is $x = 2$.

PRACTICE EXERCISES

1. Solve the following equations by using algebra tiles or by drawing a diagram of how you would use the tiles. Write the solutions.

a) $3x-2=x+4$

b) $3x-5=2x-7$

c) $3+4x=9-2x$

d) $-3x-2=7-6x$

Lesson 4 SOLVING EQUATIONS

NOTES

Algebra can be used to solve problems that occur in everyday situations. A variable is used to represent an unknown that you are trying to find. The situation described by the statement "Jenna is 2 years older than Amy and the sum of their ages is 32" can be represented as an equation using algebra. The equation would be $x+2+x=32$.

The **distributive property** is often used to simplify an equation. When using this property, the term outside of the brackets is multiplied by each term inside the brackets to remove them. For example, the equation $2(x+4)=7$ is simplified to $2x+8=7$ by applying the distribution property.

When solving equations, move the variables to one side of the equation and the numbers to the other. Lastly, divide by the coefficient in front of the variable to get your answer.

Use opposite, or **inverse**, operations as you work toward the answer.

Example 1

Solve and verify the equation $5x=21+2x$

Verify means to perform a check.

Solution

$5x=21+2x$

$5x-2x=21+\cancel{2x}-\cancel{2x}$

$3x=21$

$\frac{\cancel{3}x}{\cancel{3}}=\frac{21}{3}$

$x=7$

Remember to substitute into brackets.

After solving an equation, you can verify your answer to make sure it is correct by substituting the value of the variable back into the equation. If your answer is correct, then the left side of the equation should equal the right side. When verifying your answer, you do not need to move terms from one side of the equation to the other.

Verify the solution for example 1.

Substitute $x=7$ into the original equation.

Left Side	=	Right Side
$5x$	=	$21+2x$
$5(7)$	=	$21+2(7)$
35	=	35

Since the left side and the right side of the equation are equal, the solution $x=7$ is correct.

NOTES

Example 2

Solve and verify.

$-2(x+5)=12$

Solution

As your first step, use the **distributive property** to multiply –2 into the brackets.

$-2(x+5)=12$

$-2x-10=12$

$-2x-\cancel{10}+\cancel{10}=12+10$

$-2x=22$

Divide by –2 since the coefficient is a negative.

$\frac{\cancel{-2}x}{\cancel{-2}}=\frac{22}{-2}$

$x=-11$

Verify

Left Side	=	Right Side
$-2(x+5)$	=	12
$-2(-11+5)$	=	12
$-2(-6)$	=	12
12	=	12

Since the left side $=$ the right side, $x=-11$ is correct.

Example 3

Solve the following equation for x.

$3x-5=6x+2$

$\frac{7}{-3}=\frac{-7}{3}=-\frac{7}{3}$ are equivalent forms of the same fraction.

Answers may be rational numbers as well as integers.

$x=\frac{7}{-3}$ is a rational number.

Solution

$3x-5=6x+2$

$3x-\cancel{5}+\cancel{5}=6x+2+5$

$3x=6x+7$

$3x-6x=\cancel{6x}-\cancel{6x}+7$

$-3x=7$

$\frac{\cancel{-3}x}{\cancel{-3}}=\frac{7}{-3}$

$x=\frac{7}{-3}$

NOTES

Example 4

Solve the following equation. Express the answer as a fraction in lowest terms and as a decimal.

$3(2x+5)=-2(-4x+7)$

Solution

First, multiply to remove the brackets.

$3(2x+5)=-2(-4x+7)$

$6x+15=8x-14$

$6x+\cancel{15}-\cancel{15}=8x-14-15$

$6x=8x-29$

$6x-8x=\cancel{8x}-\cancel{8x}-29$

$-2x=-29$

$\frac{\cancel{-2}x}{\cancel{-2}}=\frac{-29}{-2}$

$x=\frac{29}{2}$

Express this solution in lowest terms.

$x=\frac{29}{2}=14\frac{1}{2}$

Expressed as a decimal, $14\frac{1}{2}=x=14.5$.

Example 5

Solve the following equation.

$\frac{7}{x}=8$

LCD stands for Lowest Common Denominator.

The **denominator** is the bottom of the fraction.

Solution

When you have a rational number in an equation, multiply each term by the LCD to reduce to eliminate fractions.

$\frac{7}{x}=8$ or $\frac{7}{x}=\frac{8}{1}$

In this case, the LCD $=x$.

$(x)\frac{7}{x}=8(x)$

$(\cancel{x}^{1})\frac{7}{\cancel{x}_{1}}=8(x)$

The x's on the left side cancel and reduce to 1.

$7=8x$

NOTES

$$\frac{7}{8}=\frac{\cancel{8}x}{\cancel{8}}$$

$$\frac{7}{8}=x$$

x is the same as $\frac{x}{1}$

Example 6

Solve the following equation.

$$\frac{3x}{4}-\frac{2x}{3}=\frac{5}{6}+x$$

Remember that **terms** are separated by addition, subtraction, and equal signs.

Solution

$$\frac{3x}{4}-\frac{2x}{3}=\frac{5}{6}+x$$

Since the LCD is 12, multiply each term by 12.

Reduce to eliminate the fractions.

Multiply and collect like terms.

$$\frac{3x}{4}\left(\frac{12}{1}\right)-\frac{2x}{3}\left(\frac{12}{1}\right)=\frac{5}{6}\left(\frac{12}{1}\right)+x\left(\frac{12}{1}\right)$$

$$\frac{3x}{\cancel{4}_1}\left(\frac{\cancel{12}^3}{1}\right)-\frac{2x}{\cancel{3}_1}\left(\frac{\cancel{12}^4}{1}\right)=\frac{5}{\cancel{6}_1}\left(\frac{\cancel{12}^2}{1}\right)+x\left(\frac{12}{1}\right)$$

Be very careful when manipulating negative numbers. It is important to check that the negative signs are moved from one side of the equation to the other properly.

$$3x(3)-2x(4)=5(2)+x(12)$$

$$9x-8x=10+12x$$

$$x=10+12x$$

$$x-12x=10+\cancel{12x}-\cancel{12x}$$

$$\frac{\cancel{-11}x}{\cancel{-11}}=\frac{10}{-11}$$

$$x=\frac{10}{-11}$$

PRACTICE EXERCISES

1. Solve each of the following equations and verify your answers.

a) $3x + x = 5x - 6$

b) $-6x + 9 = 3x$

c) $5 - 6x = 2x + 5$

d) $2(x + 1) = 3(x - 1)$

e) $41 = 0.5x + 0.7x - 7$

2. Solve each of the following equations, rounding answers to the nearest tenth.

a) $2.5x - 4 + 1.3x = 3$

b) $1.2x + 3.5(2.5 - x) = 41$

c) $5.9 - (3x + 2.5) = 0.5x$

3. Solve each of the following equations. Express your answer as a fraction in lowest terms.

a) $14 = \frac{-3}{x}$

b) $\frac{x}{4} - \frac{2}{3} = 3$

c) $\frac{5x}{3} - 3 = 8 + \frac{x}{2}$

d) $-2(3x - 1) = 2(-4x + 3)$

Lesson 5 SOLVING WORD PROBLEMS BY CREATING EQUATIONS

Word problems can be solved by creating an equation containing a variable to represent the problem and solving for the variable.

NOTES

A **variable** is used to represent an unknown number or quantity.

A **variable** is used to represent any unknown that you need to find. There may be more than one unknown in a given problem, so you may need to use more than one algebraic expression that includes variables to represent them. Consider the following problem.

The length of a rectangle is 5 cm more than the width, and the perimeter of the rectangle is 50 cm. What is the width of the triangle? What is the length of the rectangle?

In this problem, you could use x to represent the width and $x + 5$ to represent the length. Using the formula for finding the perimeter of a rectangle, the equation to solve the problem is $2(x)+2(x+5)=50$.

After the equation is solved, you can substitute the value for x back into the expressions representing the unknown width and length and answer the problem with a sentence.

Example 1

A string measuring 50 cm is cut into three pieces. One piece is twice as long as the shortest piece, and the other piece is 10 cm longer than the shortest piece. What is the length of each piece of string?

Solution

Identify a math expression to represent each part of the string.

Let x = the shortest piece of string
$2x$ = the length of the second piece
$10 + x$ = the length of the third piece

It is a good strategy to let the part that other parts are being related to be x. In this case, the other parts are being compared with the shortest piece of string. Look for key words. "Twice" means to multiply by 2. "Longer than" means to add. The total length of the string is 50 cm, so you add all of the parts and make them equal to 50 cm.

The resulting equation will be
$x+2x+10+x=50$
Add the like terms on either side of the equation.
$4x+10=50$

NOTES

Subtract 10 from both sides of the equation.

$4x + \cancel{10} - \cancel{10} = 50 - 10$

$4x = 40$

Lastly, divide by the coefficient in front of the variable to solve.

$\frac{4x}{4} = \frac{40}{4}$

$x = 10$

Now take the answer for x and substitute it back into the math expressions used to identify the different pieces of string.

If $x = 10$, the shortest piece is 10 cm.
Therefore, $2(10) = 20$, so the second piece is 20 cm.
Finally, $10 + 10 = 20$, so the third piece is also 20 cm.

Complete your work on the problem by writing a sentence answering the question asked in the problem.

The length of one piece of string is 10 cm, another is 20 cm, and the third is 20 cm.

Example 2

The perimeter of a rectangular garden is 44 m. The length of the garden is 8 m longer than the width. What are the dimensions of the garden.

Solution

Let $x =$ the width of garden
$x + 8 =$ the length of the garden

$x + 8$

x x

$x + 8$

The perimeter of a rectangle is found with the formula $P = 2l + 2w$. If you substitute the algebraic expressions and the given value for perimeter into this formula, you get
$44 = 2(x + 8) + 2(x)$.

Use the **distributive property** to remove the brackets.
$2(x + 8) = 2x + 16$

Now solve for x.

$44 = 2x + 16 + 2x$

$44 = 4x + 16$

$44 - 16 = 4x + \cancel{16} - \cancel{16}$

$28 = 4x$

$\frac{28}{4} = \frac{\cancel{4}x}{\cancel{4}}$

$7 = x$

NOTES

Width $= x$ Length $= x + 8$

$= 7$ m $= 7 + 8$

$= 15$ m

Thus, the width is 7 m and the length is 15 m.

Substitute $x = 7$ into the original expressions for width and length.

Example 3

A jar contains nickels, dimes, and quarters that total $4.15. There are three more nickels than quarters and twice as many dimes as quarters. How many of each type of coin are in the jar?

Solution

Let $x =$ the number of quarters

$3 + x =$ the number of nickels

$2x =$ the number of dimes

With coin problems, multiply the number of coins by the coin value to get their total value.

You know the total value of the coins in the jar, so you must multiply the number of coins of each type by their value to get the total value for that type.

It may be easier to express the equation in cents rather than dollars, but it can be solved by either method.

$$25(x)+5(3+x)+10(2x)=415$$
$$25x+15+5x+20x=415$$
$$50x+15=415$$
$$50x+\cancel{15}-\cancel{15}=415-15$$
$$50x=400$$
$$\frac{\cancel{50}x}{\cancel{50}}=\frac{400}{50}$$
$$x=8$$

Quarters $= x$ Nickels $= 3 + x$ Dimes $= 2x$

$= 8$ $= 3 + 8$ $= 2 \times 8$

$= 11$ $= 16$

The jar contains 8 quarters, 11 nickels, and 16 dimes.

Use the **distributive property** to remove the brackets and then add like terms.

NOTES

Example 4

The sum of three consecutive odd integers is 111. What are the three integers?

Solution

Let $x =$ the first odd integer
$x + 2 =$ the second odd integer
$x + 4 =$ the third odd integer

$$x+(x+2)+(x+4)=111$$
$$3x+6=111$$
$$3x=105$$
$$x=35$$

$$\begin{aligned}\text{The first odd integer} &= x\\ &= 35\end{aligned}$$
$$\begin{aligned}\text{The second odd integer} &= x+2\\ &= 35+2\\ &= 37\end{aligned}$$
$$\begin{aligned}\text{The third odd integer} &= x+4\\ &= 35+4\\ &= 39\end{aligned}$$

Thus, the three integers are 35, 37, and 39.

PRACTICE EXERCISES

1. Four consecutive whole numbers have a sum of 298. What are the numbers?

2. Find two consecutive numbers where 259 is the sum of the first number and triple the second number.

3. Ellen is 4 years older than twice Bob's age. One-third of Bob's age plus 6 equals Raymond's age. The sum of their three ages is 50. How old is Raymond?

4. The perimeter of an isosceles triangle is 35 cm. The base is 4 cm less than one of the equal sides. Find the length of each side.

5. The sum of two numbers is 53. One number is 7 more than the other. Find the numbers.

6. Amy emptied the coins from the vending machine at school and collected a total of $11.85. If there were 4 more quarters than loonies and triple the number of dimes than loonies, how many of each coin were there?

7. The perimeter of a rectangular field is 76 m. The length is 1 m less than double the width. Find the dimensions of the field.

Lesson 6 SOLVE AND GRAPH INEQUALITIES

Inequalities are equations that use >, <, ≥, ≤, or ≠ in place of the equal sign. Inequalities are solved in the same way that equations are solved: all the variables are moved to one side of the equation and all of the numbers to the other side. However, there is one important difference.

RULE: When you multiply or divide both sides of an inequality by a negative, *reverse* the inequality sign.

NOTES

Remember that > means greater than and ≥ means greater than or equal to, < means less than and ≤ means less than or equal to, and ≠ means not equal to.

Example 1

Solve and graph the solution to $2x-2 \le 3x+1$.

Solution

$$2x-\cancel{2}+\cancel{2} \le 3x+1+2$$

$$2x \le 3x+3$$

$$2x-3x \le \cancel{3x}-\cancel{3x}+3$$

$$-1x \le 3$$

$$\frac{\cancel{-1}x}{\cancel{-1}} \ge \frac{3}{-1}$$

Treat the inequality as an equal sign that divides the equation into two sides.

Notice that when you divide by a negative, ≤ is reversed to ≥.

$x \ge -3$

The solution is then graphed on a number line for the set of rational numbers.

When creating your number line, start by placing the solution number –3 in the middle of the line and then write the next 3 numbers in the sequence on either side of the middle number.

Draw a circle at the place on the number line that indicates –3. If you shade in the circle, you are saying that –3 is part of the solution. If you do not shade the circle, you are saying that the solution begins at –3, but does not include –3.

When making a number line that includes decimals or fractions, remember that the intervals between values should always be equal.

Next, draw your arrow in the direction of the numbers that satisfy your solution. You can check to make sure your arrow goes in the proper direction by taking numbers from either side of the solution number and substituting them for x in the final solution.

For example, $-4 \ge -3$, is not true, so do not point the arrow in the direction of – 4.

NOTES

Now, $-2 \geq -3$, is true, so point the arrow in the direction of -2.

−6 −5 −4 −3 −2 −1 0

Example 2

Graph the solution to $x < 5$.

Solution

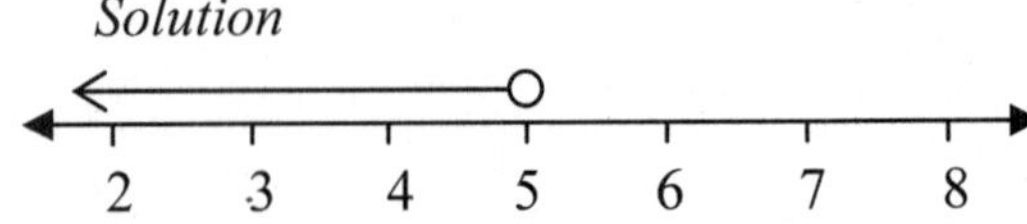

The circle is only shaded in when the inequality is $\leq$ or $\geq$.

Notice that the circle is not shaded in for this inequality.

Example 3

Solve $2x - 3 > 5$ and then identify which of the numbers –3, –4, –7, and 7 belongs to the solution set.

Solution

$2x > 8$

$x > 4$

The only number that is greater than 4 is 7.

PRACTICE EXERCISES

1. Solve the following inequalities and then graph them on a number line.

a) $-4 > 4x$

b) $-6 \geq 3 - x$

c) $2x + 2 > x + 4$

2. Solve the following inequalities.

a) $4x + 2 \geq 2x - 2$

b) $2(x-1) < 3(x+2)$

c) $3(4-2x) > 2(x+1)-2$

3. Identify which of the numbers 0, 2, –6, and –10 belong to the solution set of $-3 < x+2$.

PRACTICE QUIZ 1

1. Write an equation to represent the following word problem:
"John has $4.45 in quarters and dimes in his desk drawer. If he has 8 more quarters than dimes, how many of each coin does he have in his drawer?"

2. Which of the following equation is an equivalent form of the equation $V = abc$?

A. $\frac{ab}{V} = c$ **B.** $a = \frac{V}{bc}$ **C.** $a = Vbc$ **D.** $a = \frac{bc}{V}$

3. Make an algebra tile diagram to show how to solve $4x + 6 = 2x - 2$.

4. In the equation $6x + 10 = 2x - 14$, the value of x is

A. –6 **B.** –3 **C.** 2 **D.** 6

5. The solution to the equation $4(3x - 8) = 10$ is

A. $-3.\overline{6}$ **B.** 3.5 **C.** $3.\overline{6}$ **D.** 4

6. In the equation $2(3x-7)=-3(-4x+2)$ for x, the value of x is

A. -4 **B.** $\frac{-4}{3}$ **C.** $\frac{4}{3}$ **D.** 4

7. The Smiths paid their school fees of $185 in three installments. The second installment was $25 more than the first installment, and the third was twice as much as the first. Create an equation to find the amount of each instalment, and then tell how much each instalment was.

8. Solve the following inequality and then graph it on a number line: $-3x \leq 2x+10$.

Lesson 7 POLYNOMIALS TERMINOLOGY

Polynomials are algebraic expressions that are formed by combining numbers, variables, and exponents into algebraic terms. An example of an algebraic term is $3x^2$.

NOTES

Terms in algebraic expressions are separated by addition and subtraction signs. The expression $-4xy^3z^4g$ is just one term since there are no addition or subtraction signs separating the algebraic expressions.

Coefficients are the numbers that are being multiplied by the variables.

A number that stands alone without any variables connected to it is called a **constant**. Examples of a constant are 8 and $\frac{2}{3}$. Notice that there are no variables connected to either of them.

A **constant** is a number that stands alone without any variables attached to it.

Polynomials with one term, two terms, and three terms have special names.

A polynomial with one term is called a **monomial**.
Examples are $8y$, $\frac{2}{7}$, and $-9y^4z$.

Monomial = a polynomial with one term

A polynomial with two terms is called a **binomial**.
Examples are $2x+3$ and $4c^2-7c$.

Binomial = a polynomial with two terms

A polynomial with three terms is called a **trinomial**.
Examples are x^2+3x-5 and x^3+5x+9.

Trinomial = a polynomial with three terms

A polynomial with four or more terms is simply referred to as a **polynomial**.
An example is $4x^3+3x^2-7x+2$.

Example 1

Identify the coefficients, variables, and constants of each of the following polynomials, and name each.

a) $2x-7$

Solution
The coefficient is 2.
The variable is x.
The constant is –7.
This polynomial is a binomial because there are two terms: $2x$ and –7.

NOTES

Terms are separated by addition or subtraction signs.

$3n^3 - 4n + 7$ has three terms.

For negative terms, remember to include the sign in front of the number when identifying the coefficient.

b) $3n^3 - 4n + 7$

Solution
The coefficients are 3 and –4.
The variable is *n*.
The constant is 7.
This polynomial is a trinomial because there are three terms: $3n^3$, $-4n$, and 7.

c) $\frac{1}{5}xyz$

Solution
The coefficient is $\frac{1}{5}$.
The variables are *x*, *y*, and *z*
There is no constant.
The polynomial is a monomial since there is only one term: $\frac{1}{5}xyz$.

PRACTICE EXERCISES

1. Identify the coefficients, variables, and constants of each of the following polynomials, and name each.

a) $6t^2 - 4t$

b) $-2a - 6 + t$

c) $-x^2y + 2x$

d) $5 - d + 3c - p$

e) $\frac{7}{8}x$

f) $x - \frac{3}{5}$

Lesson 8 EVALUATING POLYNOMIALS BY SUBSTITUTION

Polynomials can be evaluated by substituting designated values for the variables into the polynomial. You must then follow the order of operations to evaluate that polynomial.

NOTES

It is important to put brackets around the numbers being substituted back into the equation.

In Example 1, when −2 is put in brackets, its square is +4. However, if you omit the brackets, -2^2 equals -4, which will lead you to a completely different, and incorrect, result.

Example 1

Evaluate each of the following polynomials for the given values.

a) $3x^2+4x-6$, when $x=-2$

Solution

$3(-2)^2+4(-2)-6$

$12-8-6$

-2

Put the value being substituted back into the polynomial in brackets so the negative sign is included wherever it is substituted.

b) $x^{-3}+y^3$, when $x=3$ and $y=-3$

Solution

$(3)^{-3}+(-3)^3$

At this point, you may decide to enter this form of the expression into your calculator to get the solution.

You may also simplify by changing the negative exponents to positive exponents and then evaluating.

$\frac{1}{(3)^3}+(-27)$

$\frac{1}{27}+(-27)$

$-26\frac{26}{27}$ or $-26.\overline{962}$

PRACTICE EXERCISES

1. Evaluate each of the following polynomials for the given values.

a) $2l + 2w$, when $l = 13$ and $w = 10$

b) πr^2, when $r = 15$

c) lwh, when $l = 12$, $w = 9$, and $h = 15$

d) $2x^2 - 7x + 12$, when $x = -4$

e) $m^2 - n^3$, when $m = -5$ and $n = -6$

f) $h^{-2} + 2p^{-3}$, when $h = -3$ and $p = -1$

Lesson 9 USING ALGEBRA TILES AND DIAGRAMS TO ADD AND SUBTRACT POLYNOMIALS

NOTES

Algebra tiles can be used to assist in the addition and subtraction of polynomials. The diagram below shows what each tile represents.

$= +x$ $= -x$ $= +1$ $= -1$ $= +x^2$ $= -x^2$

By using tiles, you can combine like terms in a hands-on fashion. When you put together a negative and a positive tile of the same size, you get zero. This is the process of simplification by adding like terms, with the remainder being the solution. Below is an example of a diagram of the polynomial $x^2 - 3x + 2$.

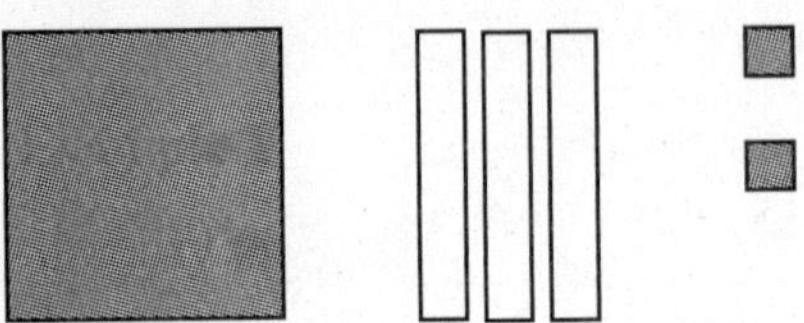

Example 1

The diagram below represents the addition of two polynomials. Draw the diagram of the simplified solution and write the algebraic expression to represent the polynomial. Show the combining of like terms to simplify the expression.

When a positive and negative like term are added together the result is zero.

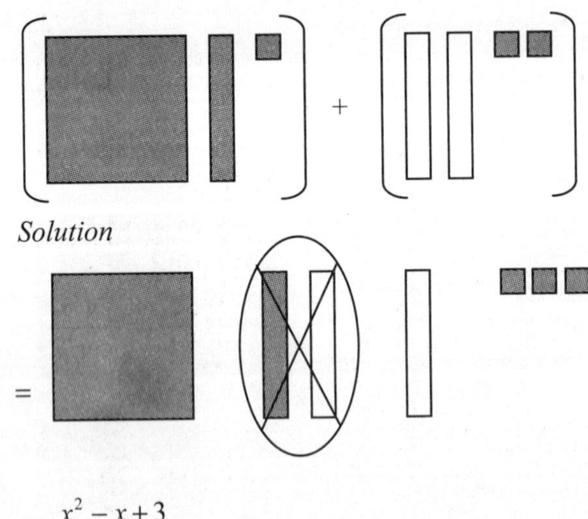

$x^2 - x + 3$

Example 2

Using the symbols for algebraic tiles, draw the diagram that represents $(2x^2 - x + 4) + (x^2 + x + 3)$. Simplify and then write the algebraic solution.

Solution

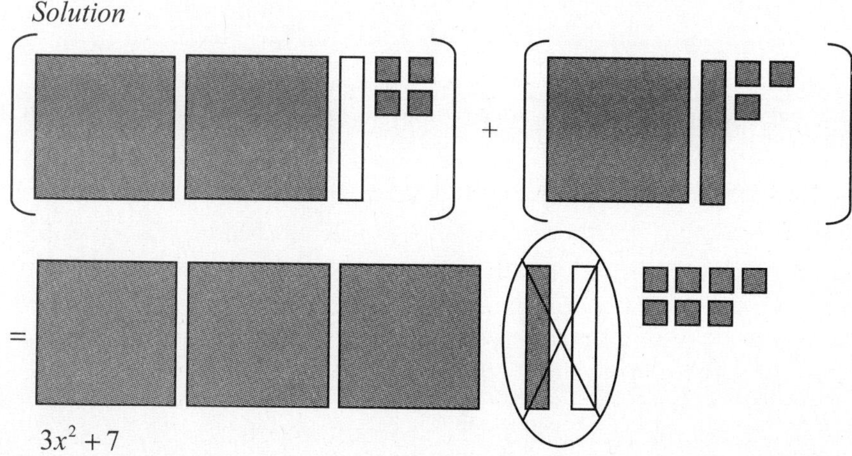

$3x^2 + 7$

NOTES

If you have algebra tiles, you may use them to add instead of drawing out the polynomials.

Remember that opposite values of like terms cancel out and equal zero.

When subtracting polynomials using tiles, change the subtraction sign to an addition sign. The polynomial to the right of the subtraction sign should have all the tiles switched to their opposite sign. This is called the **additive inverse**. Once you have done this, you can combine like terms.

Subtraction means to add the opposite.

Example 3

Draw the diagram that represents $(2x^2 - 3x - 2) - (-x^2 + 2x - 1)$. Simplify and write the algebraic solution.

Solution

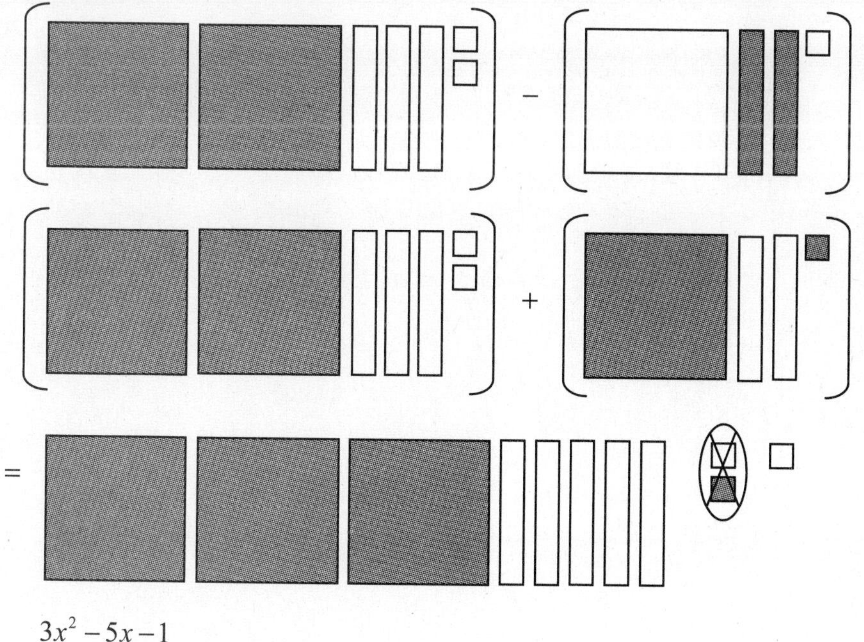

$3x^2 - 5x - 1$

PRACTICE EXERCISES

1. Draw an algebra tile diagram to represent each of the following additions or subtractions of polynomials. Then, use your diagram to simplify each expression and write the algebraic form of the solution.

a) $\left(x^2+3x-6\right)+\left(-x^2+4\right)$

b) $\left(2x^2+x-2\right)+\left(5-3x^2\right)$

c) $\left(-2x^2+x-2\right)-\left(x+3-3x^2\right)$

d) $(x+3)-\left(x^2-2x\right)-\left(5-x^2\right)$

Lesson 10 ADDING AND SUBTRACTING POLYNOMIALS

NOTES

The skills that were used to add and subtract polynomials using algebra tiles can now be applied to the algebraic form of the polynomials. When adding polynomials, drop the brackets and add like terms.

Example 1

Add the following polynomials.

$\left(-x^2-7x-4\right)+\left(5x^2+8x-1\right)$

Solution

$=-x^2-7x-4+5x^2+8x-1$

$=-x^2+5x^2-7x+8x-4-1$ Group like terms together.

$=4x^2+x-5$

Like terms must have the same variables and the same exponents.

When subtracting polynomials, change the subtraction sign to an addition sign and switch the signs of the terms on the right of the subtraction sign to their opposites.

Example 2

Subtract the following polynomials.

$\left(2x^2-4x+6\right)-\left(4x^2-4x+1\right)$

The signs of the terms of the polynomial to the right of the subtraction sign are switched to their opposite sign before like terms are added.

Solution

Change subtraction to addition, and then add the opposite.

$\left(2x^2-4x+6\right)+\left(-4x^2+4x-1\right)$

$=2x^2-4x+6-4x^2+4x-1$

$=2x^2-4x^2-4x+4x+6-1$ Group like terms together.

$=-2x^2+5$

PRACTICE EXERCISES

1. Simplify each of the following polynomials.

   a) $(3x^2+4x-8)+(-2x^2+8x-9)$

   b) $(x^2-7x-3)+(-2x+11)$

   c) $(3x-4x^2)-(5+3x^2)$

d) $\left(-5x^2-6x+1\right)-\left(-2x^2+7-8x\right)$

e) $(3x-5)-(3-6x)+(8x-7)$

f) $\left(6x^2-5x+7\right)-\left(-2x^2-4x-6\right)-(x-5)$

Lesson 11 MULTIPLYING, DIVIDING, AND FACTORING POLYNOMIALS USING ALGEBRA TILES

NOTES

The multiplication of polynomials using algebra tiles is similar to finding the area of a rectangle. You can arrange the tiles to represent length and width and then multiply them by one another to obtain the solution.

In the diagram below, the numbered tile represents the width and the variable tiles represent the length.

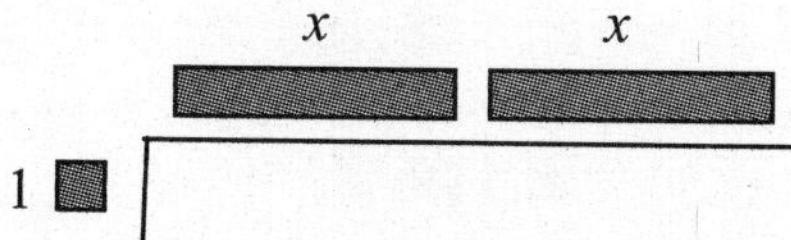

When you multiply these tiles, fill in the blank space to create the area of the rectangle, which represents the solution.

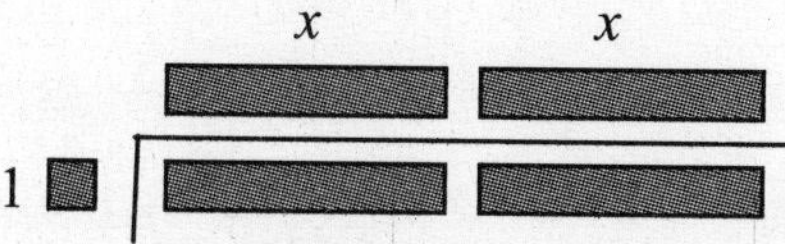

Notice that edge 1 is multiplied by edge $2x$ to get the area $2x$.

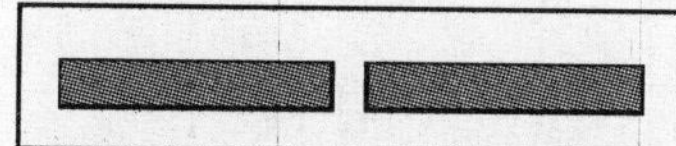

The diagram below illustrates the multiplication of $(2x)(3)$.

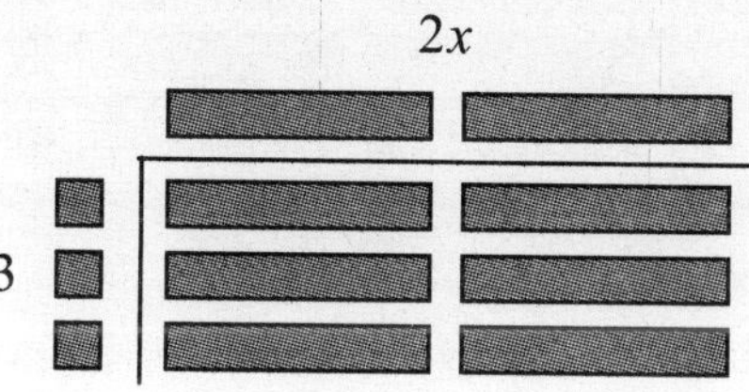

Multiply 1 by x and 1 by x again to get the answer for the first row. Repeat for the second and third rows.

After multiplication is complete, you have the following rectangular area:

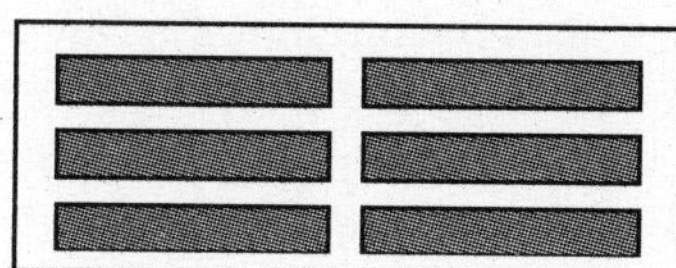

Now you can add like terms to identify the solution, $6x$.

NOTES

Multiply the edge of the length by the edge of the width to get the area.

Example 1

a) $2(x+2)$

Solution

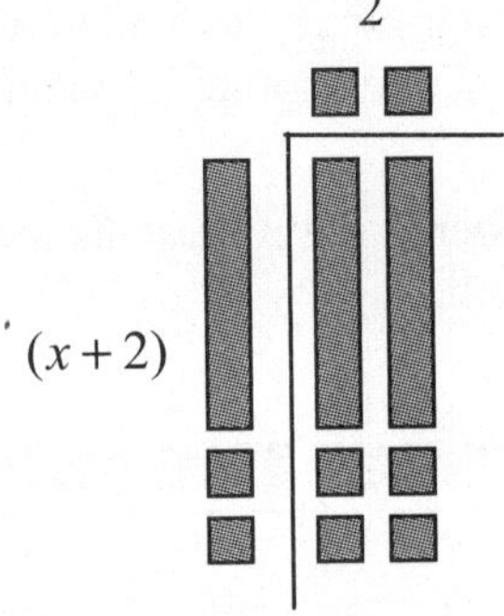

The answer is $2x+4$.

b) $(x+3)(2x+1)$

Solution

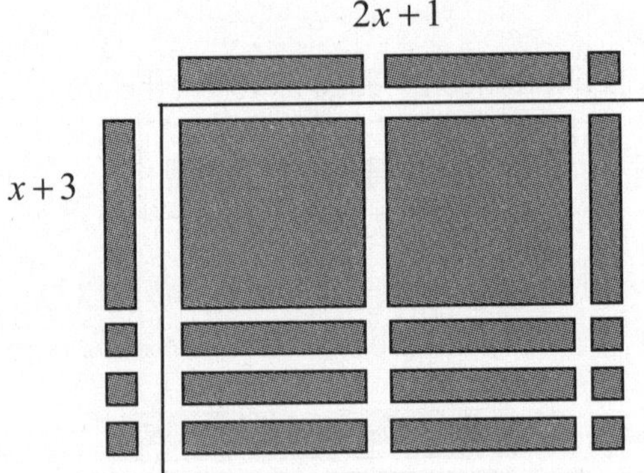

Remember that $(x)(x)=x^2$, so you must use the algebraic tiles that represent x^2 in the multiplication of these polynomials. The answer is $2x^2+7x+3$.

A **factor** is a number that divides evenly into a given number.

Algebra tiles can also be used in the factoring of a given polynomial. A factor is a number that divides evenly into a given number. Factors of 12 are 1, 2, 3, 4, 6, and 12. All of these numbers divide evenly into 12. When algebra tiles are arranged as a rectangle to represent a polynomial, the length and width of the rectangle are factors of the polynomial. If you had a rectangle arranged as the following one, you would say that the factors are 2 and 6 because the width is 2 units long and the length is 6 units long.

2

6

NOTES

Example 2

Identify the factors of the following polynomials by identifying the polynomials that represent the length and the width.

a)

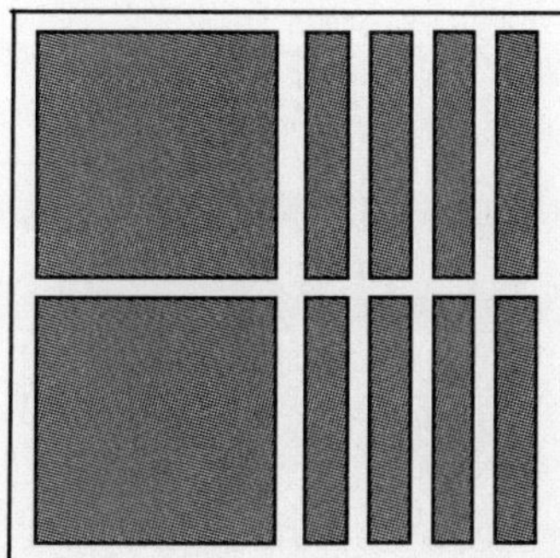

Solution

The polynomial is $2x^2 + 8x$. The left edge has a length of $2x$ and the top has a length of $x + 4$. You can say that $2x$ and $x + 4$ are factors of $2x^2 + 8x$. Since $A = l \times w$, you can also say that $(2x)(x + 4) = 2x^2 + 8x$.

You can check your factoring by multiplying the factored answer. The result should be the original polynomial.

The order in which you write polynomials that are being multiplied does not change the answer: $(3x + 1)(x + 2)$ is the same as $(x + 2)(3x + 1)$.

b)

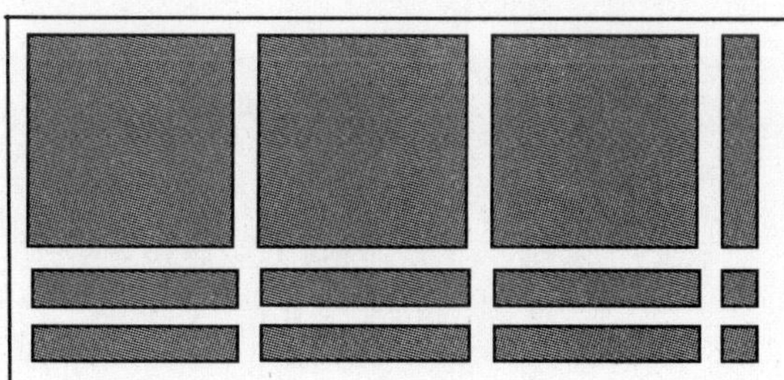

Solution

The polynomial is $3x^2 + 7x + 2$. The factors are $3x + 1$ and $x + 2$. Thus $(3x + 1)(x + 2) = 3x^2 + 7x + 2$.

PRACTICE EXERCISES

1. Draw an algebra tile diagram that represents the multiplication of the following polynomials, and then write the polynomial that represents the area.

a) $3(x+4)$

b) $2x(x+6)$

c) $(x+1)(x+3)$

d) $(2x+3)(x+4)$

2. Given the following diagrams, identify the factors representing the length and width of each polynomial, and then write the equation in the form of $A = l \times x$.

a)

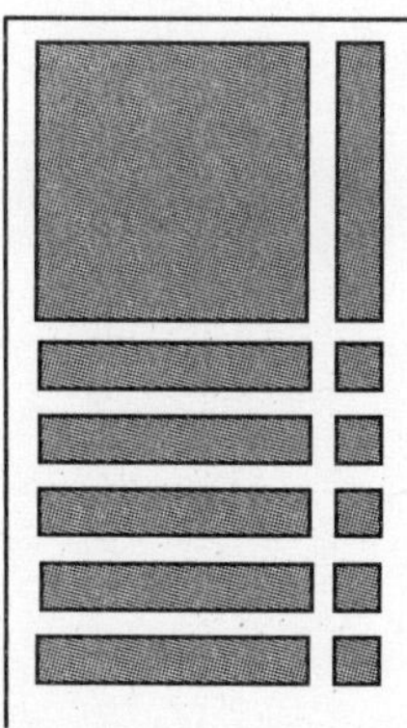

b)

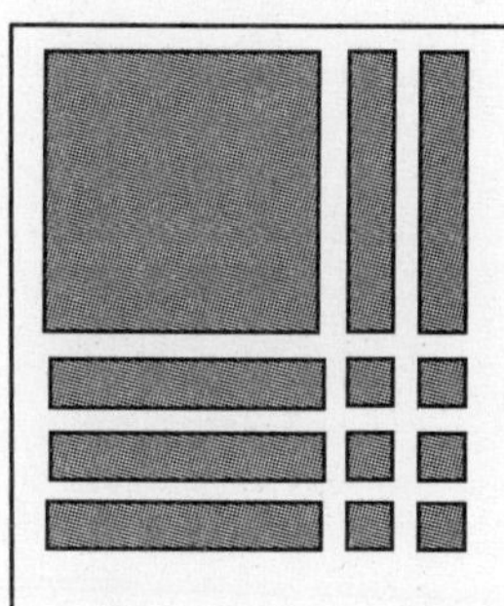

c)

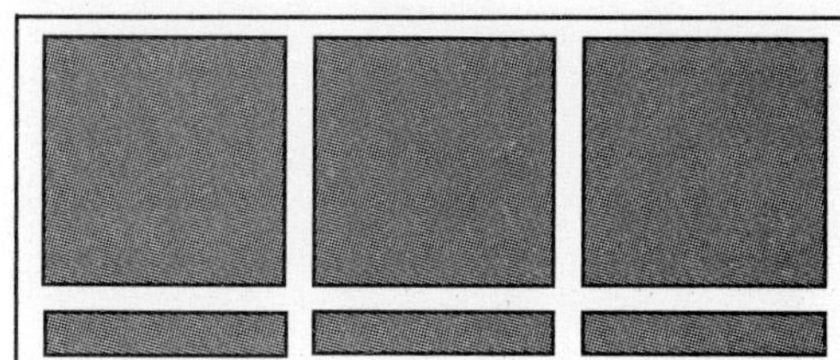

d)

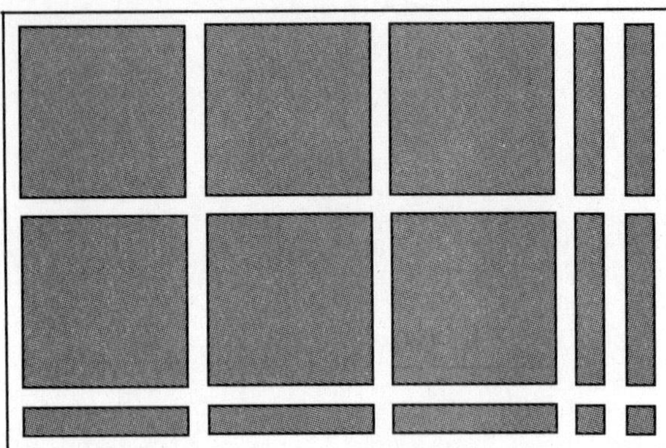

Lesson 12 MULTIPLYING POLYNOMIALS

NOTES

You can multiply polynomials with long-hand multiplication. Simply treat each term as a separate digit, multiply the terms out, and add the rows just as you would digits. This is called vertical multiplication.

Example 1

Multiply the monomials $(2x)$ and $\left(3x^2\right)$.

Solution

When multiplying monomials, multiply the coefficients together and add exponents of the same base together.

$(2)(3)(x)\left(x^2\right) = 6x^{1+2} = 6x^3$

When multiplying terms with the same base, add the exponents.

Example 2

Multiply a monomial and a trinomial: $3\left(2x^2 - 6x + 4\right)$.

Solution

Apply the **distributive property** and multiply the term outside the brackets by each term inside the brackets.

$(3)\left(2x^2\right) + (3)(-6x) + (3)(4)$

or

$$\begin{array}{r} 2x^2 - 6x + 4 \\ \times \quad\quad\quad 3 \\ \hline 6x^2 - 18x + 12 \end{array}$$

Notice that addition signs are written between each group being multiplied. Minus six (– 6) can be written as negative six (–6) in the expansion when applying the distributive property.

$6x^2 - 18x + 12$

NOTES

Binomials are polynomials with two terms.

Terms are separated by addition and subtraction signs.

The acronym **FOIL** is often used to remember how to multiply binomials.

First terms
Outer terms
Inner terms
Last terms

Example 3

Multiply a binomial and a binomial: $(x+2)(x-3)$.

Solution

The distributive property is applied so that the first term is multiplied by the expression in the second bracket and the second term is then multiplied by the expression in the second bracket. Then, like terms are added to get the simplified solution.

$$(x)(x-3)+(2)(x-3)$$
$$=x^2-3x+2x-6$$

or

$$\begin{array}{r} x+2 \\ \times x-3 \\ \hline 3x-6 \\ +x^2+2x+0 \\ \hline \end{array}$$

The multiplication of two binomials can also be done by multiplying according to the following order: **F**irst terms, **O**uter terms, **I**nner terms, and **L**ast terms. The bolded letters for each step form the acronym **FOIL**.

First

$(x+2)(x-3)$
↑ ↑
$x \times x = x^2$

Outer

$(x+2)(x-3)$
↑ ↑
$x \times -3 = -3x$

Inner

$(x+2)(x-3)$
↑ ↑
$2 \times x = 2x$

Last

$(x+2)(x-3)$
↑ ↑
$2 \times -3 = -6$

$$x^2-3x+2x-6$$
$$=x^2-x-6$$

Example 4

Multiply $(2x-1)(3x+2)$.

NOTES

Solution

$(2x)(3x)+(2x)(2)+(-1)(3x)+(-1)(2)$

$=6x^2+4x-3x-2$

$=6x^2+1x-2$

or

$$\begin{array}{r} 2x-1 \\ \underline{3x+2} \\ 4x-2 \\ \underline{6x^2-3+0} \\ 6x^2+1x-2 \end{array}$$

PRACTICE EXERCISES

1. Find the product of each of the following expressions.

a) $(3x^2)(-4x^3)$

b) $(x^2y)(4x^3y^2)$

c) $(3mn^3)(-9m^4)$

d) $\left(\frac{2}{3}a^3b^4\right)\left(\frac{3}{5}a^2b^5\right)$

2. Find the product of each of the following expressions.

a) $(-2)(x^2-x-6)$

b) $(3x)(4x^2-2x-3)$

c) $(3xy)(-5x^2+2xy-3y^2)$

d) $(7ab)(-2b^3+6ab^2-4a^5)$

3. Find the product of each of the following expressions.

a) $(x+5)(x+6)$

b) $(2x+5)(x-3)$

c) $(2x-3)(x-4)$

d) $(3x-7)(-x+8)$

e) $2(x+4)(3x+2)$

Lesson 13 FACTORING POLYNOMIALS

NOTES

Factors are numbers that divide evenly into a given number with no remainder.

With polynomials, the GCF can be
1. a coefficient only
2. a coefficient and a variable
3. one or more variables only

To form the GCF, follow this order:
1. Coefficient (number)
2. Variable(s) (letter)

When factoring polynomials, your first step should be to look for the Greatest Common Factor (**GCF**). To find the greatest common factor, you can list all the factors of each term and then choose the highest one common to all terms.

Example 1

Find the (GCF) of 12 and 18.

Solution

List all the factors of each number and pick the highest one common to both.

The factors of 12 are 1, 2, 3, 4, 6, and 12.

The factors of 18 are 1, 2, 3, 6, 9, and 18.

The GCF is 6.

The same process can be used to find the GCF for polynomials.

Example 2

Find the GCF of $4x^2$ and $12x^3y$.

Solutions

Factors of $4x^2$ are 1, 2, 4, x, and x.

Factors of $12x^3y$ are 1, 2, 3, 4, 6, 12, x, x, x, and y.

The GCF for the coefficient is 4. For the variable, take the greatest number of a variable that occurs in each term. Since the greatest number of *x's* that occur in each term is 2, the GCF for the variables is $x \times x = x^2$. Do not include *y* because it is not common to both terms; thus, it is not a common factor. The GCF of $4x^2$ and $12x^3y$ is $4x^2$.

Example 3

Find the GCF of $-3x^2y^2$, $6xy^3$, $15x^3y^3$.

Solution

$-3x^2y^2 = -1, 3, x, x, y, y$

$6xy^3 = 1, 2, 3, 6, x, y, y, y$

$15x^3y^3 = 1, 3, 5, 15, x, x, x, y, y, y$

The GCF is $3xy^2$.

To factor a polynomial, first find the GCF of each term. Next, divide each term by the GCF. Finally, multiply the GCF and the quotient. This is the factor of the original polynomial.

Example 4

Factor $6x^3 + 3x^2$.

Solution

$6x^3 = 1, 2, 3, 6, x, x, x$

$3x^2 = 1, 3, x, x$

The GCF is $3x^2$.

Divide each term by the GCF.

$$\frac{6x^3}{3x^2} + \frac{3x^2}{3x^2} = 2x + 1$$

Multiply the quotient by the GCF.

$3x^2(2x + 1)$ is the factored solution.

NOTES

Circle the GCF for the coefficient and for the variables to help you identify the GCF of the polynomial.

A **quotient** is the answer to a division question.

NOTES

When factoring trinomials, first look for a GCF.
If there is no GCF, then write the trinomial as a product of two binomials. Factoring is the inverse operation of multiplying.

Consider the following product of binomials:

$(x+3)(x-5)=(x)(x)+(x)(-5)+(3)(x)+(3)(-5)$

Use the FOIL method of multiplication.

$(x+3)(x-5)=x^2-5x+3x-15$

$(x+3)(x-5)=x^2-2x-15$

Notice that the first two terms of the binomials are multiplied to get the first term of the trinomial: $(x)(x)=x^2$.

The last two terms of the binomials are multiplied to give you the last term in the trinomial: $(3)(-5)=-15$.

The answer to a multiplication problem is called the **product**.

The last term in the trinomial is called the **product**.
Since the middle term in the trinomial is found by adding the like terms together, the middle term in the trinomial is called the **sum**.

The answer to an addition problem is called the **sum**.

Example 5

Factor x^2+6x+8.

Solution

First look for a GCF. If there is no GCF, then identify the **product** and **sum** values in the trinomial.

Sum = 6
Product = 8

Factors are two numbers that are multiplied to give the product.

Then, list all the factors of the product until you find two numbers that multiply to a product of 8 and add to a sum of 6.

Product	Sum
$1\times8=8$	$1+8=9$
$2\times4=8$	$2+4=6$
$-1\times-8=8$	$-1+(-8)=-9$
$-2\times-4=8$	$-2+(-4)=-6$

NOTES

The only pair of numbers that adds to 6 is 4 and 2.
Now, create your factored solution of two binomials.
Since $(x)(x) = x^2$, we know the first term in the binomials.
Therefore, you have
$(x + \_\ )(x + \_\ )$

The two numbers that fit the product and sum are inserted for the second term in each binomial. The order does not matter, but the proper sign of the number must be inserted.
$(x+2)(x+4)$

Now, you can check your solution by using FOIL.

Use FOIL to check your solution.

$(x+2)(x+4) = x^2 + 4x + 2x + 8$

$(x+2)(x+4) = x^2 + 6x + 8$

You can also check by using vertical multiplication.

$$\begin{array}{r} x+2 \\ \times x+4 \\ \hline 4x+8 \\ x^2+2x+0 \\ \hline x^2+6x+8 \end{array}$$

Example 6

Factor $x^2 - 11x + 18$.

Solution
Sum = -11
Product = 18 Factor the product.

Product	Sum
$1 \times 18 = 18$	$1 + 18 = 19$
$2 \times 9 = 18$	$2 + 9 = 11$
$3 \times 6 = 18$	$3 + 6 = 9$
$-1 \times -18 = 18$	$-1 + (-18) = -19$
$-2 \times -9 = 18$	$-2 + (-9) = -11$
$-3 \times -6 = 18$	$-3 + (-6) = -9$

The two numbers that work are -2 and -9.
The factored answer is $(x-2)(x-9)$.

NOTES

After factoring out the GCF, try to factor the trinomial that remains by identifying the product and sum.

Example 7

Factor completely $3m^2 - 18m + 15$.

Solution

First, look for a GCF.

The GCF is 3.

Divide each term by 3.

$$\frac{3m^2}{3} - \frac{18m}{3} + \frac{15}{3} = m^2 - 6m + 5$$

The first stage of factoring is $3(m^2 - 6m + 5)$.

Now, see if the trinomial can be factored any further.

$m^2 - 6m + 5$

Sum = – 6

Product = 5

Product	Sum
$1 \times 5 = 5$	$1 + 5 = 6$
$-1 \times -5 = 5$	$-1 - 5 = -6$

The factored trinomial is $(x-1)(x-5)$.

The completely factored final solution includes the GCF with the factored trinomial.

The final solution is $3(x-1)(x-5)$.

PRACTICE EXERCISES

1. Factor each of the following expressions.

a) $10x+15$

b) $12x^2-4x$

c) $18x^3+12x^2-6x$

d) $21x^2y-14xy^2+28x^3y^3$

e) $2m^3n^4-8m^2n^3$

2. Simplify, and then factor, the following expressions.

a) $12x-15+6x-18$

b) $6n^2-3n+n^2-18n+7$

c) $9-5m+m^2+6m^2+5+12m$

3. Factor each of the following expressions.

a) $x^2 + 8x + 15$

b) $x^2 + 15x + 56$

c) $x^2 - 7x + 12$

d) $x^2 - 5x - 14$

e) $a^2 - 10a - 24$

f) $a^2 + 23a - 24$

g) $n^2 + 17n + 30$

h) $n^2 + 8n - 20$

i) $n^2 + 7n + 10$

4. Completely factor each of the following expressions.

a) $2x^2 - 10x + 8$

b) $m^3 - 2m^2 - 48m$

c) $5c^2 - 55c + 150$

Lesson 14 DIVIDING A POLYNOMIAL BY A MONOMIAL

NOTES

When dividing a polynomial by a monomial, divide each term by the polynomial by the monomial.

Example 1

Find the quotient of $\frac{4x^3+8x^2-16x}{2x}$.

Solution

Divide each term in the numerator by the denominator.

$$\frac{4x^3+8x^2-16x}{2x}$$
$$=\frac{4x^3}{2x}+\frac{8x^2}{2x}-\frac{16x}{2x}$$
$$=2x^2+4x-8$$

Example 2

Find the quotient of $\frac{4n^2+12n-20}{-4}$.

Solution

$$\frac{4n^2+12n-20}{-4}$$
$$=\frac{4n^2}{-4}+\frac{12n}{-4}-\frac{20}{-4}$$
$$=-n^2-3n+5$$

PRACTICE EXERCISES

Find the quotient of each of the following expressions.

1. a) $\dfrac{12x^2 - 8x}{4x}$

b) $\dfrac{12x^3 - 20x^2}{-2x^2}$

c) $\dfrac{-28 + 14x}{-7}$

d) $\dfrac{15x^4 - 30x^3 + 35x^2}{5x^2}$

e) $\dfrac{4n^2 - 12n - 6}{4}$

f) $\dfrac{2a^2 + 15 - 3a}{-3}$

PRACTICE QUIZ 2

1. Identify the following parts of the polynomial expression $-6x^2+3y-8$.

a) Coefficients

b) Variables

c) Constant

2. Evaluate the polynomial expression $2x^3-4x^2+7$ for the value $x=-2$.

3. Use algebra tile diagrams to show the simplification of $(4x-3x^2+1)-(2x^2-4x-3)$.

4. Simplify $\left(8x^2-3x-12\right)-\left(-6x^2+4x-8\right)$.

5. Simplify the following expression.

a) $-4\left(5g^2-9g+\dfrac{3}{4}\right)$

b) $(4x-3)(2x+5)$

6. Factor each of the following polynomials

a) $m^2+3m-40$

b) $n^2 - 10n + 25$

7. Find the quotient of $\dfrac{15x - 20 - 30x^3}{-5}$.

Lesson 15 USING EQUATION SKILLS TO SOLVE PROBLEMS

NOTES

You can see that as problems become more and more complex, there is more benefit to using algebra skills to solve them. Remember the following key skills:

- use a variable to represent an unknown that you are trying to find
- write an equation that represents the problem
- solve for the variable
- give the solution to the problem in a complete sentence

Example 1

It takes one water hose 2 min to fill a hot tub and another hose 3 min to fill the same hot tub. How long will it take to fill the hot tub if both hoses are used at the same time?

Solution

Let $x =$ the time it takes both hoses to fill the tub

Since we are given that the first hose takes 2 min to fill the tub, we can quickly calculate that it will fill $\frac{1}{2}$ of the tub in 1 min, and therefore we can further reason that it will fill $\frac{x}{2}$ tubs in x minutes

Using the same reasoning, the second hose will fill $\frac{x}{3}$ tubs in x minutes.

Together, the two hoses will fill one whole tub. Thus, an equation can be created where the fraction of the tub filled by the first hose is added to the fraction filled by the second hose so the sum equals one full tub.

$$\frac{x}{2}+\frac{x}{3}=1$$

Remember to multiply each term by the LCD to eliminate the fractions.

Eliminate the fractions and multiply.

$$\left(\frac{\overset{3}{\cancel{6}}}{1}\right)\left(\frac{x}{\underset{1}{\cancel{2}}}\right)=\left(\frac{\overset{2}{\cancel{6}}}{1}\right)\left(\frac{x}{\underset{1}{\cancel{3}}}\right)=(1)\left(\frac{6}{1}\right)$$

$$3x+2x=6$$

$$5x=6$$

$$\frac{5x}{5}=\frac{6}{5}$$

$$x=1.2$$

$$1.2\text{ min}\times\frac{60\text{ s}}{1\text{ min}}=72\text{ s}$$

It will take 1.2 min or 72 s for both hoses to fill the hot tub.

NOTES

Example 2

Jenna received 77%, 69%, 81% and 76% on her science tests. What mark does she need on her fifth test in order to achieve an average of 80%?

Solution

Let $x =$ her mark on the fifth test.

To find the average, add the test marks together and divide by the number of tests.

$$\frac{77+69+81+76+x}{5}=80$$

$$\frac{303+x}{5}=80$$

$$\left(\frac{\overset{1}{\cancel{5}}}{1}\right)\frac{(303+x)}{\underset{1}{\cancel{5}}}=\left(\frac{5}{1}\right)80 \qquad \text{Reduce}$$

$$303+x=400$$
$$x=97$$

Jenna needs a mark of 97% on her fifth test in order to achieve an average of 80%.

PRACTICE EXERCISES

1. Conveyor belt A fills a truck with gravel in 15 min. Conveyor belt B fills the same truck in 20 min. If the company wants to speed up the process and have both conveyors fill the truck at the same time, how long will it take them to fill it?

2. So far this term, Colleen has received the following marks on her math tests: 74%, 90%, and 86%. What mark will she need on her fourth test to achieve an average of 85%?

3. A particular swimming pool is filled by means of three pipes. Individually, the first pipe can fill the pool in 8 h, the second can fill it in 12 h, and the third pipe can fill it in 24 h. When all three pipes are in use at the same time, how long does it take to fill the pool?

REVIEW SUMMARY

- When writing an equation from a word problem, remember to look for key words that represent math symbols.
- When manipulating equations, use inverse operations to isolate the desired variable on one side of the equation.
- When using algebra tiles to solve equations, put positive and negative tiles of the same size together to cancel like terms (the zero principle of elimination).
- When solving equations with brackets, simplify first.
- If an equation has a denominator, multiply all terms by the LCD to reduce the denominators to 1.
- When solving word problems, identify math expressions for all unknowns. Use the expressions to aid in creating an equation to solve the problem.
- When multiplying or dividing each side of an inequality by the same negative number, reverse the inequality sign.
- When graphing inequalities, use ○ or ● to show if the value on the number line is included.
- Constants are terms that stand alone with no variable.
- Coefficients are the numbers being multiplied by a variable.
- When substituting a value into an expression, make sure to put brackets around the number being inserted.
- When subtracting using algebra tiles, switch the subtraction sign to addition and change the tiles to its right to their opposite signs.
- When multiplying polynomials using algebra tiles, let one polynomial represent the length of a rectangle and the other represent the width.
- When factoring using algebra tiles, the length and width represent factors of the polynomial when it is arranged in a rectangle.
- When factoring, look for the greatest common factor (GCF) first.

- When factoring trinomials, identify the numbers that represent the sum and the product. Use the factors of the product to find two numbers that give both the sum and product of the trinomial.
- When dividing a polynomial by a monomial, divide each individual term in the polynomial by the monomial.
- For combined rate problems, make x the numerator of each rate, and then make the sum of these fractions equal 1. Solve the equation.
- To find an average, divide the sum of the terms by the number of terms.

PRACTICE TEST

Use the following table to answer the first question.

n	1	2	3	4	5
Value of math expression	3	5	7	9	11

1. Which of the following math expressions relates the values in the table?

A. $2n-1$ **B.** $2n+1$ **C.** $3n-2$ **D.** $3n+3$

2. Which of the following pairs of expressions is equivalent?

A. $2(n-4)$, $2n-4$

B. $2(n-4)$, $2n+4$

C. $2(n-4)$, $2n-8$

D. $3(n+2)$, $3n+8$

3. If the length of a rectangle is represented by $2x+1$ and the width of the same rectangle is represented by $2x-3$, then the perimeter of the rectangle would be represented by

A. $4x-2$ **B.** $8x-2$ **C.** $8x-6$ **D.** $8x-4$

Use the following information to answer next question.

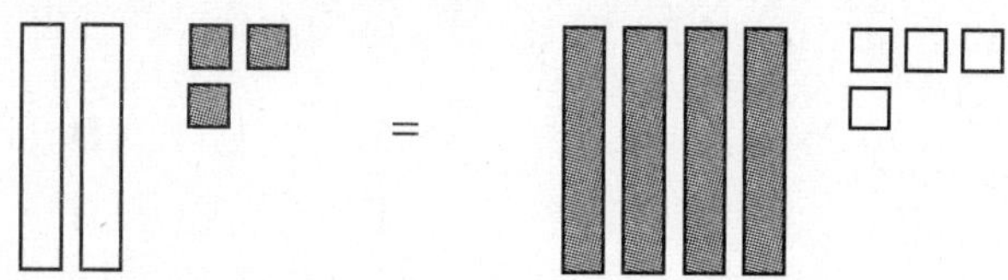

4. Which of the following equations is represented by the group of tiles above?

A. $2x-3=-4x+4$ **B.** $-2x+3=4x-4$ **C.** $3x-2=-4+4x$ **D.** $3x-2=4-4x$

5. The formula for the volume of a rectangular prism is $V=lwh$. If the volume of a rectangular prism is 864 cm^2, its length is 12 cm, and its width is 8 cm, then its height is

A. 9 cm **B.** 8 cm **C.** 7 cm **D.** 6 cm

6. The solution to $3(2x-14)=-12$ is

A. $x=-5$ **B.** $x=\frac{1}{6}$ **C.** $x=5$ **D.** $x=6$

7. Which of the following graphs represents the solution to the inequality $4x-7 \geq 5x-9$?

A.

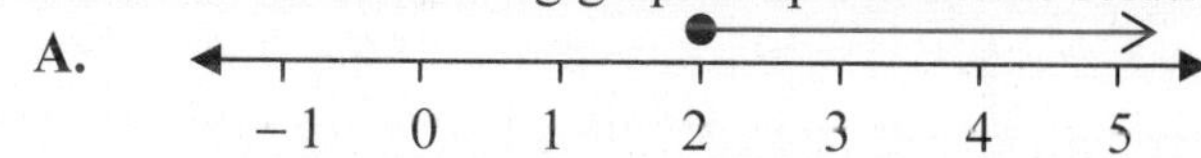

B.

-1 0 1 2 3 4 5

C.

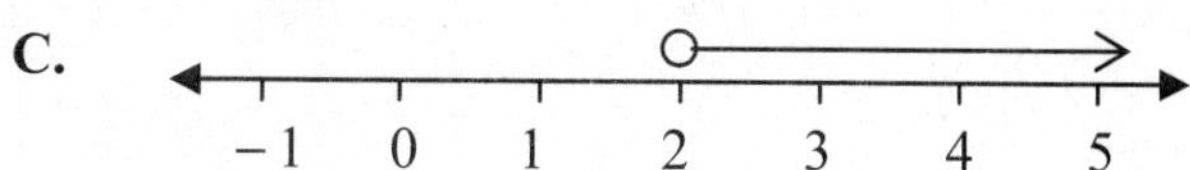

D.

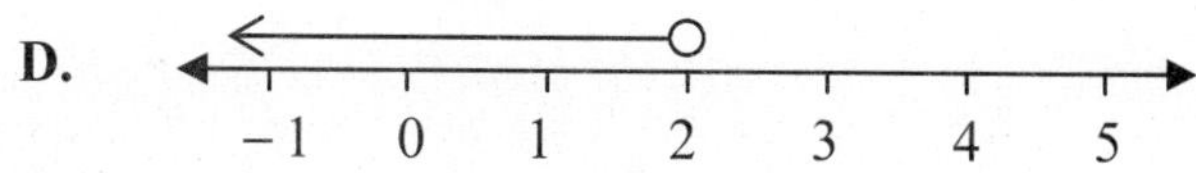

8. The solution of the equation $\frac{-1}{4} = \frac{1}{8} - \frac{x}{2}$ is

A. $x = -0.5$ **B.** $x = -0.75$ **C.** $x = 0.5$ **D.** $x = 0.75$

9. The largest coefficient in the polynomial $10x^2 - 13x + 20$ is

A. –13 **B.** 130 **C.** 13 **D.** 20

10. When factored, $9p - 3$ is

A. $3(3p)$ **B.** $9(p-3)$ **C.** $3(3p-1)$ **D.** $3(3p-3)$

11. Jim is 3 times as old as Ed. Six years ago, the sum of their ages was 48. How old are they now?

12. Simplify $(3 - 7x + 5x^2) - (8x - 9x^2 - 4)$.

13. Expand and simplify $(2x-7)(4x+5)$.

14. Expand and simplify $-5p\left(4p^3+5p-7p^2\right)$.

15. Completely factor $3x^2+3x-36$.

16. Find the quotient of $\dfrac{32x^2y^3-40x^4y^2}{-8xy^2}$.

17. An outdoor pool can be filled with a black hose or a green hose. The green hose takes 30 min to fill the pool. The black hose takes 15 min to fill it. If both hoses are used at the same time, how long does it take to fill the pool?

18. A sequence of numbers is given as 1, 1, 2, 3, 5, 8, 13, _____ , _____.
Find the next two numbers in the sequence.

19. Write an equation to represent for the following statement.
"The sum of three consecutive numbers is 33."

20. Draw a algebra tile diagram to represent the following equation $3x-2=-2x-5$.

SHAPE AND SPACE

When you are finished this unit, you should be able to . . .

- explain the meaning of sine, cosine, and tangent ratios in right triangles (SO 1)
- use sine, cosine, and tangent ratios to solve missing sides and angles in right triangles (SO 2)
- use a calculator to find sine, cosine, and tangent ratios for an unknown side or angle (SO 3)
- solve problems by drawing a right triangle to represent the problem and then solve for the desired side or angle (SO 4)
- identify the relationship between the volume of a prism and volume of a pyramid (SO 5)
- identify the relationship between the volume of a cylinder and volume of a cone (SO 5)
- solve design problems in three dimensions by calculating and applying rate of volume to surface area for a rectangular prism (SO 6)
- solve design problems in two dimensions by calculating and applying rate of area to perimeter (SO 7)
- give a definition for similar triangles (SO 8)
- find missing sides in similar triangles (SO 8)
- solve problems involving similar triangles (SO 8)
- give a definition for congruent triangles (SO 9)
- identify why triangles are congruent by applying the properties of SSS, SAS, ASA (SO 9)
- classify triangles as congruent or similar (SO 10)
- given a 3-D model, draw its front, top, and side views (SO 11)
- given the front, top, and side views, draw a 3-D sketch on isometric dot paper (SO 12)
- recognize and draw the locus of points in solving problems (SO 13)
- draw a shape given a reflection, transformation, or rotation (SO 14)
- draw a shape given a combination of reflections, rotations, and transformations (SO 15)
- draw the dilation image of a shape (SO 16)
- given a final image, identify the translation that was done to the original shape to get the final image (SO 15)
- show that a triangle and its dilation image are similar (SO 16)
- show that triangles that have been translated, rotated, or reflected are congruent to the original triangle (SO 17)

PREREQUISITE SKILLS AND KNOWLEDGE

Prior to beginning this unit, you should be able to. . .

- calculate a missing side in right triangle using the Pythagorean theorem
- determine the area and perimeter of quadrilaterals and circles
- calculate the surface area and volume of any right prism or cylinder
- understand the definitions of surface area and volume and apply them to solve problems
- calculate the area of irregular shapes
- measure and calculate the surface area and volume of three-dimensional objects
- identify a polygon as a square, trapezoid, parallelogram, rectangle, rhombus, square, or kite
- build three-dimensional objects, given a net
- identify enlargements and reductions of drawings or shapes
- draw scale diagrams
- solve problems using scale diagrams

Lesson 1 THE TANGENT RATIO AND RIGHT TRIANGLES

Trigonometry deals with the relationships between the angles of right triangles and the ratios of specific sides to the angles. When working with trigonometry, you must be able to identify the hypotenuse, side opposite, and side adjacent to the **angle under discussion**.

NOTES

The **side opposite** is the side that is across from the angle under discussion. Start from the vertex of the angle and go directly across the triangle to the opposite side.

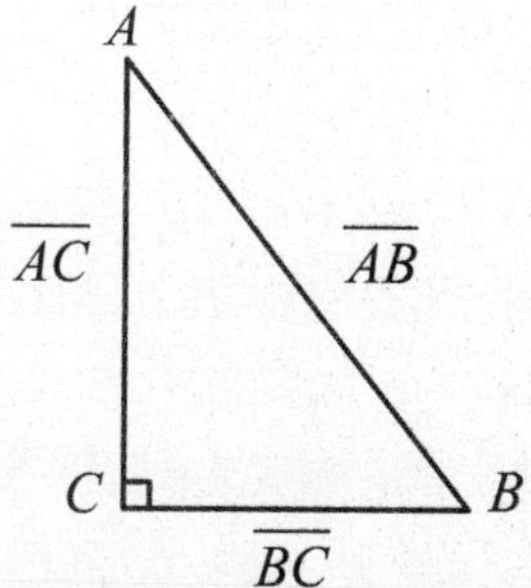

The **vertex** is the point where two sides join.

The **angle under discussion** is the angle you are starting from.

In looking at the diagram of ΔABC above, you can see that the side opposite of angle B is $\overline{AC}$. The side opposite of angle A is $\overline{CB}$.

The **hypotenuse** is the side opposite a right angle.

Since angle C is a right angle, its opposite side, $\overline{AB}$, has a special name: the **hypotenuse**. In any right triangle, the side opposite of the right angle is always called the hypotenuse. The **adjacent** side is one of the sides that forms the angle, but it is never hypotenuse.

The opposite and adjacent sides change depending on which angle is under discussion. In the diagram of triangle ABC above, angle B is formed by the joining of $\overline{AB}$ and $\overline{CB}$. The adjacent side of angle B is $\overline{CB}$ because $\overline{AB}$ is the hypotenuse. Angle A is made formed by joining $\overline{AB}$ and $\overline{AC}$. The adjacent side to angle A is $\overline{AC}$ because $\overline{AB}$ is the hypotenuse.

NOTES

Example 1

Use the diagram below to answer the following question.

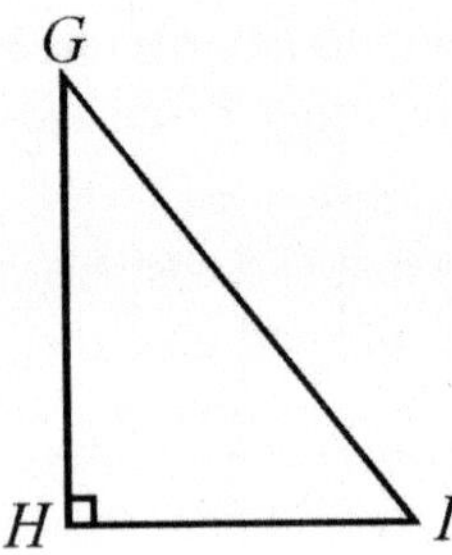

For ΔGHI, identify the

a) hypotenuse
b) side opposite to angle G
c) side adjacent to angle G
d) side opposite to angle I
e) side adjacent to angle I

Solution

A side identified as $\overline{GI}$ is the same as $\overline{IG}$.

a) The hypotenuse is the side opposite of the right angle: $\overline{GI}$.

b) The side across from angle G is $\overline{HI}$.

c) Angle G is made by the connection of $\overline{GH}$ and $\overline{GI}$. Since $\overline{GI}$ is the hypotenuse, $\overline{GH}$ is the adjacent side.

d) The side across from angle I is $\overline{GH}$.

e) Angle I is formed by the connection of $\overline{HI}$ and $\overline{GI}$. Since $\overline{GI}$ is the hypotenuse side, $\overline{HI}$ is the adjacent side.

Acute angles are those that are less than 90°.

Identification of the opposite or adjacent side depends on the angle under discussion. The angles under discussion are always acute angles in a right triangle.

The tangent ratio in a right triangle, where angle A is an acute angle can be identified as $\tan A = \dfrac{\text{length of the side opposite } \angle A}{\text{length of the side adjacent to } \angle A}$.

NOTES

Example 2

Use the diagram below to answer the following questions.

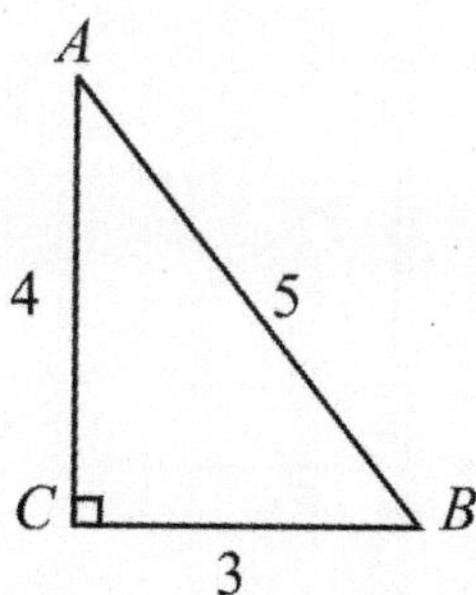

a) Find the ratio for tan A.
b) Find the ratio for tan B.

Solution

a) $\tan A = \frac{3}{4}$

b) $\tan B = \frac{4}{3}$

Angles have set ratios to the lengths of their sides. When working with trigonometry, make sure that your calculator is in degree mode. You can then use your calculator to get the side ratio that relates to the various acute angles.

For example, if you type tan 30° into your calculator, you will get 0.577 (rounded to 3 decimal places).

Written as a ratio, $\tan 30° = \frac{0.577}{1}$.

This is illustrated in the diagram below.

0.577

30°

1

$\text{Tan } \theta = \frac{\text{opposite}}{\text{adjacent}}$

The tangent of any 30° angle can always be reduced to a ratio of $\frac{0.577}{1}$.

This represents a constant ratio between the opposite and adjacent sides of any 30° angle.

NOTES

Example 3

Diagram and explain the meaning of tan 35°. Round the decimal value to three decimal places.

Solution

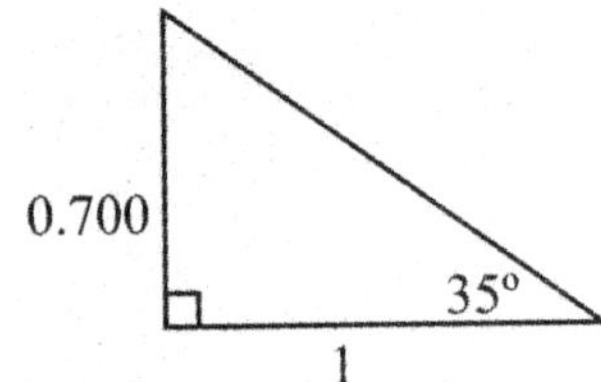

$\tan 35° = \frac{0.700}{1}$. This means that whenever you take tan 35° of a right triangle, the ratio of the side opposite the 35° angle to the side adjacent to it will always reduce to the ratio $\frac{0.700}{1}$.

You can also say that the side opposite is 0.700 times as long as the side adjacent.

The tangent ratio may also be used to help find unknown sides in a right triangle.

Example 4

For triangle ABC below, find the length of $\overline{BC}$ to the nearest tenth of a centimetre.

Solution

Start from the given angle of 25°. Identify the ratio for tan 25°.

$$\tan 25^\circ = \frac{\overline{BC}}{\overline{AC}}$$

Tangent $A = \dfrac{\text{opposite side}}{\text{adjacent side}}$

Replace the known values from the triangle.

$$\tan 25^\circ = \frac{\overline{BC}}{4}$$

$$\tan 25^\circ \times 4 = 1.9$$

$$\overline{BC} = 1.9$$

Make sure your calculator is in degree mode.

You can also find the length of $\overline{BC}$ using your calculator.

First, find tan 25° to 3 decimal places.

$$0.466 = \frac{\overline{BC}}{4}$$

Write the decimal equivalent to tan 25° as a fraction.

$$\frac{0.466}{1} \times \frac{\overline{BC}}{4}$$

Cross-multiply. Remember that one cross equals the other.

$$0.466 \times 4 = 1 \times (\overline{BC})$$

$$1.9 = \overline{BC}$$

The length of $\overline{BC}$ is 1.9 cm.

NOTES

Example 5

For triangle *MNO* below, find the length of $\overline{NO}$ to the nearest tenth of a centimetre.

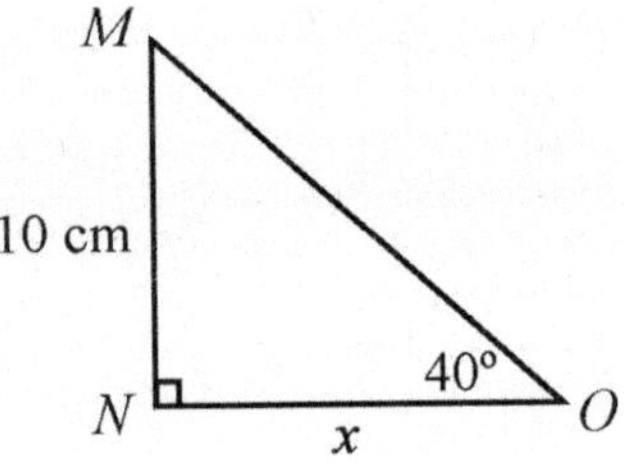

Solution

$\tan 40° = \dfrac{\overline{MN}}{\overline{NO}}$

$\tan 40° = \dfrac{10}{\overline{NO}}$

Find the decimal equivalent to tan 40°.

$0.839 = \dfrac{10}{\overline{NO}}$

$\dfrac{0.839}{1} = \dfrac{10}{\overline{NO}}$

Cross-multiply.

$0.839 \times (\overline{NO}) = 1 \times 10$

Divide both sides by 0.839 to get the solution to $\overline{NO}$.

$\dfrac{0.839 \times (\overline{NO})}{0.839} = \dfrac{10}{0.839}$

$\overline{NO} = 11.9$

The length of side $\overline{NO}$ is 11.9 cm.

The calculator may also be used to assist in finding any angle of a right triangle, given the tangent ratio for its sides.

NOTES

Example 6

For triangle *ABC* below, find the measure of angle *A* to the nearest degree.

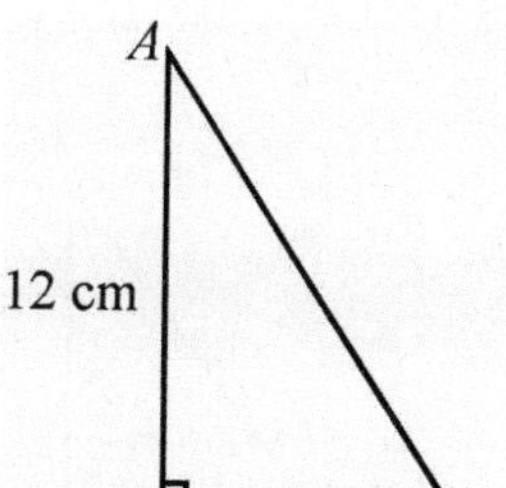

Solution

$\tan A = \frac{BC}{AB}$

Since the angle under discussion is angle *A*, identify its opposite and adjacent sides.

$\tan A = \frac{8}{12}$

When finding the angle using the ratio of its sides, use the $\tan^{-1}$ button on your calculator.

$\angle A = \tan^{-1}\left(\frac{8}{12}\right)$

$\angle A = 33.69$

$\angle A = 34°$

The measure of angle *A* is 34°.

PRACTICE EXERCISES

1. Answer the following questions relating to the triangles below.

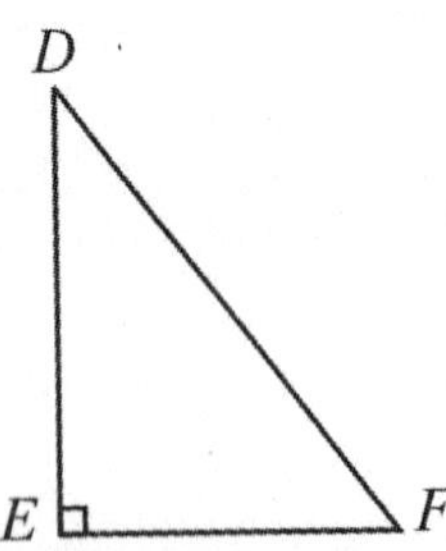

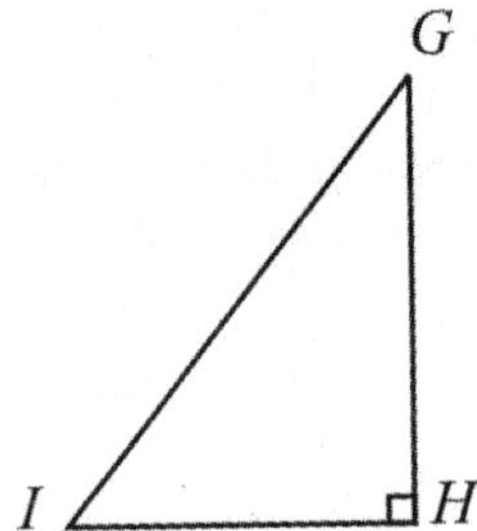

a) Identify the following parts of triangle *DEF*.

i) Hypotenuse

ii) Side opposite to angle *F*

iii) Side adjacent to angle *F*

b) Identify the following parts of triangle *GHI*.

i) Side opposite to angle *I*

ii) Side adjacent to angle *I*

iii) Side opposite to angle *G*

iv) Side adjacent to angle *G*

2. Diagram and explain the meaning of tan 60º. (Make sure your calculator is in degree mode).

3. Draw triangle *ABC* in which angle *B* is equal to 90º and tan *A* has each of the values given below.

a) $\frac{4}{7}$

b) $\frac{2}{3}$

c) $\frac{12}{7}$

d) $\frac{5}{9}$

4. For each of the tangents given below, find the value to three decimal places.

a) tan 27°

b) tan 63°

c) tan 80°

d) tan 45°

5. Write the ratio for tan *A* and tan *B* in each of the following triangles.

a)

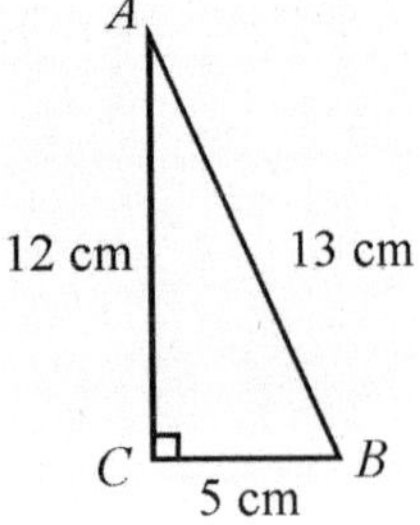

b)

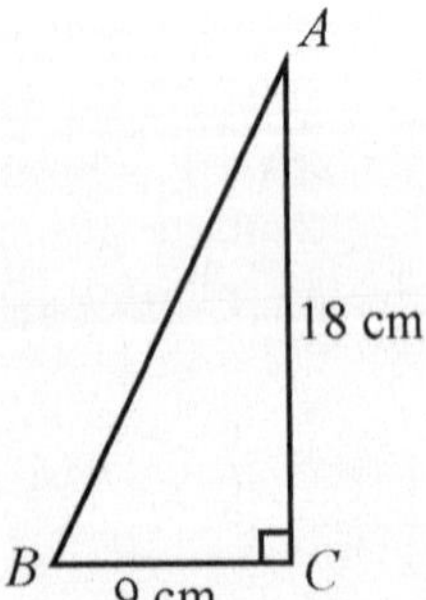

6. For each of the following triangles, find the length of side x to the nearest tenth. Use $\tan^{-1}$ to find the angles.

a)

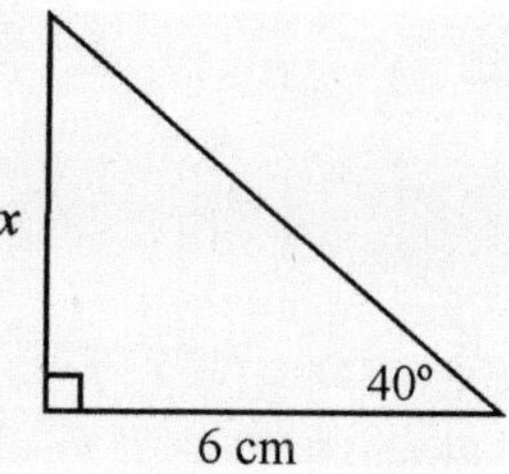

b)

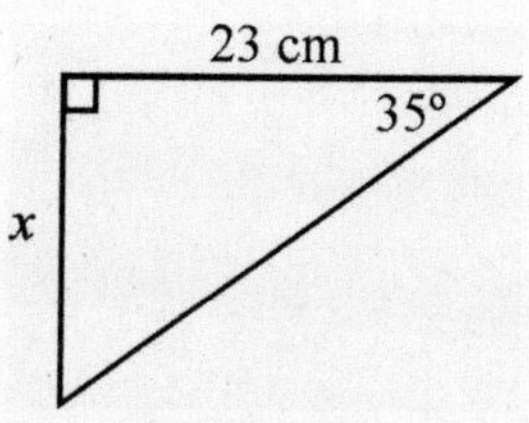

c)

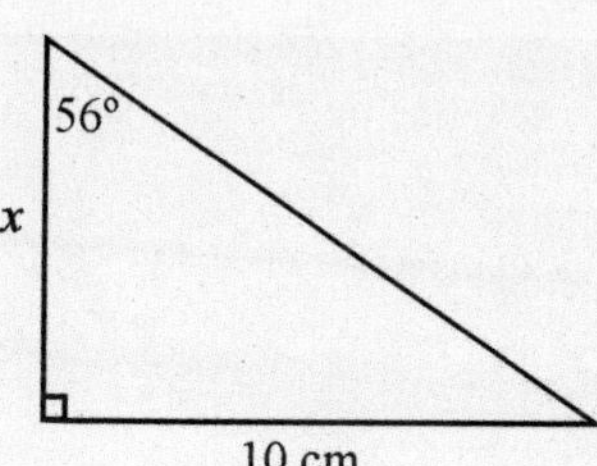

d)

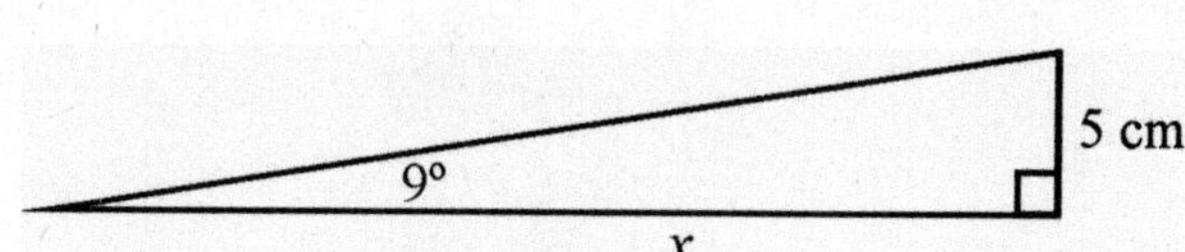

7. Determine angle B to the nearest degree.

a) $\tan B = 0.876$

b) $\tan B = 0.236$

c) $\tan B = 23.845$

d) $\tan B = \frac{5}{9}$

e) $\tan B = \frac{15}{7}$

f) $\tan B = \frac{8}{3}$

8. For each of the following triangles, identify tan B and angle B to the nearest degree.

a)

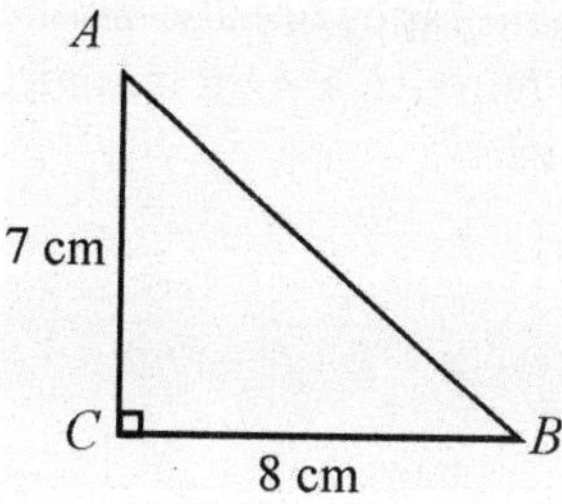

b)

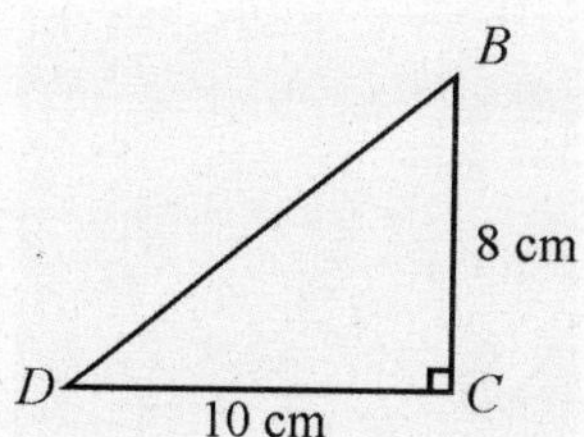

c)

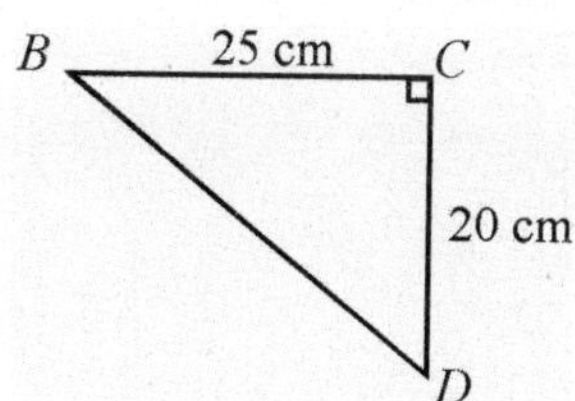

Lesson 2 THE SINE AND COSINE RATIO AND RIGHT TRIANGLES

NOTES

All the same skills that were used with tangent ratios are also applied to sine and cosine ratios. The sine and cosine ratios in a right triangle, where angle A is an acute angle, can be identified as

$$\sin A = \frac{\text{length of the side opposite } \angle A}{\text{hypotenuse}}$$

$$\cos A = \frac{\text{length of the side adjacent } \angle A}{\text{hypotenuse}}$$

Example 1

For triangle ABC, identify the ratios for sin A, sin B, cos A, and cos B.

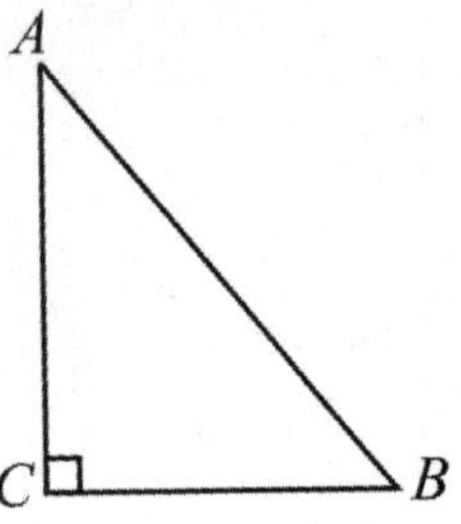

Solution

$\sin A = \frac{\overline{CB}}{\overline{AB}}$ $\sin B = \frac{\overline{AC}}{\overline{AB}}$

$\cos A = \frac{\overline{AC}}{\overline{AB}}$ $\cos B = \frac{\overline{BC}}{\overline{AB}}$

NOTES

Example 2

Determine sin 35°, rounded to three decimal places.
Draw a diagram to help explain the result.

Solution

$$\sin 35° = \frac{\text{opposite}}{\text{hypotenuse}}$$

$$\sin 35° = \frac{0.574}{1}$$

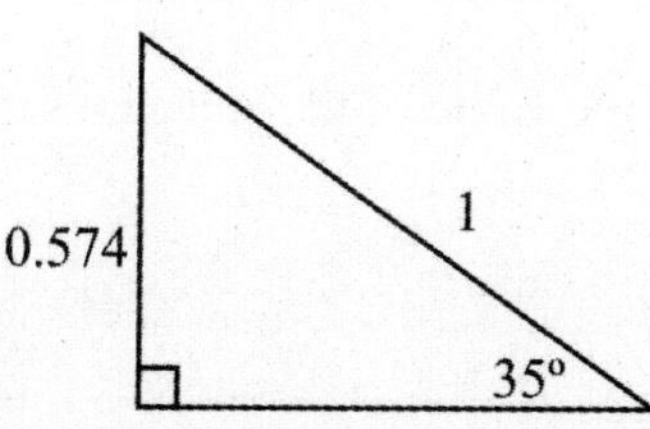

For a 35° angle, the ratio of the opposite side divided by the hypotenuse will always reduce to 0.574 divided by 1. In other words, the side opposite a 35° angle is 0.574 times the length of the hypotenuse.

Example 3

For the following triangle, find the value of the side labelled x, rounded to the nearest tenth.

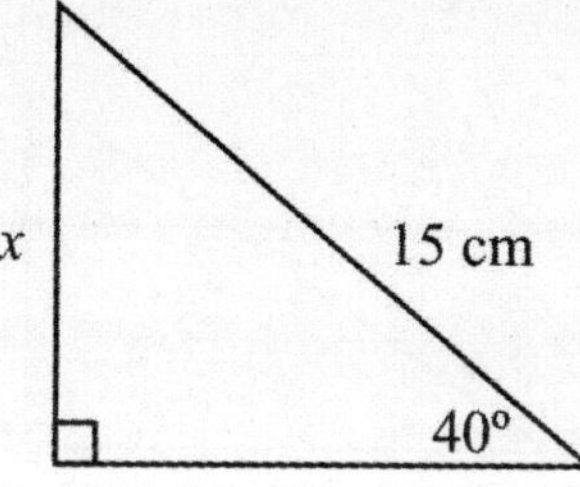

Solution

In this case, the angle under discussion is 40°, and it is given that the hypotenuse is 15 cm. With this information, you can use sine to find the value of the opposite side, which is labelled x.

$$\sin 40° = \frac{x}{15}$$

$$\frac{0.643}{1} = \frac{x}{15}$$ Cross-multiply to solve for x.

$$x = \frac{0.643 \times 15}{1}$$

$$x = 9.6\,\text{cm}$$

$$\sin\theta = \frac{\text{opposite}}{\text{hypotenuse}}$$

NOTES

$\cos\theta = \frac{\text{adjacent}}{\text{hypotenuse}}$

Example 4

For the following triangle, find the value of the side labelled x, rounded to the nearest tenth.

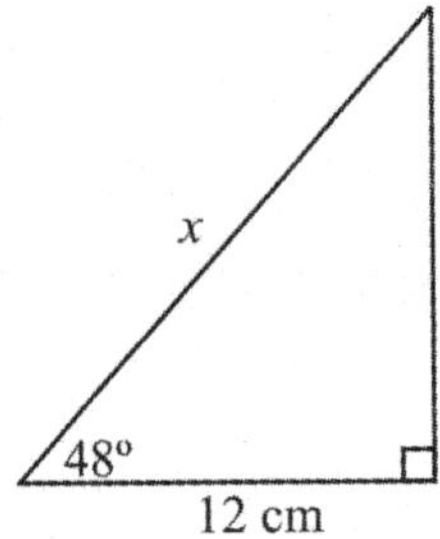

Solution

Here, use cosine and the value of the adjacent side to find the measure of the hypotenuse.

$$\cos 48° = \frac{12}{x}$$

$$\frac{0.669}{1} = \frac{12}{x}$$ Cross-multiply to solve for x.

$$x = \frac{1\times 12}{0.669}$$

$$x = 17.9 \text{ cm}$$

Example 5

For right triangle DEF, find angle D, rounded to the nearest whole number.

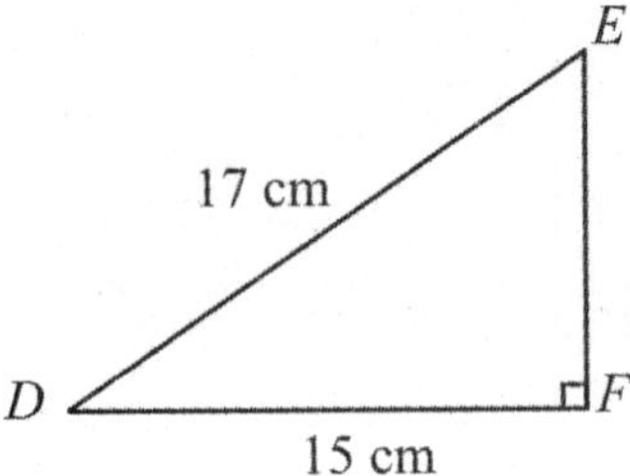

$\cos\theta = \frac{\text{adjacent}}{\text{hypotenuse}}$

Solution

From angle D, you can identify $\overline{DF}$ as adjacent and $\overline{DE}$ as the hypotenuse. The measures of these sides can be used to find cosine and thus, angle D.

$$\cos D = \frac{\text{adjacent}}{\text{hypotenuse}}$$

$$\cos D = \frac{15}{17}$$

$$\angle D = \cos^{-1}\left(\frac{15}{17}\right)$$

$$\angle D = 28°$$

NOTES

Example 6

For right triangle *DEF*, find angle *D*, rounded to the nearest whole number.

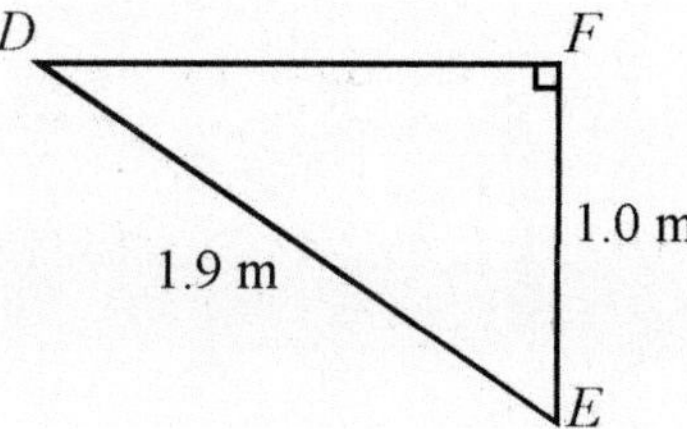

Solution

From angle *D*, you can identify $\overline{EF}$ as opposite and $\overline{DE}$ as the hypotenuse. The measure of these sides can be used to find sine and thus, angle *D*.

$$\sin D = \frac{\text{opposite}}{\text{hypotenuse}}$$

$$\sin D = \frac{1.0}{1.9}$$

$$\angle D = \sin^{-1}\left(\frac{1.0}{1.9}\right)$$

$$\angle D = 32°$$

$$\sin\theta = \frac{\text{opposite}}{\text{hypotenuse}}$$

When finding angles using sine or cosine, remember to use the inverse functions $\sin^{-1}$ or $\cos^{-1}$.

PRACTICE EXERCISES

1. For triangle ΔJKL below, state the following ratios:

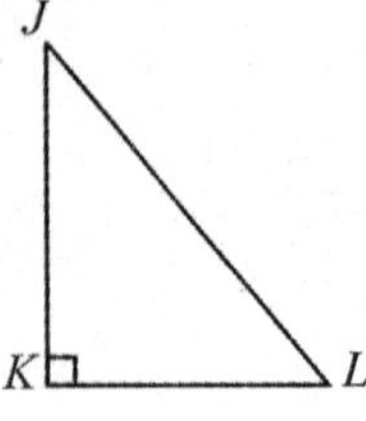

a) $\sin J$

b) $\cos J$

c) $\sin L$

d) $\cos L$

2. Determine cos 80°, rounded to three decimal places. Draw a diagram to help explain the result.

3. For each triangle below, find the value of x, rounded to the nearest tenth.
To determine whether you will use sine or cosine, start from the angle under discussion and decide if you are using the opposite side and the hypotenuse or the adjacent side and the hypotenuse.

a)

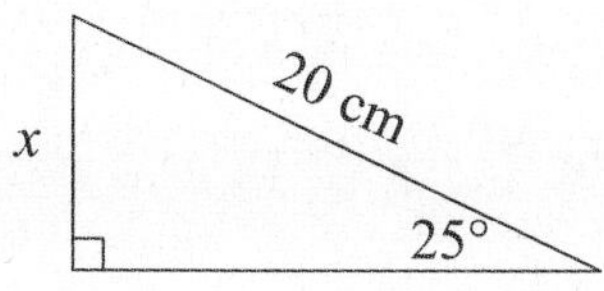

b)

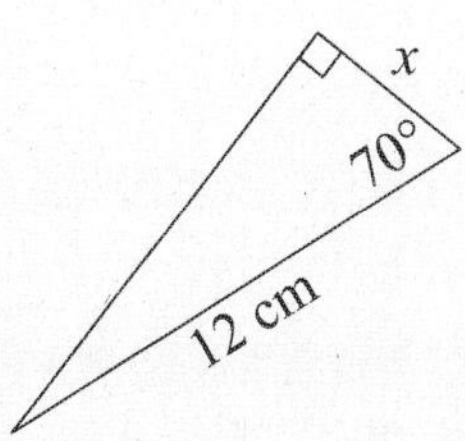

c)

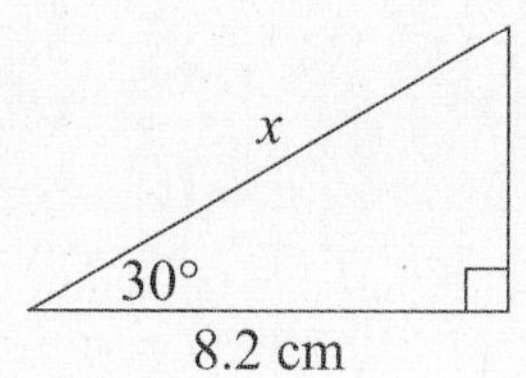

d)

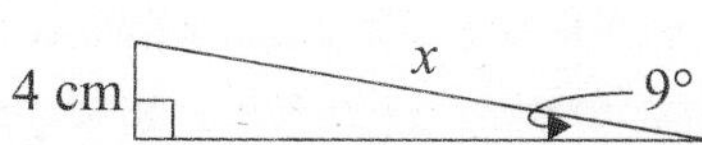

e)

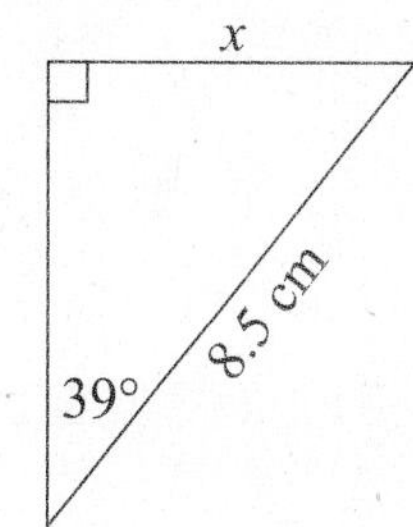

4. For the following right triangles, find angle D, rounded to the nearest whole number.

a)

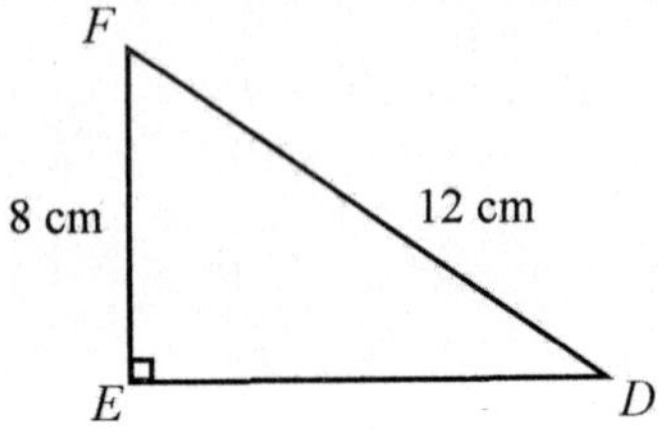

b)

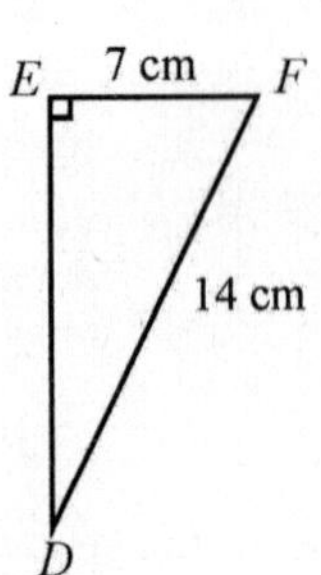

c)

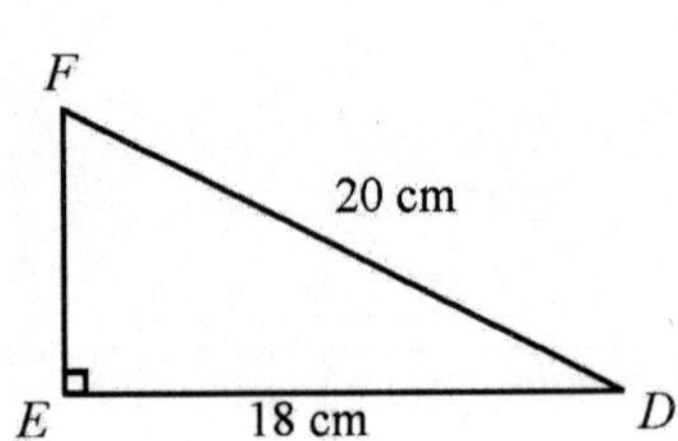

d)

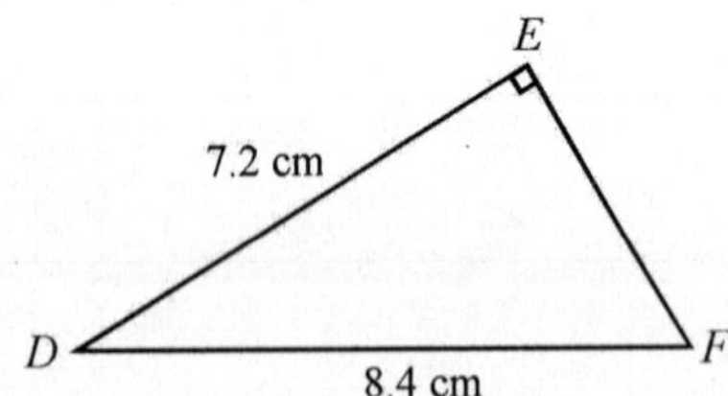

Lesson 3 SOLVING PROBLEMS INVOLVING RIGHT TRIANGLES

While you are solving problems involving right triangles, you may wish to write **SohCahToa** across the top of your page. SohCahToa stands for sine = opposite divided by hypotenuse, cosine = adjacent divided by hypotenuse, and tangent = opposite divided by adjacent. The first letter of each word is used to assist you in remembering the ratios for the trigonometric ratios.

NOTES

Use SohCahToa to remember the trigonometric ratios.

Now that you have three ratios to use, you must decide which one to use in a particular problem involving missing angles and sides of right triangles. You should always draw a diagram to assist you in these types of problems.

Soh

$$\sin\theta = \frac{\text{opposite}}{\text{hypotenuse}}$$

Cah

$$\cos\theta = \frac{\text{adjacent}}{\text{hypotenuse}}$$

Toa

$$\tan\theta = \frac{\text{opposite}}{\text{adjacent}}$$

Example 1

A 12 m ladder is leaning against a building. The angle formed where the ladder meets the ground is 40°. How far is the base of the ladder from the building? How far is the top of the ladder from the ground?

Solution

Draw a diagram and use variables to indicate the measure of the sides you are trying to find.

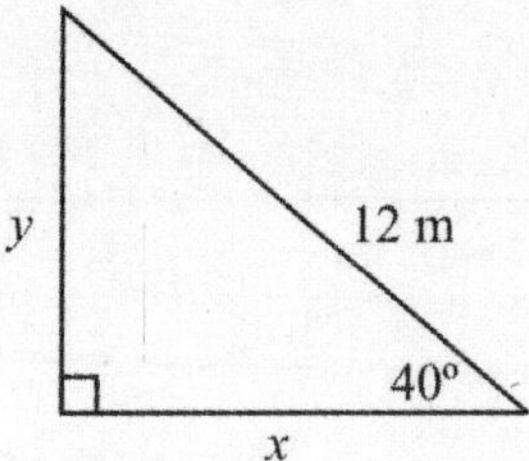

When solving for side x, start from the angle under discussion, which is 40°. Identify the sides you have to work with. Side x is the adjacent side, and the side measuring 12 m is the hypotenuse. The trigonometric ratio that uses adjacent and hypotenuse is cosine.

$$\cos 40^\circ = \frac{x}{12}$$

$$\frac{0.766}{1} = \frac{x}{12}$$ Cross-multiply to solve for x.

$$x = \frac{0.766 \times 12}{1}$$

$$x = 9.2 \text{ m}$$

The base of the ladder is 9.2 m from the building.

NOTES

When solving for y, from the angle under discussion, you have the hypotenuse as 12 m and the opposite side as y.

SohCahToa

$$\sin 40° = \frac{y}{12}$$

$$y = 7.7 \text{ m}$$

The top of the ladder is 7.7 m from the ground.

When solving right triangle problems, you will often see reference to the angle of elevation or the angle of depression. The **angle of elevation** is the angle formed from the horizontal looking upward, as in the diagram below.

Angle of elevation equals the **angle of depression**.

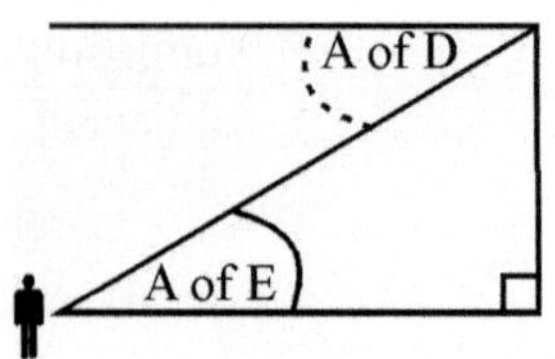

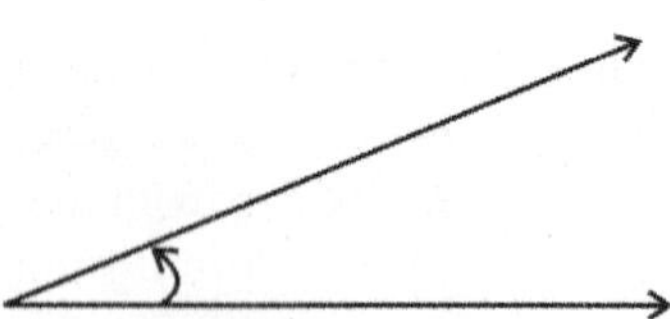

The **angle of depression** is the angle formed from the horizontal looking downward, as in the diagram below.

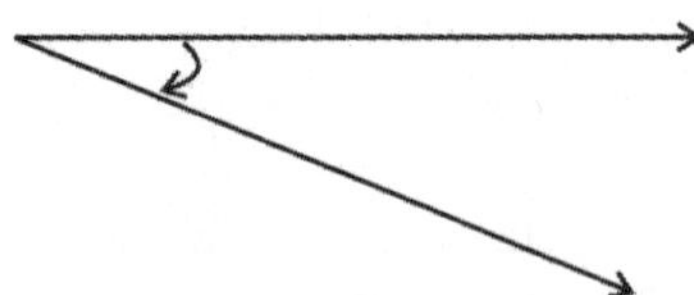

Example 2

Find the angle of elevation of a ramp that is 15 m long if the top end of the ramp is 2 m above the ground.

Solution

Draw a diagram and use a variable to indicate the measure of the angle you are trying to find.

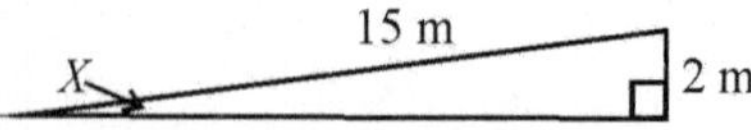

$$\sin\theta = \frac{\text{opposite}}{\text{hypotenuse}}$$

Start from the angle X, which is the angle under discussion. Identify the 2 m side as the opposite and the 15 m side as the hypotenuse. The trigonometric ratio that uses opposite and hypotenuse is sine.

$\sin X = \frac{2}{15}$

$\angle X = \sin^{-1}\left(\frac{2}{15}\right)$

$\angle X = 8°$

The angle of elevation of the ramp is 8°.

NOTES

When finding angles using sine or cosine, remember to use the inverse functions $\sin^{-1}$ or $\cos^{-1}$.

PRACTICE EXERCISES

1. A radio tower is 200 m high. The sun's rays make an angle of 30° from the top of the tower to the ground. Calculate the horizontal length of the tower's shadow to the nearest tenth of a metre.

2. The foot of a 6 m ladder is 1.8 m from the building it is leaning against. What angle, rounded to the nearest whole number, is formed where the ladder meets the ground?

3. The longest side of a certain rectangle is 20 cm. The diagonal of the rectangle forms a 33° angle with this side.
   a) Calculate the width of the rectangle to the nearest tenth of a centimetre.

   b) Calculate the length of the diagonal to the nearest tenth of a centimetre.

4. A kite is flying at the end of a 17 m string. The string makes an angle of 65° with the ground. What is the kite's vertical height above the ground?

5. The top of a building has an angle of elevation of 10° from a point 100 m away. How tall is the building?

6. A jet is flying at a speed of 60 m/s. It increases its altitude at the rate of 7.5 m/s. At what angle, to the nearest whole number, is it climbing?

Lesson 4 VOLUME OF CONES AND PYRAMIDS

NOTES

Volume is calculated in cubic units or units^3.

Volume of a cylinder
$V = \pi r^2 h$

Volume of a cone
$V = \frac{1}{3}\pi r^2 h$

Volume can be referred to as the space inside a three-dimensional object. The volumes of cones and cylinders have a special relationship.

The formula used to find the volume of a cylinder is $V = \pi r^2 h$.

The base of a cylinder and the base of a cone are both circular. If you compare a cone and a cylinder of the same base and height, you will find that it takes 3 cones to fill the cylinder with water. You can say that the volume of the cylinder is 3 times that of the cone, or that the cone has a volume $\frac{1}{3}$ the volume of the cylinder.

Therefore, the formula for a volume of a cone is $V = \frac{1}{3}\pi r^2 h$.

This formula can also be written as $V = \frac{\pi r^2 h}{3}$.

The following diagram illustrates that the *r* in the formula represents the base radius of the cone. The *h* represents the height of the cone. Notice that the height and the base radius form a right angle.

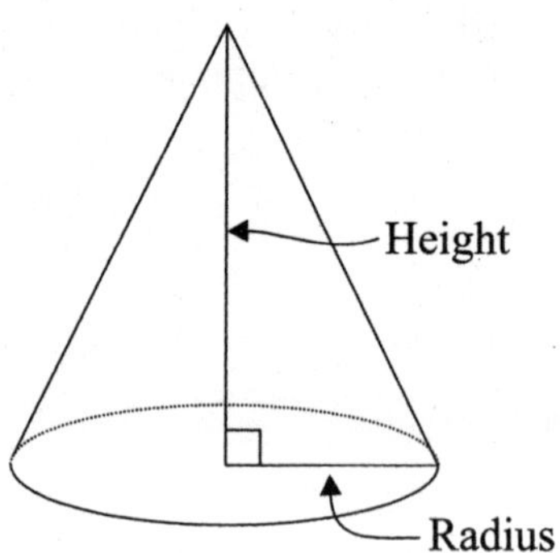

NOTES

Example 1

A cone-shaped funnel has a radius of 6 cm and a height of 4.5 cm. What is the volume of the funnel, to the nearest tenth of a cubic centimetre?

Solution

Draw a diagram to visualize what you are finding.

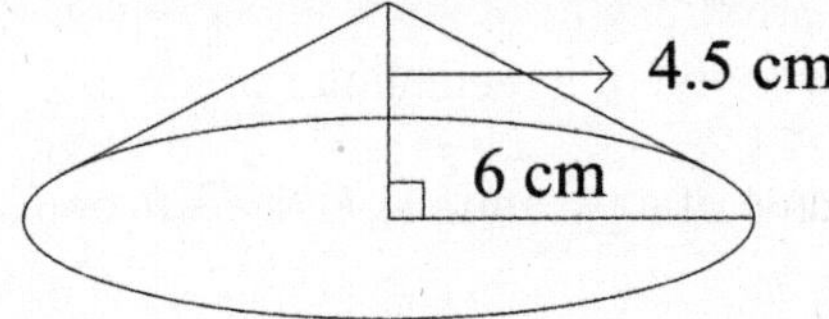

$V = \frac{\pi r^2 h}{3}$

Substitute what you know into the formula and solve for the missing variable.

Use the button for π on your calculator, rather than 3.14, to get more accurate solutions.

$V = \frac{\pi(6^2)(4.5)}{3}$

$V = 169.6 \text{ cm}^3$

The volume of the funnel is 169.6 cm^3.

Volume = units^3

Example 2

The volume of a cylinder is 75 cm^3. What is the volume of a cone that just fits inside the cylinder?

Solution

It takes 3 cones to equal the volume of a cylinder of the same height and base.

The volume of one cone can be calculated by $75 \div 3 = 25$.

Therefore, the volume of the cone will be 25 cm^3.

NOTES

The relationship between a pyramid and a rectangular prism of the same height and base is similar to the relationship between a cone and a cylinder of the same base and height.

If you turned 3 identical pyramids upside down and filled them with water, they would equal the volume of 1 rectangular prism that had the same base area and height as the pyramids.

Volume of rectangular prism =
$V = lwh$

Volume of pyramid =
$V = \frac{1}{3}lwh$ or $V = \frac{lwh}{3}$

The formula for the volume of a rectangular prism is $V = lwh$.

The formula for volume of a pyramid is $V = \frac{1}{3}lwh$ or $V = \frac{lwh}{3}$.

The formula for the volume of a pyramid is $\frac{1}{3}$ the volume of a rectangular prism of the same base area and height.

In the diagram below, you can see that the height forms a right angle with the base of the pyramid.

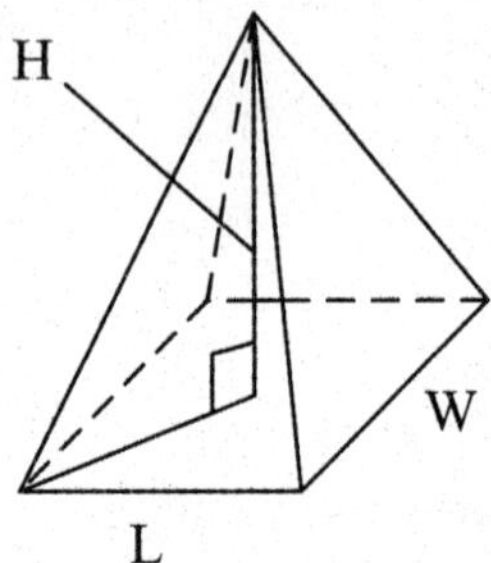

Example 3

A certain pyramid has a base measuring 15 m by 12 m and a height of 9 m. Determine its volume to the nearest tenth of a cubic metre.

Solution

$V = \frac{lwh}{3}$

Substitute and solve.

$V = \frac{(15)(12)(9)}{3}$

$V = 540.0 \text{ m}^3$

The volume of the pyramid is 540.0 m^3.

Example 4
What is the volume of a rectangular prism with the same base and height as the pyramid in Example 3?

Solution
Since the pyramid and the prism have the same base and height, it will take 3 pyramids to equal the volume of the rectangular prism.

Thus, the volume of the rectangular prism is $540 \times 3 = 1\,620\,\text{m}^3$.

NOTES

PRACTICE EXERCISES

1. Determine the volume of each of the following cones. Round your answers to the nearest tenth of a centimetre. Remember that the formula for volume of a cone is $V = \frac{\pi r^2 h}{3}$.

a) A cone with a base radius = 6 cm and height = 4 cm

b) A cone with a base radius = 11.5 cm and height = 7.4 cm

c) A cone with a base diameter = 16.4 cm and height = 13 cm

d) A cone with a base diameter = 9.6 cm and height = 9.4 cm

2. A farmer piles his grain in the shape of a cone. The pile has a base radius of 20 m and a height of 5.5 m. What is the volume of grain, to the nearest tenth of a cubic metre?

3. If a cylinder has a base radius of 7 cm and a height of 12 cm, what is the volume of a cone that has the same base radius and height? Round your answer to the nearest tenth of a centimetre.

4. Determine the volume of each of the following pyramids. Round your answer to the nearest tenth of a metre. Remember that the formula for volume of a rectangular pyramid is $V = \frac{lwh}{3}$.

a) A pyramid with a base = 6 m by 7 m and height = 10 m

b) A pyramid with a base = 4 m by 9 m and height = 6.5 m

c) A pyramid with a base = 3.5 m by 8 m and height = 9.8 m

5. A rectangular prism has a length of 5 cm, a width of 3 cm, and a height of 8 cm. What are the dimensions of a pyramid that is $\frac{1}{3}$ the volume of this prism?

6. A pyramid has a square base of 210 m and a height of 155 m. Find the volume of the pyramid.

7. The volume of a pyramid is 124 cm^3. If the base is 5 cm by 8 cm, what is the height, to the nearest tenth of a centimetre?

PRACTICE QUIZ 1

1. Find sin 47° to three decimal places. Use a diagram to help explain its meaning.

2. Given the following trigonometric ratios, find angle *A* to the nearest degree.

a) $\sin A = \frac{3}{5}$

b) $\tan A = \frac{7}{3}$

c) $\cos A = \frac{1}{8}$

3. For each of the following triangles, find the length of side x to the nearest tenth.

a)

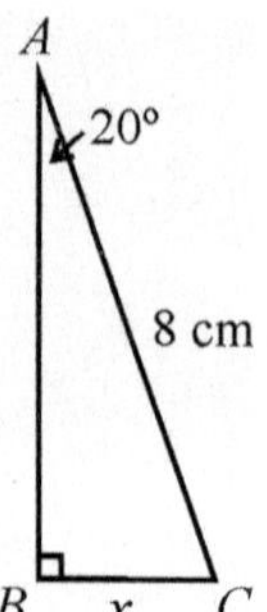

b)

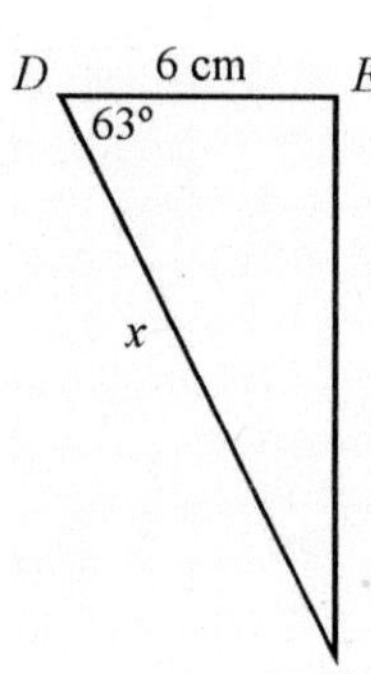

4. For each of the following triangles, find the measure of angle B to the nearest degree.

a)

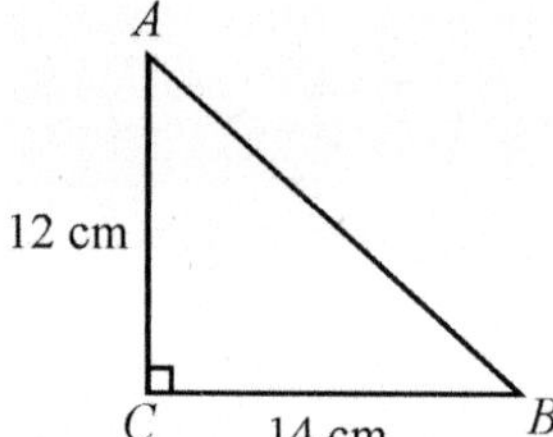

b)

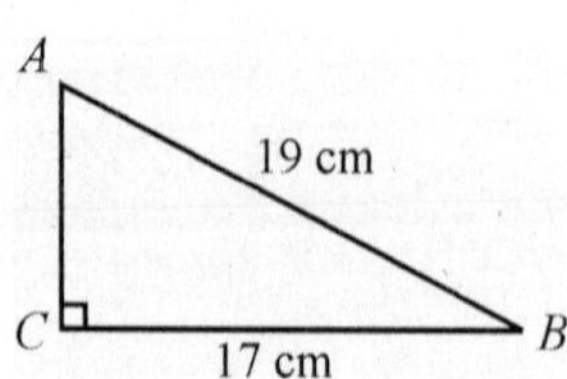

5. A ramp has a vertical rise of 0.5 m for every horizontal distance of 3 m. Find the angle of elevation of the ramp to the nearest whole number.

6. From a point 10 m from the base of a building, the angle of elevation from the ground to the top of the building is 40°. Find the height of the building to the nearest tenth of a metre.

7. If the volume of a cylinder is 575 cm^3, what is the volume of the largest cone that will fit inside of the cylinder?

8. If a rectangular-based pyramid has a volume of 216 cm^3, a length of 9 cm, and a height of 3 cm, what is the width?

Lesson 5 SOLVING DESIGN PROBLEMS INVOLVING THREE-DIMENSIONAL OBJECTS

NOTES

In this lesson, you will compare the volume of a rectangular prism to its surface area. The surface area of a rectangular prism is calculated by finding the area of all of the sides and then adding them together.

The formula for finding the surface area of a rectangular prism is $A = 2(lw)$.

In a rectangular prism, which has the shape of a closed box, the top and bottom have the same area, the front and back have the same area, and the two sides have the same area. Many different box shapes can be created with the same volume but with different surface areas. Knowing this can be very useful; for example, a company that sells cereal may design a box in such a way to minimize the surface area of a box so that the cost of making it is reduced.

Example 1

A cookie box is in the shape of a rectangular prism. List all the whole number dimensions possible given that the box has a volume of 32 cm^3. Since the company is trying to minimize packaging costs, identify the surface area of each possibility. What dimensions will give the smallest surface area?

Solution

The possibilities can be presented in a table.

Length (cm)	Width (cm)	Height (cm)	Volume $V = lwh$ (cm^3)	Surface Area $A = 2(lw)+2(hw)+2(hl)$ (cm^2)
1	1	32	32	130
1	2	16	32	100
2	2	8	32	72
1	4	8	32	88
2	4	4	32	64

The dimensions that will give the smallest surface area are 2 cm by 4 cm by 4 cm.

The shape closest to a cube will have the smallest surface area.

As the length, width, and height become closer in value to each other, the surface area of the rectangular prism decreases. As the rectangular prism approaches a cubical shape, its surface area decreases.

PRACTICE EXERCISES

1. List the possible whole number dimensions of a rectangular prism with a volume of 40 cm^3. Which of these dimensions produces the smallest surface area, and what is it?

2. A building is to be built so that it has a volume of 900 m^3. What whole number dimensions would produce the least surface area? What is this surface area?

3. a) What is the maximum number of boxes measuring 6 cm by 3 cm by 2 cm that can be packed into a shipping crate measuring 24 cm by 8 cm by 11 cm?

   b) If the dimensions of the shipping crate are doubled, how many boxes will fit inside?

Lesson 6 SOLVING TWO-DIMENSIONAL PROBLEMS

We encounter problems involving perimeter and area everyday. For example, you need to know the perimeter of the school running track to calculate the total distance you run during phys ed class. You need to know the area of your bedroom wall if you are going to paint it or cover it with wallpaper.

NOTES

Example 1

Joe has 20 m of fence with which to enclose a garden. List all the possible whole number dimensions for a rectangular garden. Which of these whole number dimensions will produce a rectangular garden with the maximum area?

Solution

Make a table to identify the possible dimensions and areas.

Length (m)	Width (m)	Area (m^2)
1	9	9
2	8	16
3	7	21
4	6	24
5	5	25

These possible garden shapes are illustrated below.

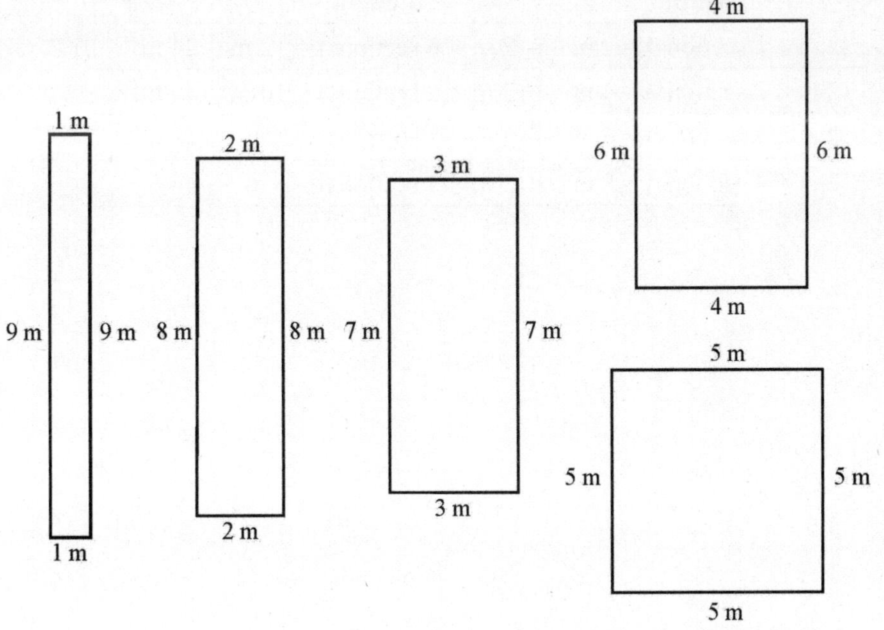

Of all rectangular shapes of the same perimeter, a **square** shape gives the maximum area.

It is important to remember that shapes may have the same total perimeter or area yet have different lengths and widths.

The 5 m by 5 m square will give the maximum amount of area for the garden.

NOTES

Draw diagrams to assist in problem solving.

Example 2

Colleen has 28 m of fence with which to make a pen for her chickens. The fence comes in 2 m sections and cannot be cut. List the possible dimensions of rectangular pens that Colleen could make. Which dimensions would create a pen with the largest area?

Solution

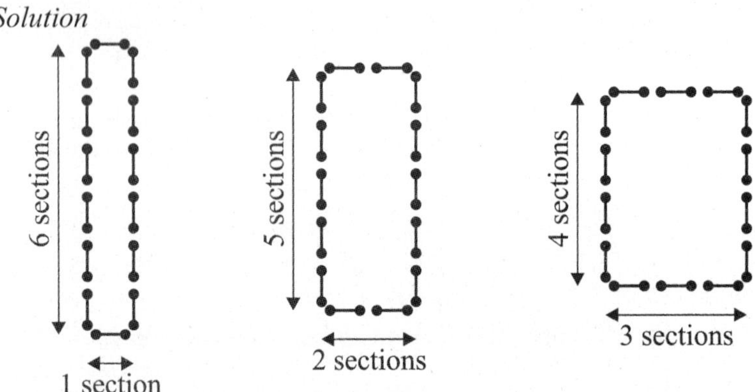

The dimensions that would produce the maximum area are 3 sections by 4 sections or 6 m by 8 m.

The maximum area would be 48 m^2.

Notice in the last two examples that when a rectangular shape is to be enclosed to produce a maximum area, the shapes closest to a square produces the largest areas.

Width	Length	Area
(2 m × 1 sections) = 2 m	(2 m × 6 sections) = 12 m	24 m^2
(2 m × 2 sections) = 4 m	(2 m × 5 sections) = 10 m	40 m^2
(2 m × 3 sections) = 6 m	(2 m × 4 sections) = 8 m	48 m^2
(2 m × 4 sections) = 8 m	(2 m × 3 sections) = 6 m	48 m^2

PRACTICE EXERCISES

1. Barrie wants to fence off an area for a rectangular garden. The fencing material comes in 1 m units that cannot be cut. If Barrie has 12 m of fencing, what are the dimensions of the largest garden he can make? Draw a diagram to aid your solution.

2. A store owner wants to make a rectangular area in one corner of his store for a special display. He has 6 m of rope to block off two sides of the area if he uses walls for the other two sides. What are the dimensions of the largest area he can rope off?

3. A lifeguard at a beach has 300 m of heavy cord to rope off a rectangular swimming area, with the beach forming one side of the rectangle. What are the dimensions of the roped-off area when the side parallel to the beach has each of the following measures?

(e.g.)

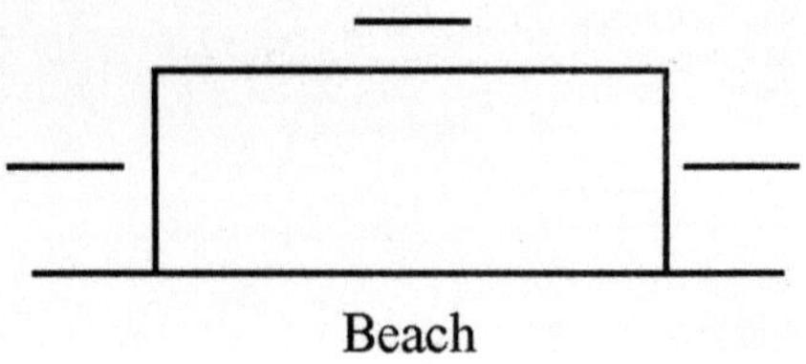

Beach

a) 100 m

b) 150 m

c) 200 m

d) 50 m

4. In the previous question, which dimensions give the largest swimming area? Is the resulting shape a square? Does enclosing only three sides make a difference when trying to determine maximum area?

Lesson 7 SIMILAR TRIANGLES

NOTES

Similar triangles have equal angles and have proportionally corresponding sides. Corresponding sides are the sides that are opposite the equivalent angles. In other words, similar triangles have the same shape, but not necessarily the same size. Equivalent fractions express the relationship of the proportional sides.

Example 1

For the following triangles, identify the corresponding sides. Write the ratio of the corresponding sides in their lowest terms. State whether or not the triangles are similar. Explain your answer.

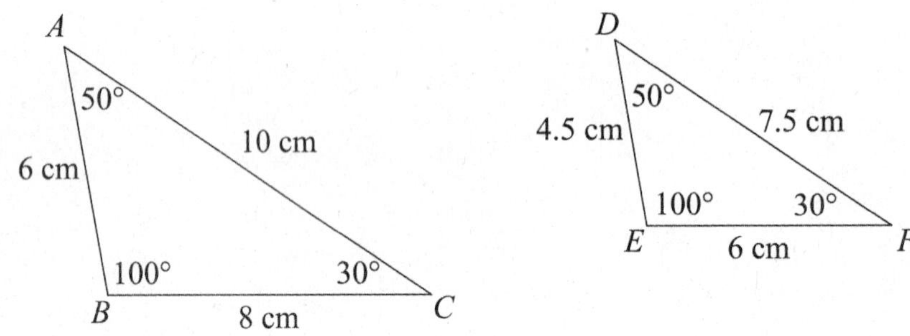

Solution

When setting up the ratios, start by placing one triangle's corresponding sides in the numerator and the other triangle's corresponding sides in the denominator.

For the given triangles, the ratio would be written as $\frac{\Delta ABC}{\Delta DEF}$.

Next, take each set of equivalent angles and determine the corresponding sides that are opposite the angles. Then, write the ratio of the sides.

In ΔABC, the 30° angle is $\angle C$; the corresponding side is $\overline{AB}$.

In ΔDEF, the 30° angle is $\angle F$; the corresponding side is $\overline{DE}$.

The ratio is $\frac{\overline{AB}}{\overline{DE}} = \frac{6\text{ m}}{4.5\text{ m}} = 1.3\text{ m}$

In ΔABC, the 50° angle is $\angle A$; the corresponding side is $\overline{BC}$.

In ΔDEF, the 50° angle is $\angle D$; the corresponding side is $\overline{EF}$.

The ratio is $\frac{\overline{BC}}{\overline{EF}} = \frac{8\text{ m}}{6\text{ m}} = 1.30$

NOTES

In ΔABC, the 100° angle is <*B*; corresponding side is $\overline{AC}$.

In ΔDEF, the 100° angle is <*E* corresponding side is $\overline{DF}$.

The ratio is $\frac{\overline{AC}}{\overline{DF}} = \frac{10\text{ m}}{7.5\text{ m}} = \frac{4}{3} = 1.3$

You can see that the triangles have equal angles and proportional sides. Therefore, ΔABC is similar to ΔDEF.

When identifying similar triangles, the order in which you write the letters should correspond with the angles that are equal to each other. Notice that angle A = angle D, angle B = angle E, and angle C = angle F.

By making an equation with the ratios of the corresponding sides, we can solve missing sides in similar triangles.

Example 2

In the similar triangles below, solve for the missing sides x and y. Show how you would use the ratios of corresponding sides.

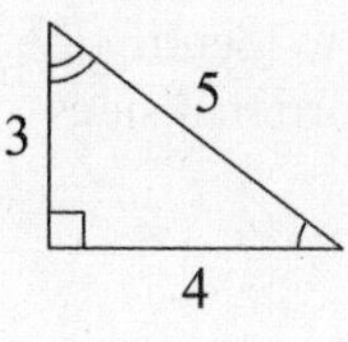

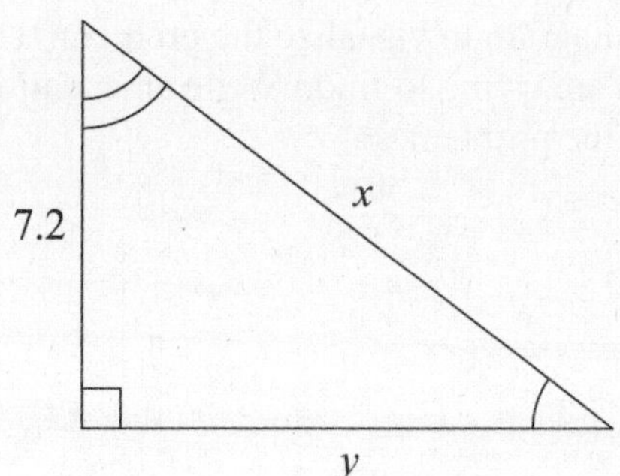

The arcs represent angles that are equal.

Solution

Identify the ratio.

$$\frac{\text{Big}\Delta}{\text{Small}\Delta}$$

$$\frac{7.2}{3} = \frac{x}{5} = \frac{y}{4}$$

You can now solve for each of the variables in turn by creating equations with these fractions. Since all the fractions are equivalent, you can set up each fraction containing a variable with the fraction containing the known values.

To solve problems involving similar triangles, draw diagrams and create proportional ratios of the corresponding sides.

NOTES

Solving for x, write

$$\frac{7.2}{3}=\frac{x}{5}$$

$(7.2)(5)=(3)(x)$ Cross-multiply.

$36=3x$

$12=x$

Solving for y, write

$$\frac{7.2}{3}=\frac{y}{4}$$

$28.8=3y$

$9.6=y$

Example 3

A person who stands 180 cm tall casts a shadow 45 cm long. A nearby telephone pole casts a shadow 300 cm long at the same time of day. What is the height of the pole in metres?

Solution

Draw a diagram to visualize the problem. Use a variable to identify the side you are trying to find. Write an equation using proportional sides to solve the problem.

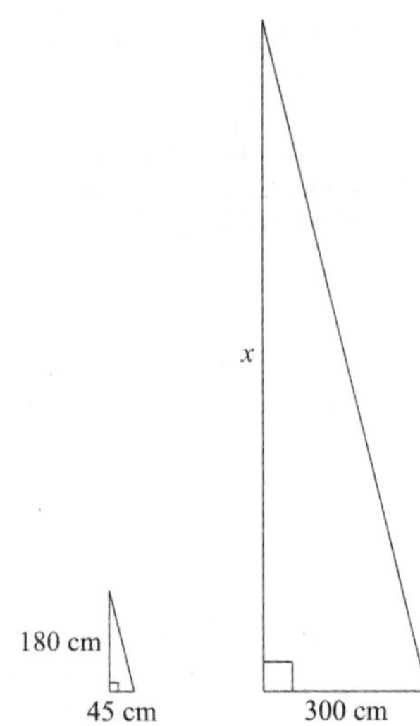

$$\frac{180}{x}=\frac{45}{300}$$

$45x=54\ 000$ (cross-multiplying)

$x=1\ 200$ cm (dividing each side by 45)

$\frac{1\ 200 \text{ cm}}{100}=12$ m (converting cm to m)

$\therefore$ The height of the pole is 12 m.

PRACTICE EXERCISES

1. For the following triangles, create ratios for the corresponding sides. State whether or not the triangles are similar triangles. Explain your answer.

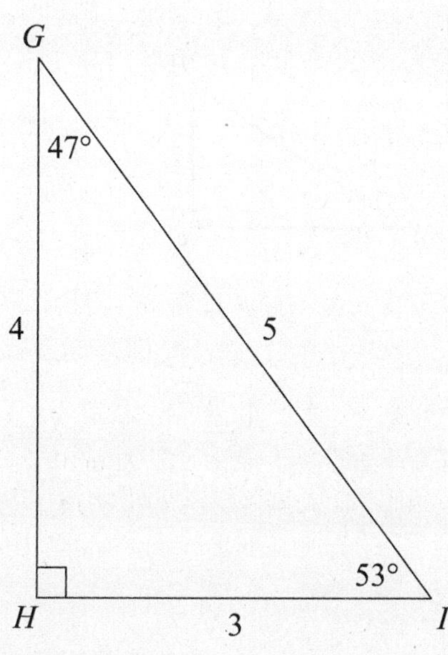

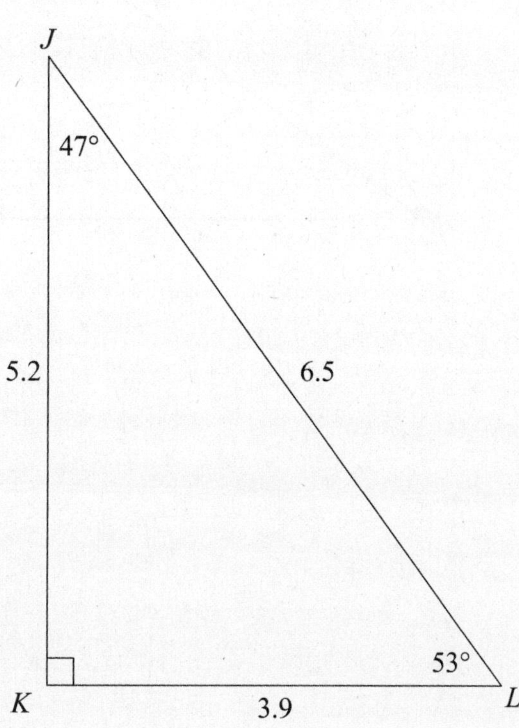

2. For each of the following sets of similar triangles, calculate the length of side x.

a)

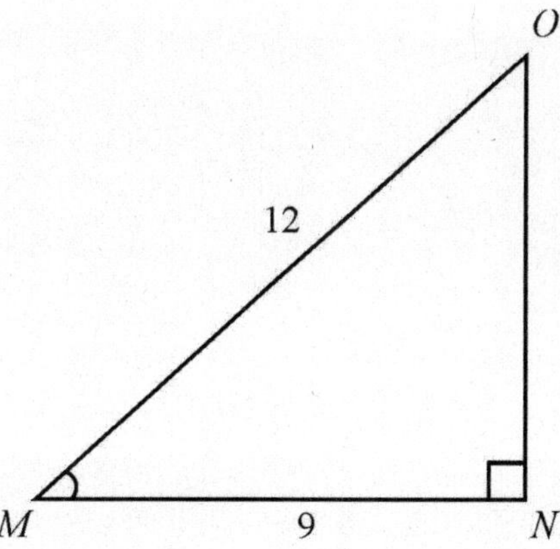

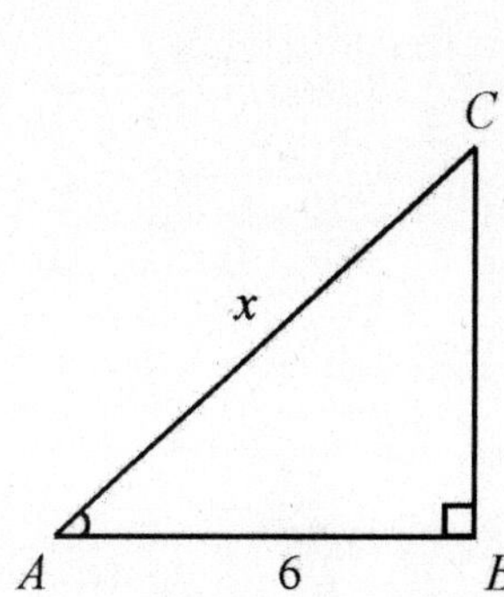

b)

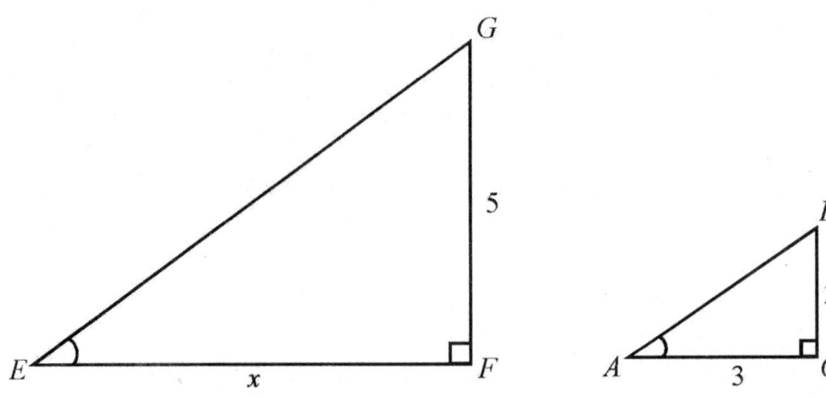

c)

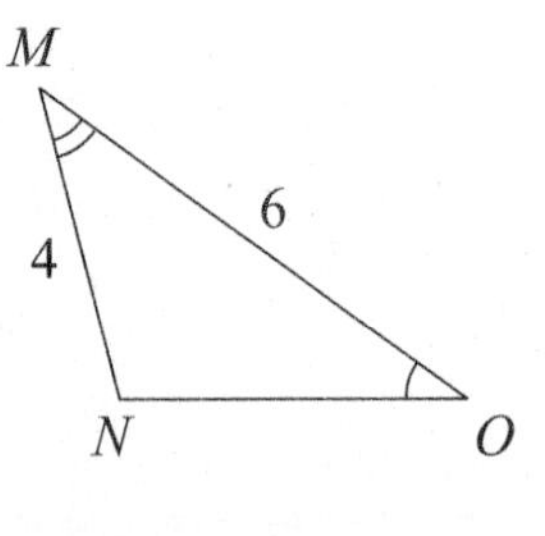

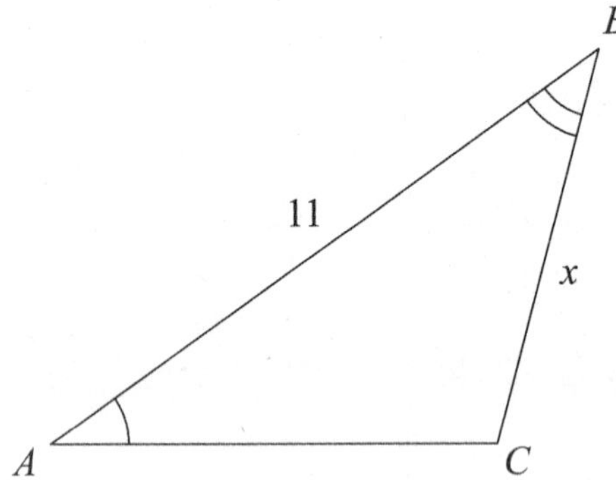

c)

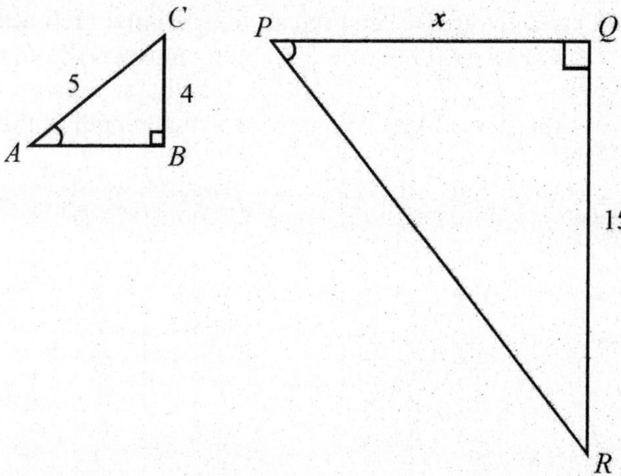

3. The length of a shadow cast by a pine tree is 5 m. A student who is 1.7 m tall casts a shadow 40 cm long at the same time of day. How tall is the tree?

4. Fred has a triangular vegetable garden. One of the sides measures 10 m and another measures 12 m; together, there sides form an angle of 50°. To prepare for planting, Fred decides to make a scale drawing of this garden. He begins by drawing a 50° angle on paper. From this, he marks off 20 cm and 24 cm to model the two sides of the actual garden. Finally, he draws a line to connect the two sides. This third line measures 19 cm long. What is the actual length of the third side of Fred's garden?

5. A 6 m tall ladder is resting against a wall. The first rung of the ladder is 30 cm from the bottom of the ladder and 24 cm vertically above the ground. How high up the wall does the ladder reach?

Lesson 8 CONGRUENT TRIANGLES

Two triangles are congruent when the angles and sides of one triangle are equal in measure to the corresponding sides and angles of the other. In other words, congruent triangles have the same shape and the same size.

One way to identify congruence would be to trace one triangle and then slide the tracing over the other triangle to show that one triangle fits exactly over the other.

Another way to show congruence, is to identify the equal angles and equal sides of congruent triangles. For ΔGHI and ΔJKL below, the equal parts of each triangle are identified using symbols.

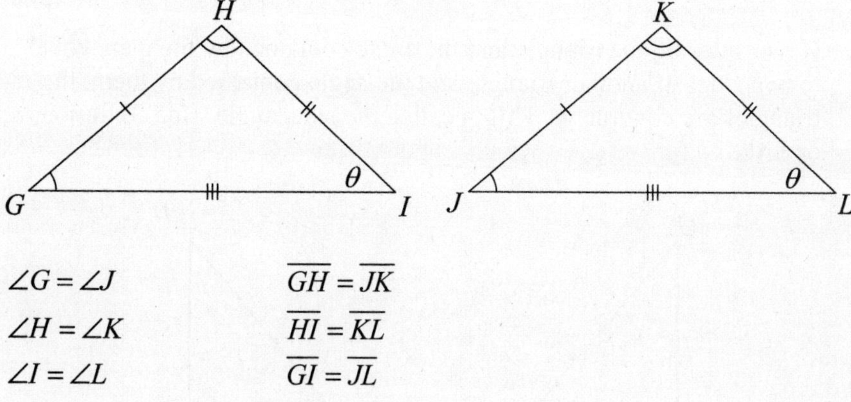

$\angle G = \angle J$ $\overline{GH} = \overline{JK}$

$\angle H = \angle K$ $\overline{HI} = \overline{KL}$

$\angle I = \angle L$ $\overline{GI} = \overline{JL}$

ΔGHI is congruent to ΔJKL.

Notice that the vertices of each triangle are listed in the same order as their corresponding equal angles.

NOTES

Congruent triangles have corresponding sides and angles that are equal.

Symbols are used to indicate that corresponding sides of triangles, or other shapes, are equal in measure.

NOTES

≅ means "is congruent"

The following three triangle relationships always prove congruency.

1. If three sides of one triangle are equal to three sides of another triangle, the triangles are congruent. This is called the side, side, side condition, or **SSS**.

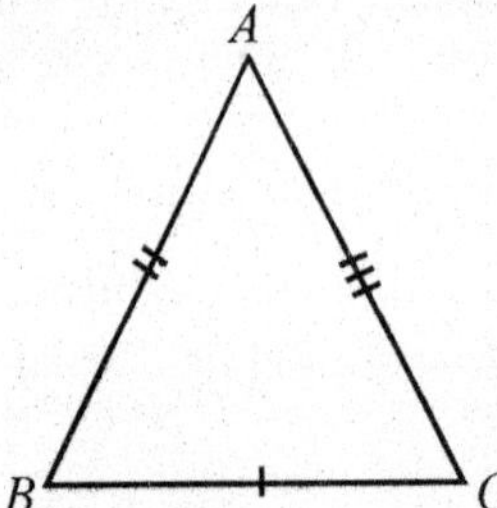

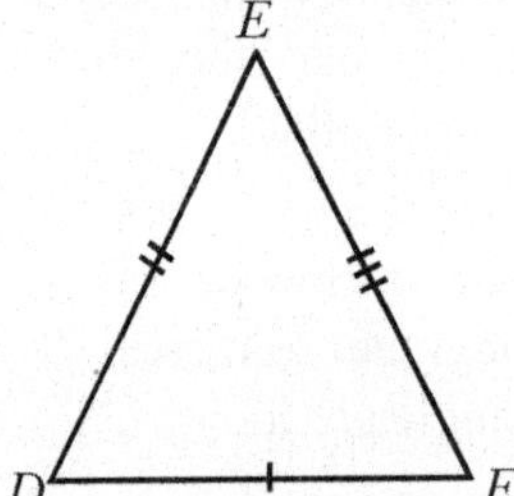

2. If two sides of one triangle and the angle contained by them are equal to two sides of another triangle and the angle contained by them, the triangles are congruent. This is called the side, angle, side condition, or **SAS**.

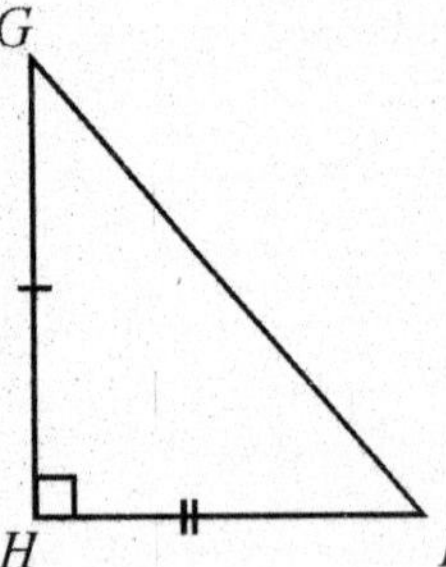

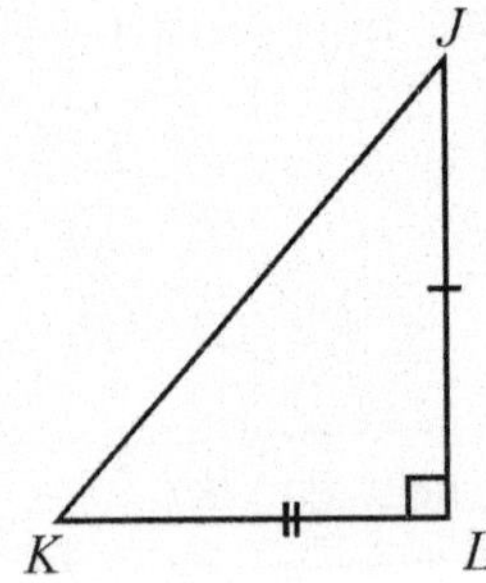

3. If two angles of one triangle and the side contained by them are equal to two angles of another triangle and the side contained by them, the triangles are congruent. This is called the angle, side, angle condition, or **ASA**.

The three proofs of triangle congruency are:

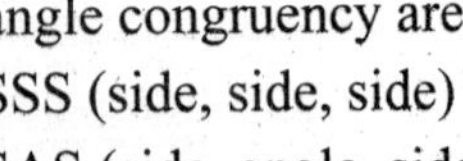

- SSS (side, side, side)
- SAS (side, angle, side)
- ASA (angle, side, angle)

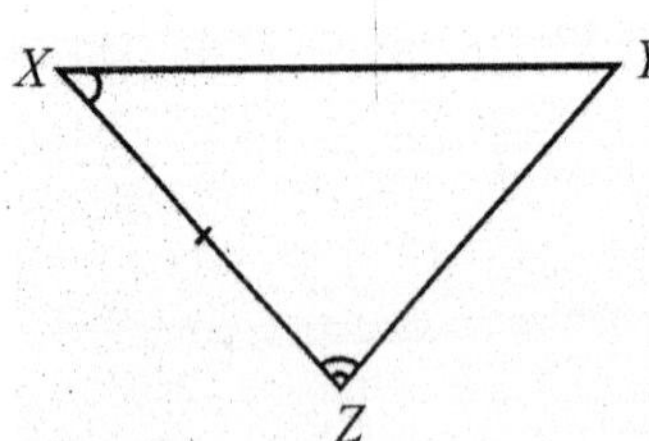

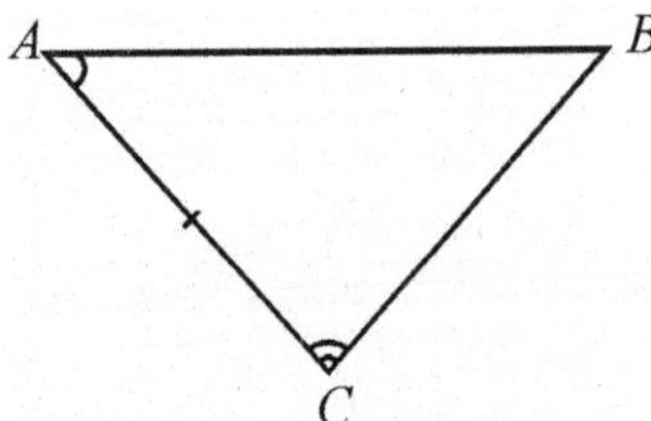

NOTES

Example 1
Are the triangles below congruent? Explain your answer.

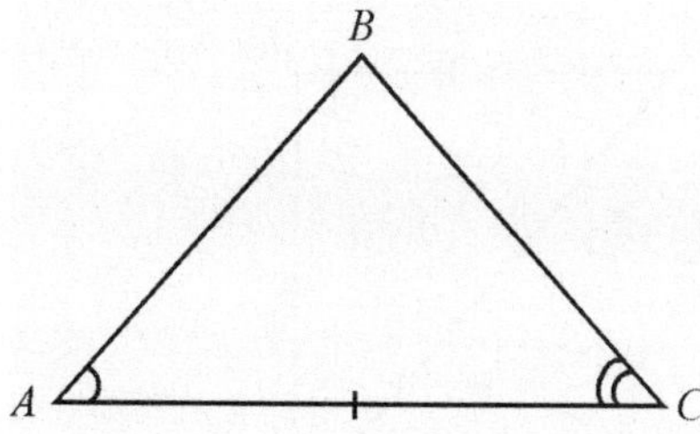

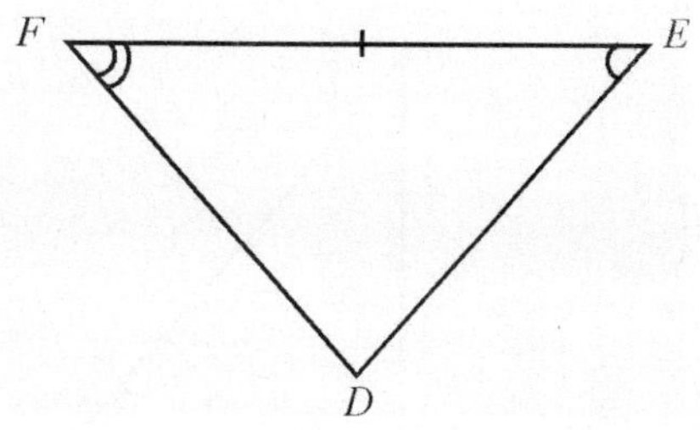

Solution
The triangles are congruent.

The reason is:
$\angle A = \angle E$
$\overline{AC} = \overline{EF}$
$\angle C = \angle F$

This satisfies the condition of ASA: two angles of one triangle are equal to two angles of the other triangle ($\angle A = \angle E$ and $\angle C = \angle F$).
The contained sides are also equal: $\overline{AC} = \overline{EF}$.
Therefore, $\Delta ABC \cong \Delta EDF$.

NOTES

Example 2
State why $\Delta GHI \cong \Delta KLJ$. List all the equal sides and angles.

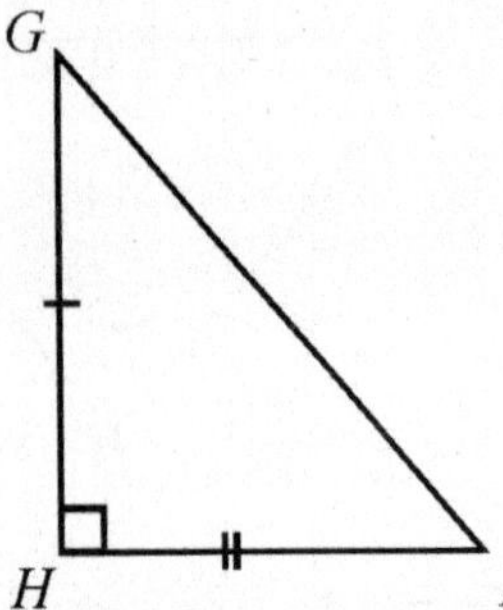

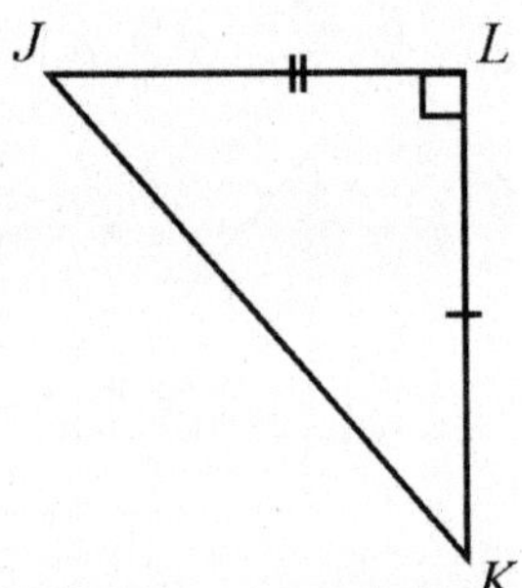

Solution
$\overline{GH} = \overline{KL}$
$\angle H = \angle L$
$\overline{HI} = \overline{LJ}$

$\cong$ means "is congruent"

Therefore, $\Delta GHI \cong \Delta KLJ$ satisfies the condition SAS.

The other equal parts are
$\overline{GI} = \overline{KJ}$
$\angle G = \angle K$
$\angle I = \angle J$

Congruent Δs = Similar Δs

Similar Δs $\neq$ Congruent Δs

You can relate congruent triangles to similar triangles. Similar triangles are not congruent triangles because the lengths of their sides are proportional, but not equal. However, you can still say that congruent triangles are similar triangles because they do have equal angles and the sides are proportional. The proportion of the sides in congruent triangles will always equal one, because when equal values are divided the answer is always one.

PRACTICE EXERCISES

1. For each of the following diagrams, state whether or not the triangles are congruent. Name the condition of congruency that supports your answer.

a)

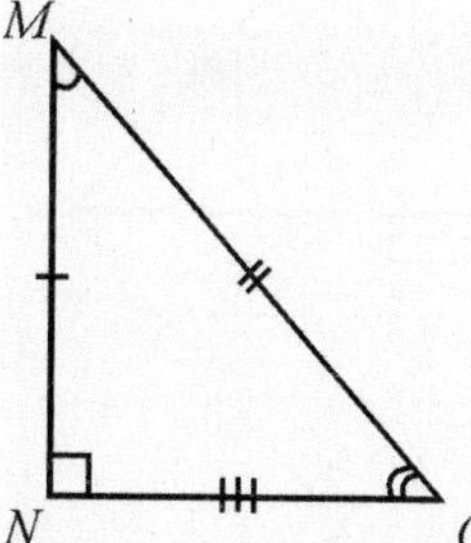

b)

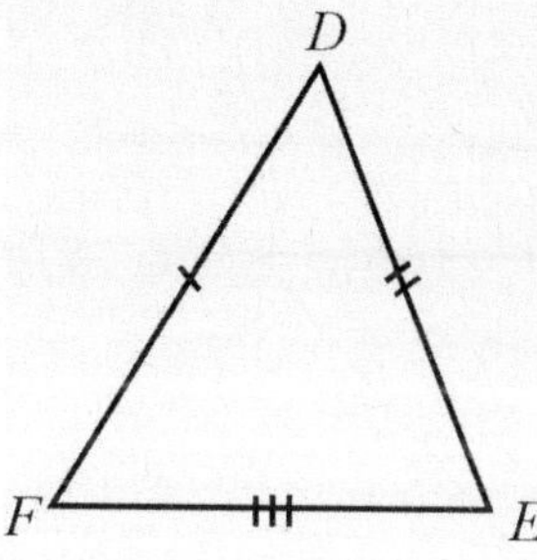

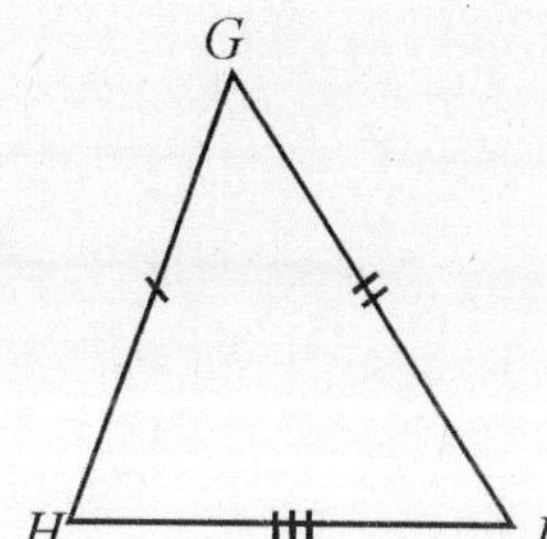

c)

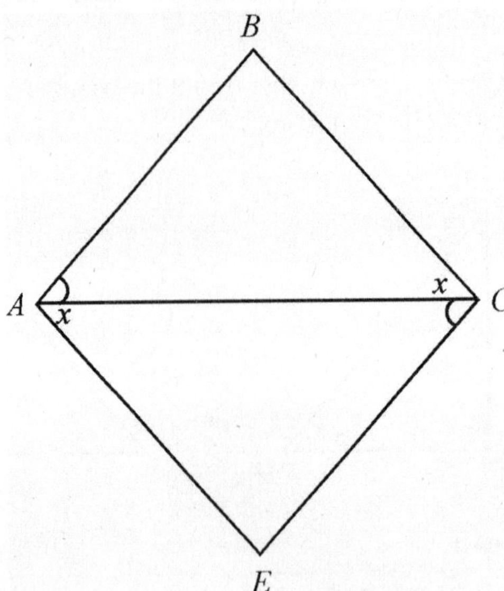

d)

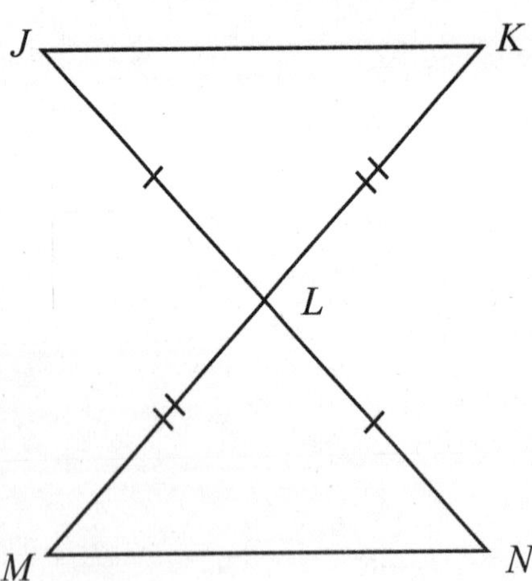

2. Name the equal sides and angles for the congruent triangles below.

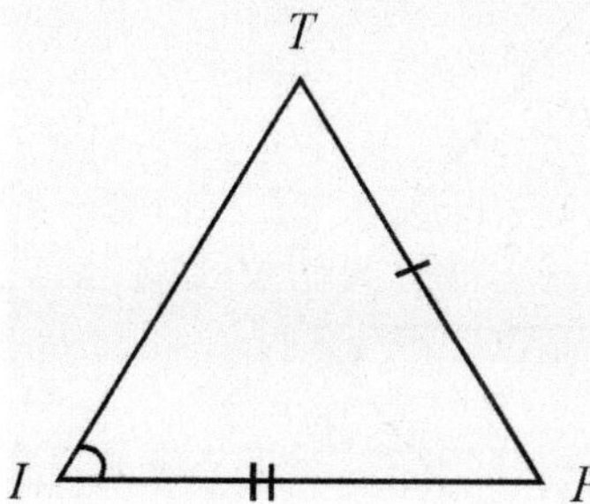

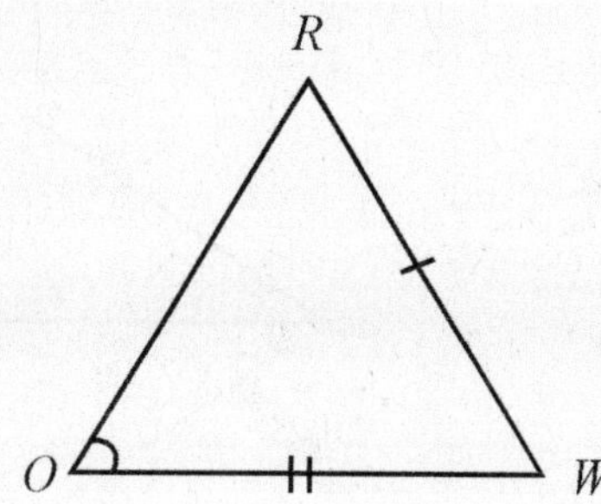

3. For each pair of triangles below list all the corresponding equal parts. Name the condition that proves the triangles are congruent.

a)

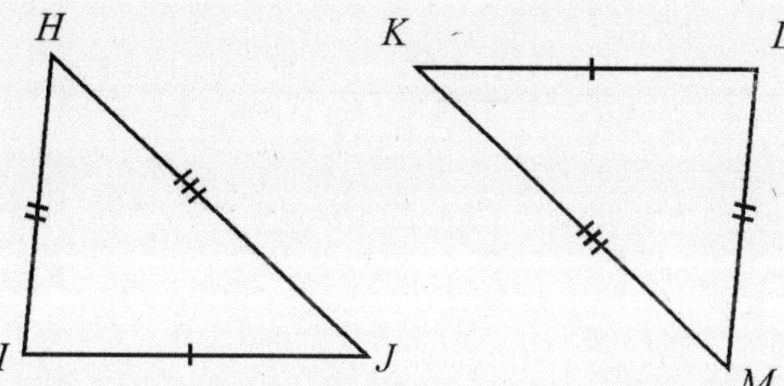

b)

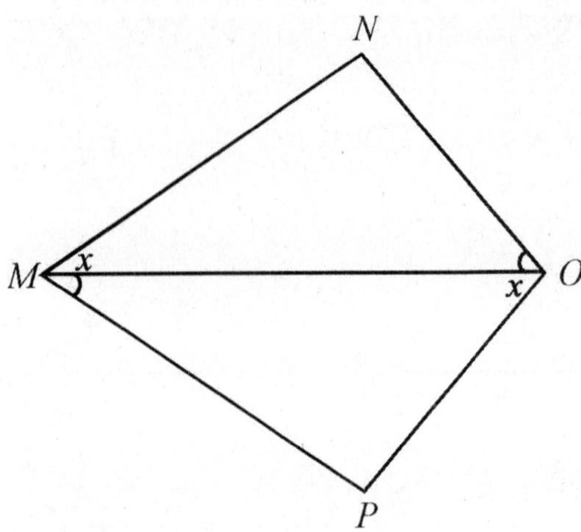

4. Explain why all congruent triangles are also similar triangles.

Lesson 9 THREE-DIMENSIONAL SKETCHES AND VIEWS OF OBJECTS

NOTES

Sometimes when people plan to build something, they first create a three-dimensional diagram or model of what the finished product should look like. Builders use this strategy when designing various styles of houses, office buildings, and other structures.

Diagrams may be two- or three-dimensional and may show a variety of views such as
- a top view that shows the object as seen from above
- front, rear, or side view that show the object from a given perspective

Diagrams usually include dimensions and show the position of objects relative to one another.

Three-dimensional models are created using a proportional scale.

Example 1

Using the following two-dimensional representations, draw the three-dimensional object that they represent. (It might be helpful to use isometric dot paper or graphing paper).

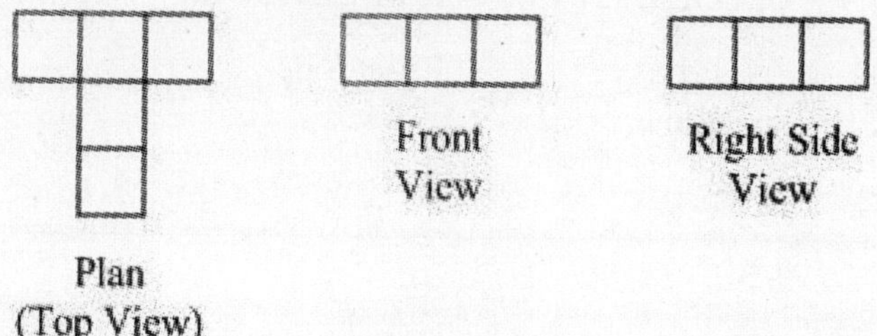

When drawing blocks on isometric dot paper, connect the dots in a diamond shape to form the top of a cube. For example,

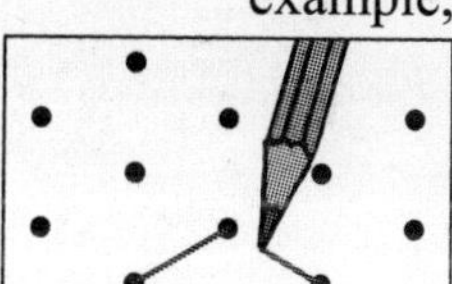

Solution

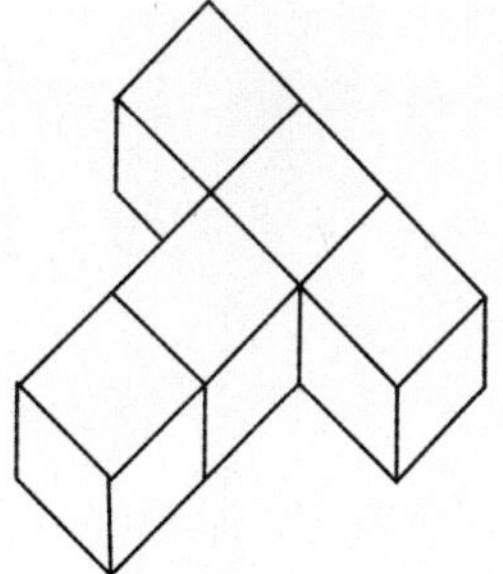

Example 2

For the following three-dimensional diagram, draw the two-dimensional plan, including the top view, front view, and right side view.

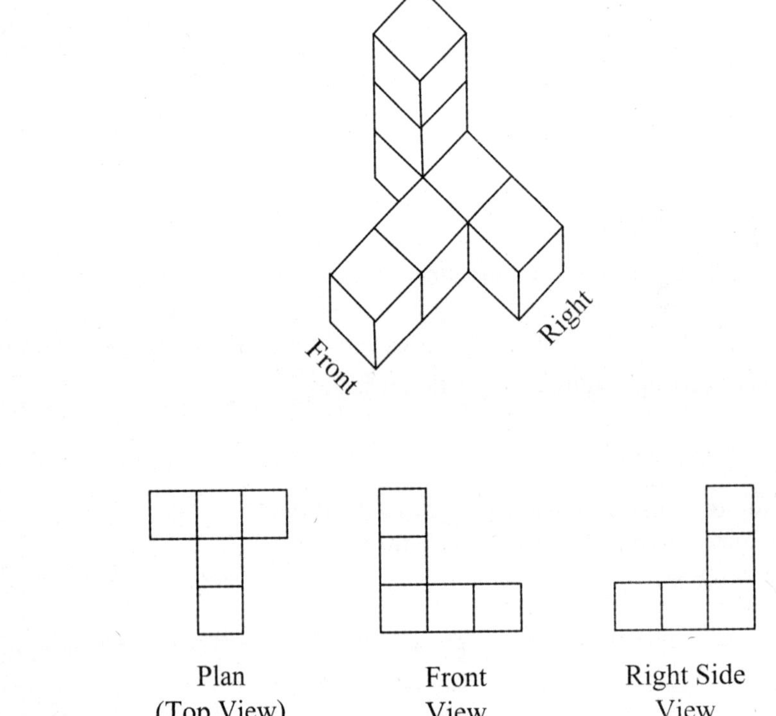

Solution

PRACTICE EXERCISES

1. For the following views, draw the three-dimensional diagram that is represented.

a)

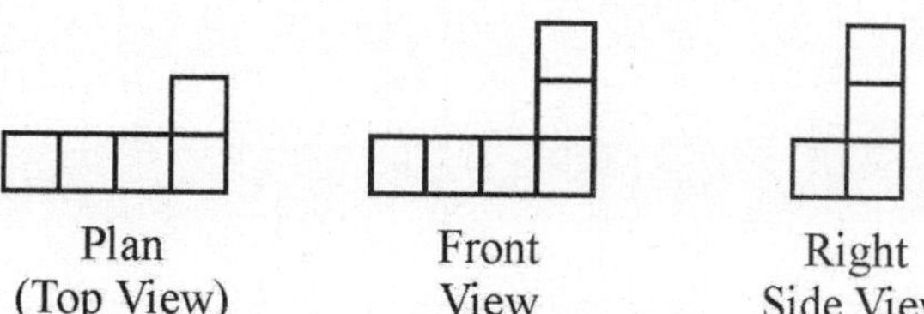

b)

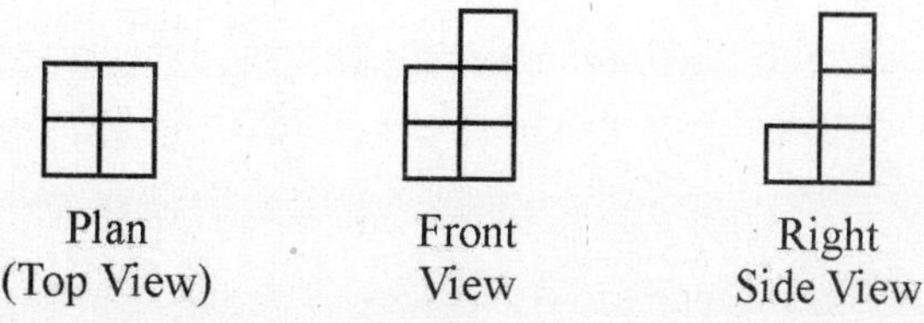

c)

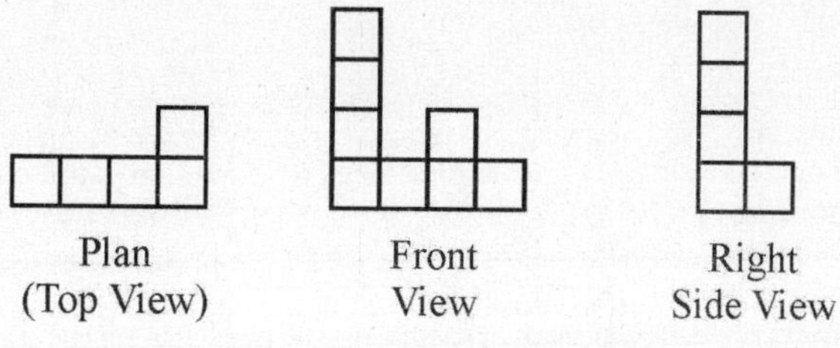

d)

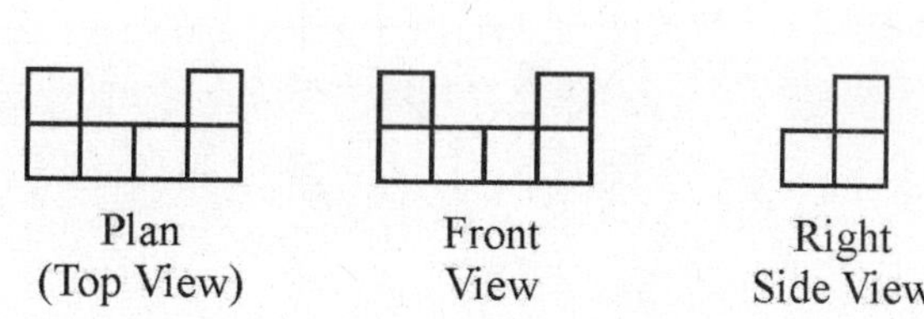

2. For each of the following three-dimensional diagrams, draw the plan (top view), front view, and right side view.

a)

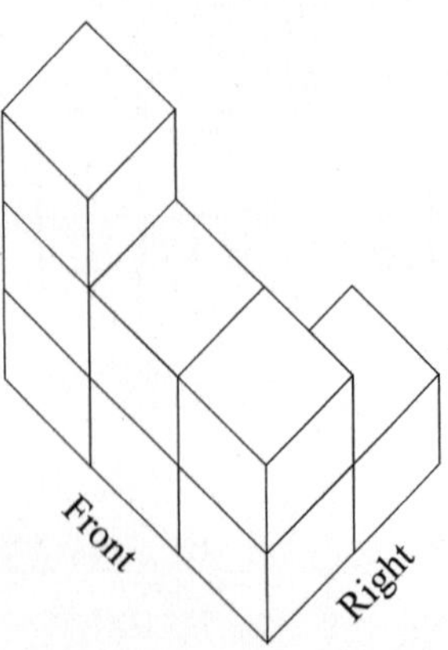

b)

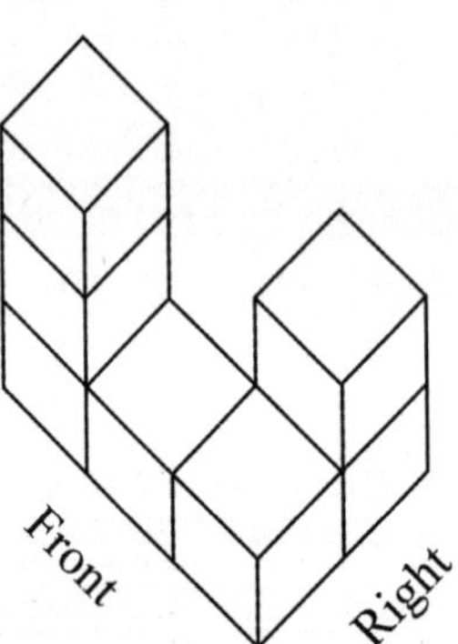

c)

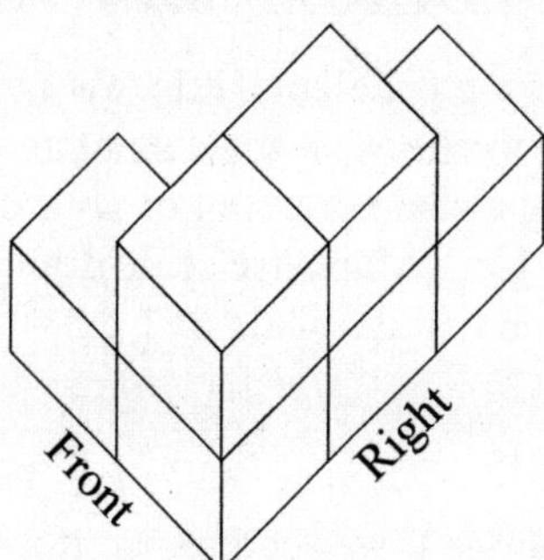

d)

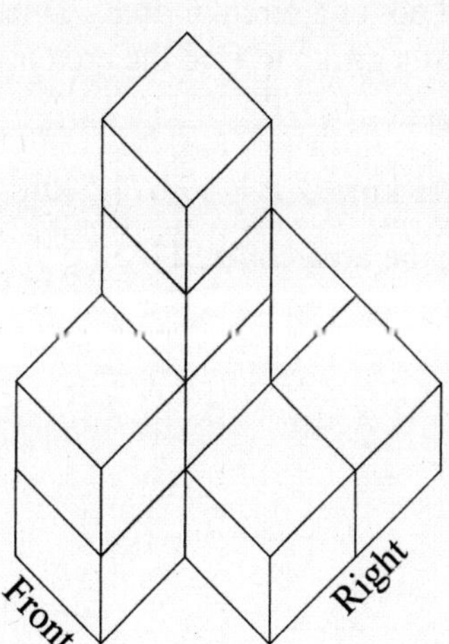

Lesson 10 DRAWING DIAGRAMS TO SOLVE PROBLEMS

NOTES

When solving problems, it is often useful to create a scale drawing. It is important to choose a scale suitable for the given problem. For example, in creating a scale drawing of your bedroom, you could use 1 cm to represent 1 m. Maps use scale drawings to show the distance between cities, often using a scale of 1 cm = 100 km.

Example 1

If a cell phone tower can transmit a signal a distance of approximately 75 km, what is the transmission area of the tower? Use a scale drawing to illustrate your answer.

Solution

The first step is to choose a suitable scale for the problem. In this case, the scale chosen is 1 cm = 25 km.

Since the tower transmits a signal a distance 75 km, you can draw a 3 cm line away from it.

Now you can see that because the tower can transmit in every direction, it will cover a circular area. This means you can use the formula for area of a circle to find the area of the tower's coverage.

$A = \pi r^2$

$A = (75 \text{ km})^2 \times \pi = 17\,671.5 \text{ km}^2$

Thus, the area covered by the tower is 17 671.5 km^2.

NOTES

Example 2

Below is a plan of a yard with a fence around it. The diagram is drawn using the scale 0.5 cm = 1 m. The owner wants to put in a lawn that is at least 1 m from the tree and at least 2 m from the fence. Shade the area that will represent the lawn.

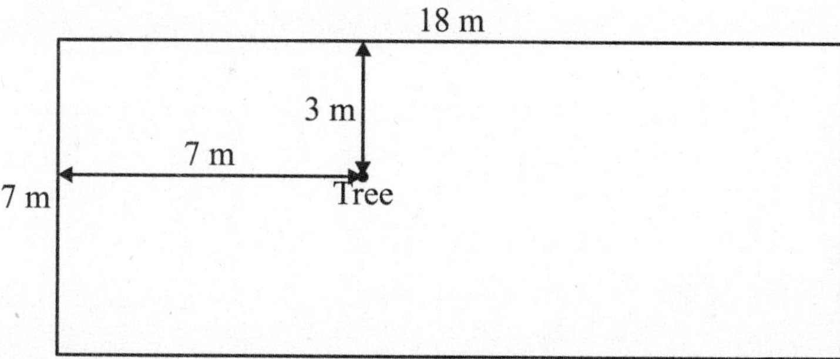

Solution

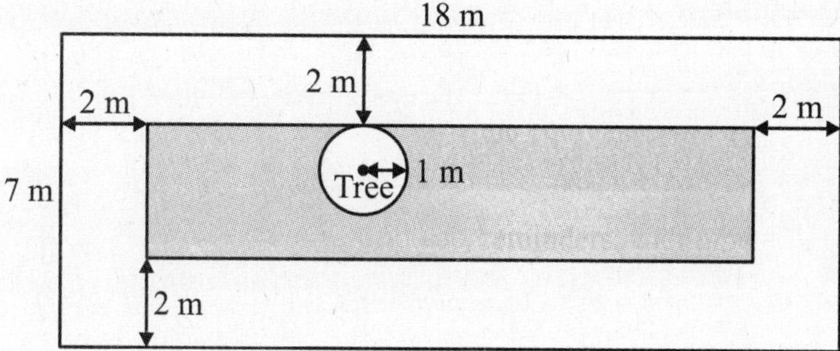

PRACTICE EXERCISES

1. A monkey is being transported in a rectangular cage that measures 160 cm by 100 cm. The monkey can reach out 60 cm all around the cage. Draw a scale diagram of the monkey's cage and surrounding area. Shade the area that the monkey can reach outside the cage.

2. In a particular campground, a washroom is to be located the same distance from section *A* as from section *B*. Section *A* and section *B* are 80 m apart. Draw a scale diagram showing the layout of the campground, including the location of the washroom.

3. Pete's backyard measures 12 m by 10 m. His dog Sparky is on a 5 m leash tied to one corner of the fence surrounding the yard. Use a scale diagram to show the area that Sparky can reach.

PRACTICE QUIZ 2

1. The triangles in each of the following diagrams are similar triangles. For each diagram, calculate the value of x and y. Round your answer to the nearest tenth.

a)

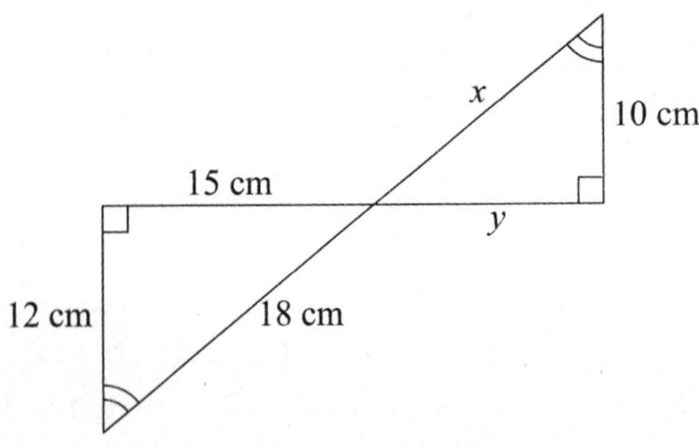

b)

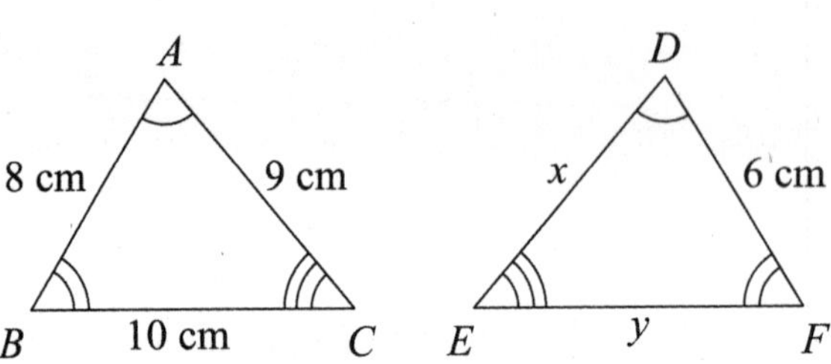

2. A company wants to sell sugar cubes in a box that has a volume of 12 cm^3. What is the smallest surface area the box can have if its dimensions are expressed as whole numbers?

3. Tannis has a lawn measuring 16 m by 16 m. She has several water sprinklers that spray in a circular pattern to a radius of 2 m. Draw a scale diagram showing how she should place the sprinkles to water the lawn, and then calculate the area of the lawn they will spray. Remember that the formula for calculating the area of a circle is $A = \pi r^2$.

4. Karwin wants to build a rectangular pen for his dog. The fencing material comes in 2 m long units that cannot be cut. If Karwin has 20 m of fencing, what are the dimensions of the largest area he can enclose?

5. Roy is 1.5 m tall and casts a 1 m shadow. At the same time of day, a light pole casts a 3.5 m shadow. Calculate the height of the light pole to the nearest tenth of a metre. You may find that drawing a diagram is helpful.

6. Are the following triangles congruent? Support your answer.

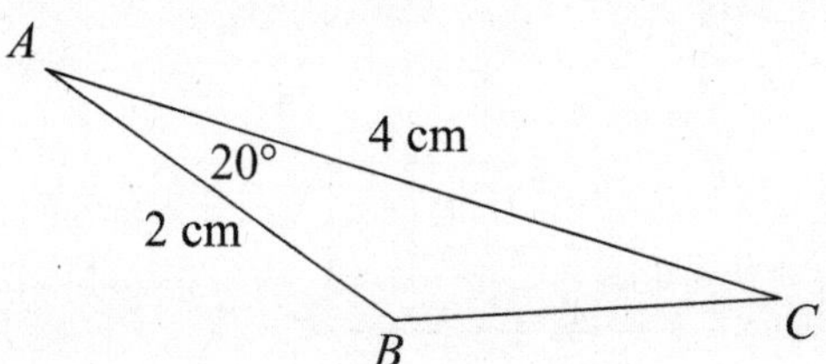

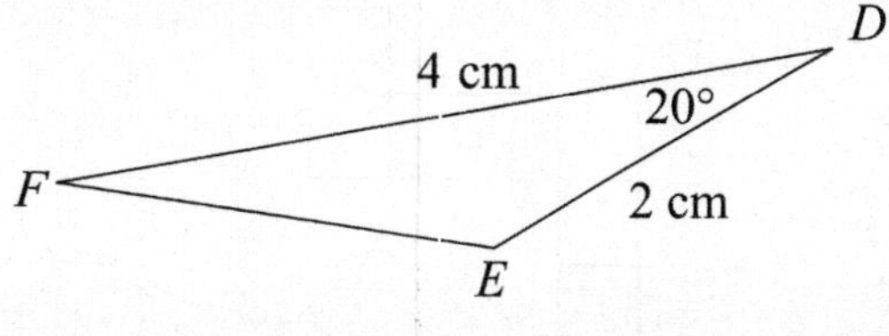

7. For the following three-dimensional diagram, draw the two-dimensional top view, front view, and side view.

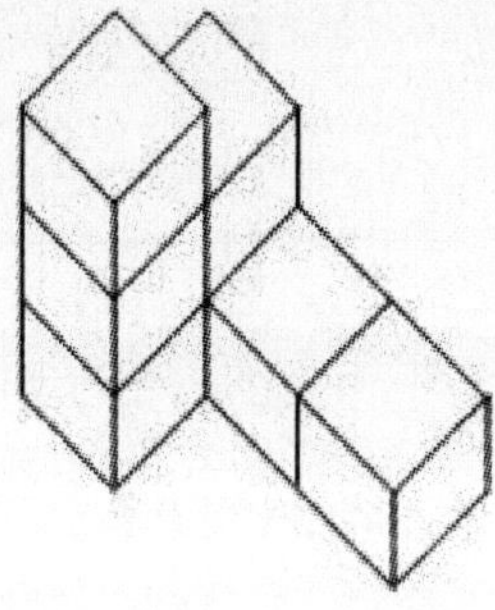

8. Given the following views, draw a three-dimensional diagram.

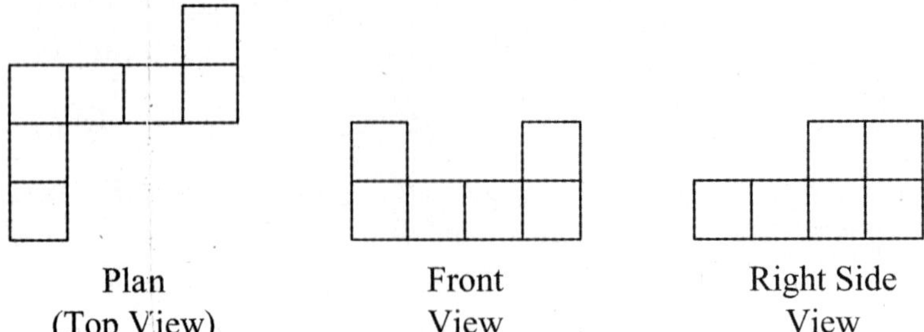

Lesson 11 TRANSFORMATIONS OF TWO-DIMENSIONAL SHAPES

A **translation** is a type of transformation that can be performed on a coordinate grid.

In a translation, an object may be moved up or down, right or left, or a combination of these. Movements to the left are made as a result of a subtraction from the original x-coordinate. Movements to the right are made as a result of an addition to the original x-coordinate. Movements up are made as a result of an addition to the original y-coordinate. Movements down are made as a result of a subtraction from the original y-coordinate.

An image that has been translated is always congruent to the original object. The angles and dimensions remain identical, the only thing that changes about the object is its location on a grid.

A **translation** is sometimes referred to as a **slide**.

NOTES

On a coordinate grid, the x-axis is a horizontal axis and the y-axis is the vertical axis.

Example 1

Draw ΔABC with vertices $A(2,3)$, $B(4,6)$, $C(6,1)$. Then translate the triangle 4 units left and 3 units down. Identify the translation image as $\Delta A'B'C'$.

Ordered pairs are always written (x, y).

Solution

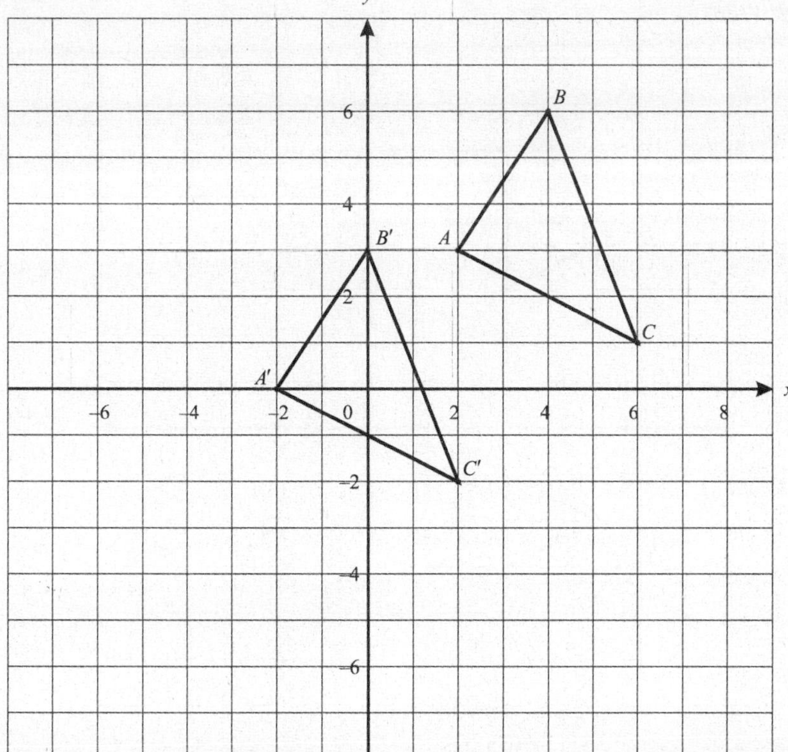

NOTES

To move a diagram on a grid to the left 4 units, subtract 4 from the x-coordinates. To move it down 3 units, subtract 3 from the y-coordinates. This will give you the coordinates of the translated image.

After a triangle has been translated, the lengths of the sides and the measures of the angles are unchanged. The original triangle and its translated image are congruent triangles.

A **reflection line** is a line of symmetry.

A **reflection** is another form of transformation. The reflection line can be thought of as the line that you fold to create a mirror image on the other side of the line. The coordinates of a reflected image are the same distance away from the mirror, or reflecting line, as in the original shape. The reflection image is on the opposite side of the reflection line as the original shape.

Primes are the small tics used to indicate that the vertices of a figure are transformations of the vertices of another figure. For example, point A' is a transformation of point A.

For instance, if the reflection line is the x-axis and the original point is at $A(2, 3)$, then the reflection image would be at $A'(2, -3)$. Point A is 3 units above the x-axis and A' is 3 units below the x-axis. The shape and the reflected image are an equal distance from the line of reflection. The figures will be symmetrical.

Example 2

Draw ΔABC with vertices $A(-5, -2)$, $B(-3, -1)$, $C(-3, -3)$. Then draw the reflection image using a line of symmetry one unit above the x-axis. The equation of that line is $y = 1$. Label the image appropriately with primes.

Solution

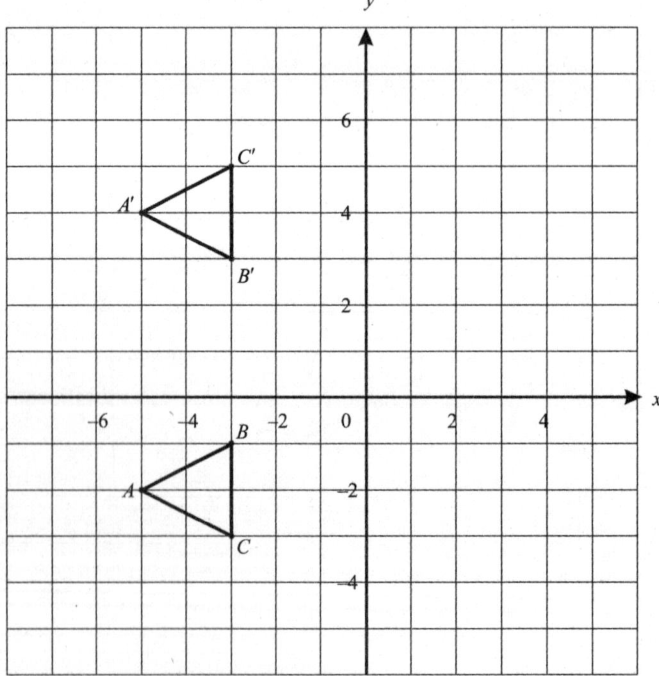

NOTES

After a triangle has been reflected, the lengths of the sides and the measures of the angles are unchanged. However, the orientation of a reflected triangle changes from the original triangle. Since all the sides and angles are equal, the original triangle and its reflected image are congruent triangles.

A **rotation** is another type of transformation. Rotations can be either clockwise or counterclockwise. Remember that one complete rotation or a complete circle is 360°. A rotation of 90° clockwise is the same as a rotation of 270° counterclockwise. If you are asked to do a rotation of 270° counterclockwise, you may decide to do a rotation of 90° clockwise because it covers a shorter distance.

Rotations can be clockwise or counterclockwise

In a 90º rotation, the slope of the lines in a figure will all change 90º, so that the final image is perpendicular to the original figure.

90º clockwise rotation = 270º counterclockwise rotation

To help you perform a rotation, you can start from the rotation point and create a "rotation stick" as you move up, down, left, or right from your original point. A rotation stick is a line that starts from the rotation point and goes to a point on the figure. Rotate the stick according to the rotation requested. The image point should be at the end of the stick.

Example 3

Draw ΔDEF with vertices $D(3, 4)$, $E(3, 1)$, $F(1, 1)$. Then, rotate it 90° counterclockwise about the point $P(0, 0)$. Label the image appropriately with primes.

Solution

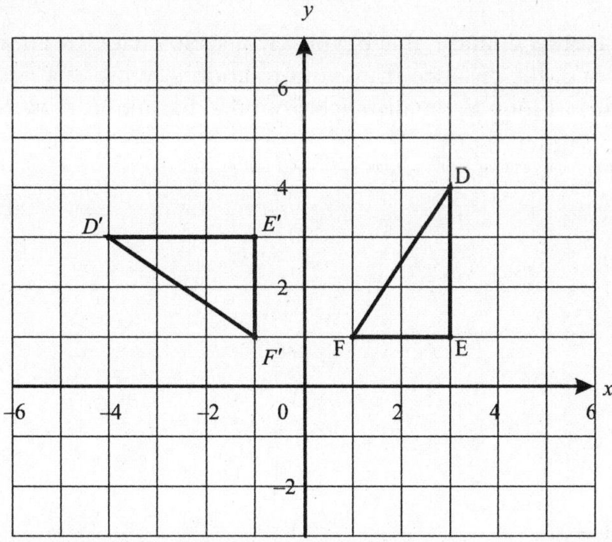

NOTES

All three points in $\Delta D'E'F'$ are the same distance from the origin (0, 0) after the 90° rotation, but the lines are now perpendicular. The slope of $\overline{DF}$ is perpendicular to the slope of $\overline{D'F'}$. The original rotation stick shows how vertex D is three units from the y-axis. Rotating the figure 90° counterclockwise transforms the image so that vertex D is now three units away from the x-axis.

To rotate point D in the last example, you would make your rotation stick by going up 4 units and right 3 units. Since you are rotating 90° counterclockwise, move the stick left 4 units and up 3 units. This gives the rotation image $D'(-4, 3)$. A rotation image is congruent to the original shape, only its positioning is different.

When an object is rotated around the origin, the vertices may be moved through the different quadrants, changing from positive to negative and back, but not changing their value.

After a triangle has been rotated, the lengths of the sides and the measures of the angles are unchanged. However, the position of the top and bottom of the rotated triangle is different than the original triangle. Since all the sides and angles are equal, the original triangle and its rotated image are congruent triangles.

Dilation images of triangles are similar triangles to the original triangle.

The last transformation that you will look at in this lesson is the **dilation**. A dilation is the proportional increase or decrease in size of a shape. Your school pictures package provides a good example of dilations. It contains both large and small pictures of you. However, while these may differ in size, they remain the same shape.

When you create a dilation image, you use a scale factor. If an image has a scale factor of 2, the distance from your dilation's centre to a point on the image is twice as long as the distance from the dilation's centre to the same point on the original figure.

NOTES

Example 4

For ΔABC that has vertices $A(1, 2)$, $B(2, 3)$, $C(3, 1)$, find the dilation image after a scale factor of 2 is applied to the dilation point $D(0, 0)$. Label the image appropriately with primes.

Solution

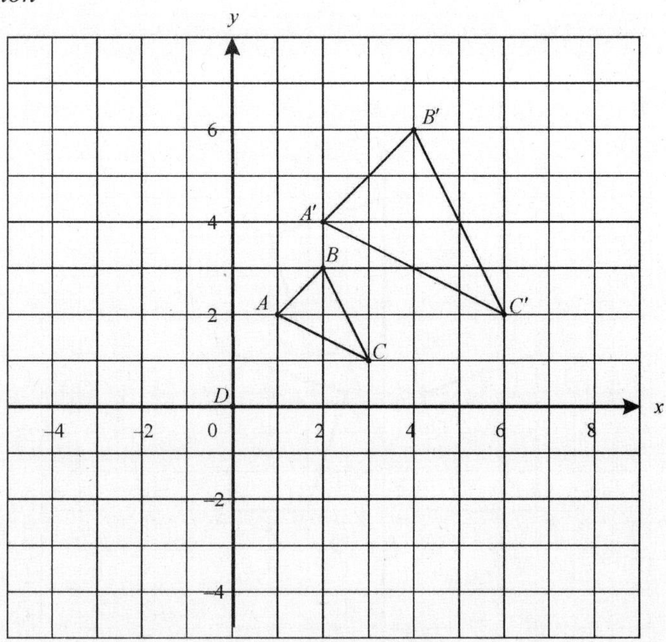

When finding the dilation image, measure $\overline{DA}$ in the original image. From the new dilation point D, and keeping your ruler at the same slope as $\overline{DA}$, find the spot where double the distance of $\overline{DA}$ is and label it A'. Apply the same steps to vertices B and C. You can also find the dilation points by multiplying the coordinates of your points by the scale factor, as long as the dilation centre is (0, 0). $A(1, 2)$ multiplied by 2 is $A'(2, 4)$.

The angles in dilation images are equal to the corresponding angles of the original image. A triangle and its dilation image are similar triangles because the corresponding angles are equal and the corresponding sides will be proportional. However, they are not congruent because they differ in size.

Dilation images of triangles are similar triangles to the original triangle.

You may also be asked to perform **combined transformations**. If you perform two translations in a row, the order you perform these does not affect the final translation image. If you start at $P(-1, 2)$ and do a translation 2 right and 1 up, followed by a translation 3 left and 2 down, you will end up at $P''(-2, 1)$. If you start at $P(-1, 2)$ and do the translation 3 left and 2 down, followed by the translation 2 right and 1 up, you will end up at $P''(-1, 2)$. This same rule applies if you do two reflections in a row. However, the rule does **not** apply if you are doing a translation followed by a reflection, or vice versa.

NOTES

Example 5

Find the image of quadrilateral *DEFG*, with vertices *D*(2, –1), *E*(1, 2), *F*(4, 3), *G*(4, –1), after it is reflected in the *y*-axis and translated 4 right and 4 up.

Identify the first image with primes (′) and the second image with double primes (″).

Solution

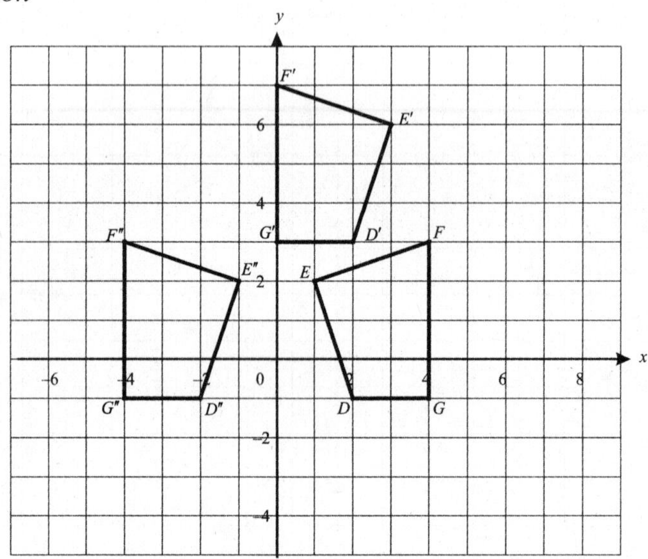

Example 6

Rotate ΔPRS 90° clockwise around point *P*. This means that *P* will not move, and *R* and *S* will rotate to new position.

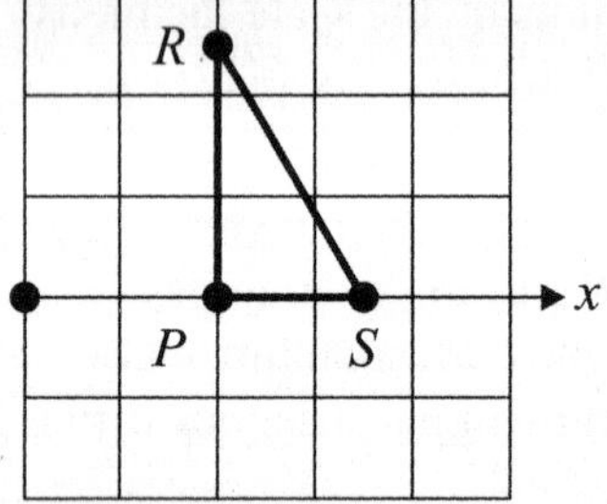

Solution

PRACTICE EXERCISES

1. Draw a triangle with the coordinates $A(3, 1)$, $B(6, 1)$ and $C(5, 3)$. Then, draw the images that result from the following transformations.

   a) 90° clockwise rotation with the centre at (0, 0). Label with primes.

   b) A reflection of the original triangle using the y-axis as a line of reflection. Label with double primes.

c) Translate the original triangle 2 units right and 4 units down. Label the triangle with triple primes.

2. For each of the above transformations, identify whether or not the original triangle and the transformation image are congruent. Explain your answer.

3. Draw a quadrilateral with vertices $P(5, 2)$, $Q(6, -2)$, $R(1, -2)$, and $S(2, 1)$. Then, draw the quadrilateral after a reflection about a line 1 unit to the left to the y-axis. Label the reflection image with primes.

4. Draw a triangle with vertices $A(-4, 6)$, $B(-2, 2)$, and $C(0, 4)$. Locate the dilation image of the triangle with the dilation centre at $O(0, 0)$ and a scale factor of $\frac{1}{2}$. Explain how you know that the triangle and its image are similar.

5. Draw a quadrilateral with vertices $P(4, 3)$, $Q(5, -2)$, $M(3, -4)$, and $N(1, -1)$. Then draw the quadrilateral after a reflection about a line 1 unit to the right of the y-axis. Finally, draw the reflected triangle after applying a translation of (3, 4). Label each triangle with appropriate primes.

6. Draw a triangle with vertices $P(4, 1)$, $Q(1, 3)$, and $R(3, 5)$. Then draw the same triangle after a rotation of 180° clockwise about the point P.

7. Draw a triangle with vertices $J(2, 2)$, $K(6, 0)$, and $L(4, -2)$. Then, draw the image of this triangle after a reflection in the y-axis followed by a reflection in the y-axis. Would the final image be different in the y-axis had been followed by a reflection in the x-axis? Explain.

Lesson 12 FINDING THE ORIGINAL SHAPE GIVEN THE TRANSFORMATION IMAGE

NOTES

When working backward from a transformation image to the original shape, do the opposite of what was done to the original shape to get the transformed image.

If you are given a point $A'(2, 3)$ that was derived after a translation of 2 units right and 3 units down, you will translate 2 units left and 3 units up from point A' to get back to the original point A. Thus, the original point is $A(0, 6)$. Similarly, if the original shape was rotated 270° clockwise, the opposite operation is to rotate 270° counterclockwise. If the original shape had been reflected on the x-axis, the opposite operation would be to reflect the image back on the x-axis.

When given a transformed point, do the opposite transformation to move back to the original position.

Example 1

The image of figure $M'N'P'Q'R'$ was formed by connecting the vertices $M'(-4, 3)$, $N'(-5, 0)$, $P'(1, -2)$, $Q'(0, 0)$, $R'(1, 2)$ after translating the original figure 3 units left. Draw the original figure $MNPQR$.

Solution

Work backward by doing the opposite translation of 3 units to the right for each of the vertices.

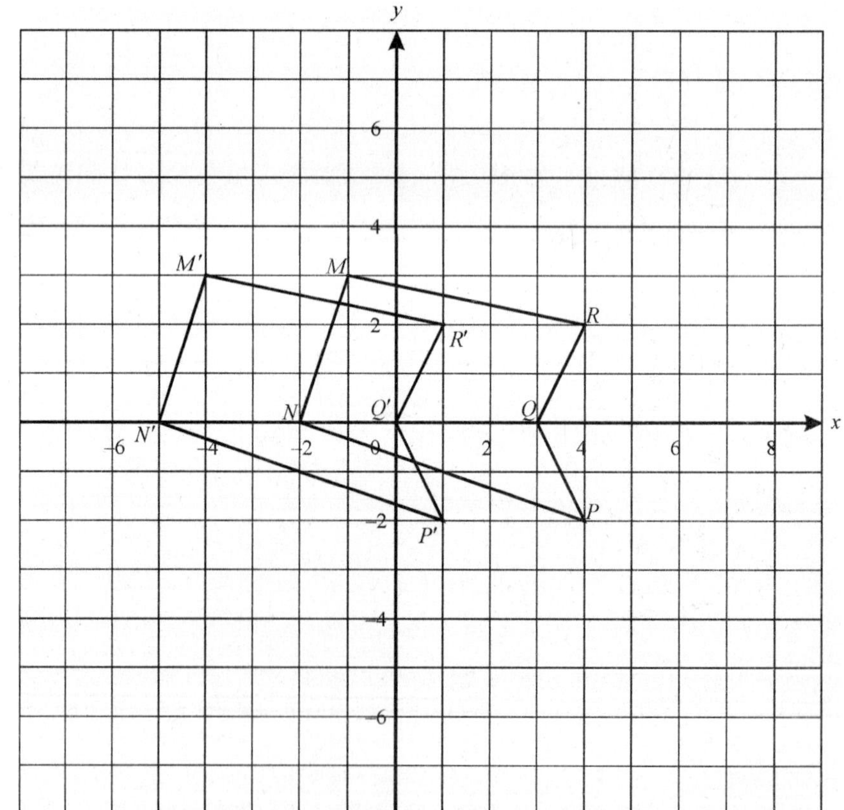

PRACTICE EXERCISES

1. Triangle $A'B'C'$ below was drawn after a reflection in the y-axis. Draw the original triangle ΔABC.

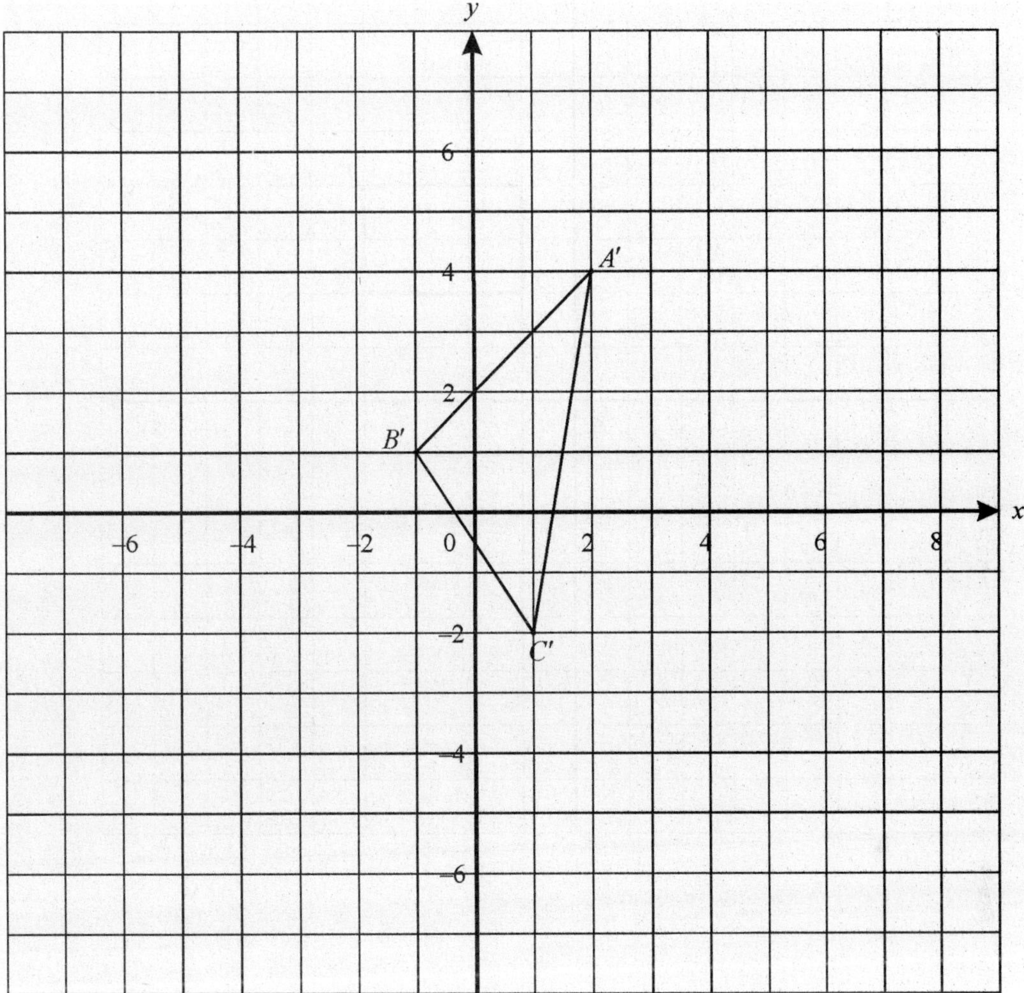

2. Rectangle $D'E'F'G'$ was drawn after a 90° counterclockwise rotation about the point $O(0, 0)$. Draw the original rectangle $DEFG$.

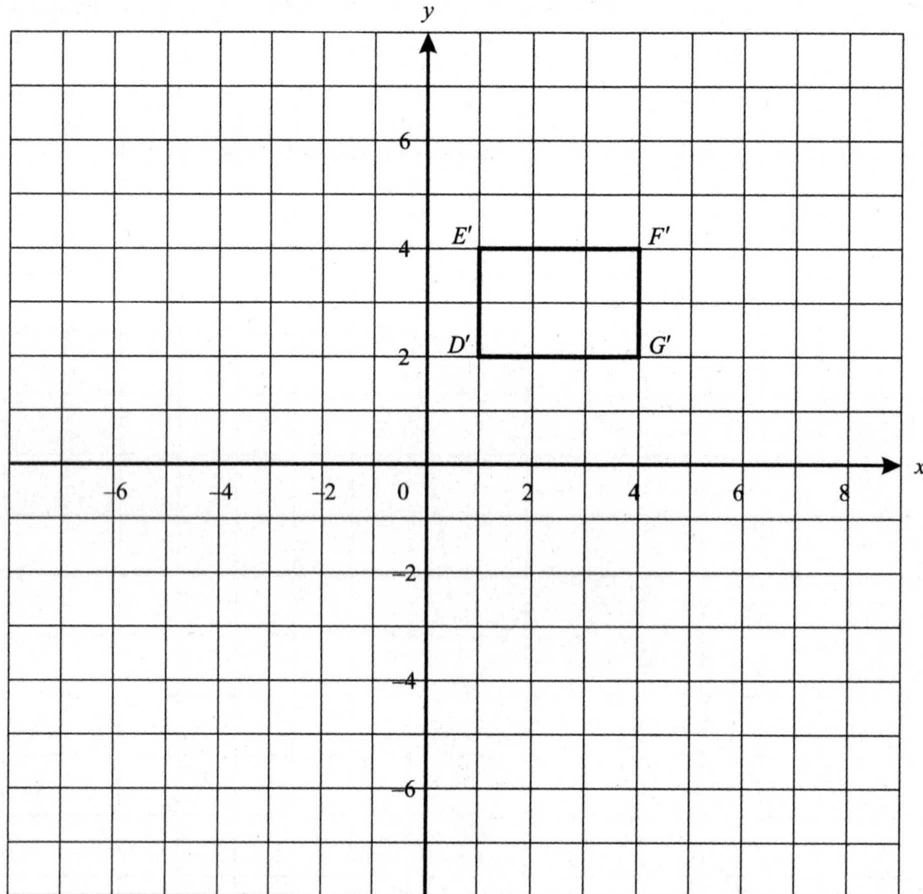

3. Triangle $J'K'L'$ below was drawn after a translation 3 units right and 2 units down. Draw the original triangle JKL.

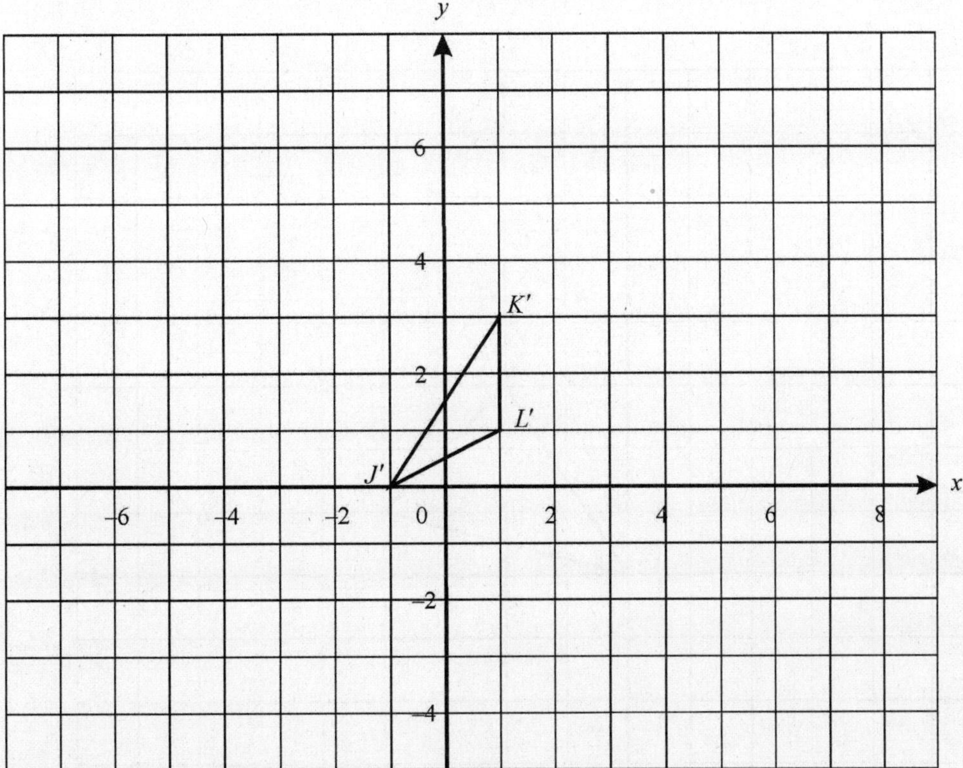

4. The triangle below was moved from its original position by adding 1 to its x-coordinates and 3 to its y-coordinates. It was then reflected over the x-axis. What are the coordinates of the vertices of the original triangle?

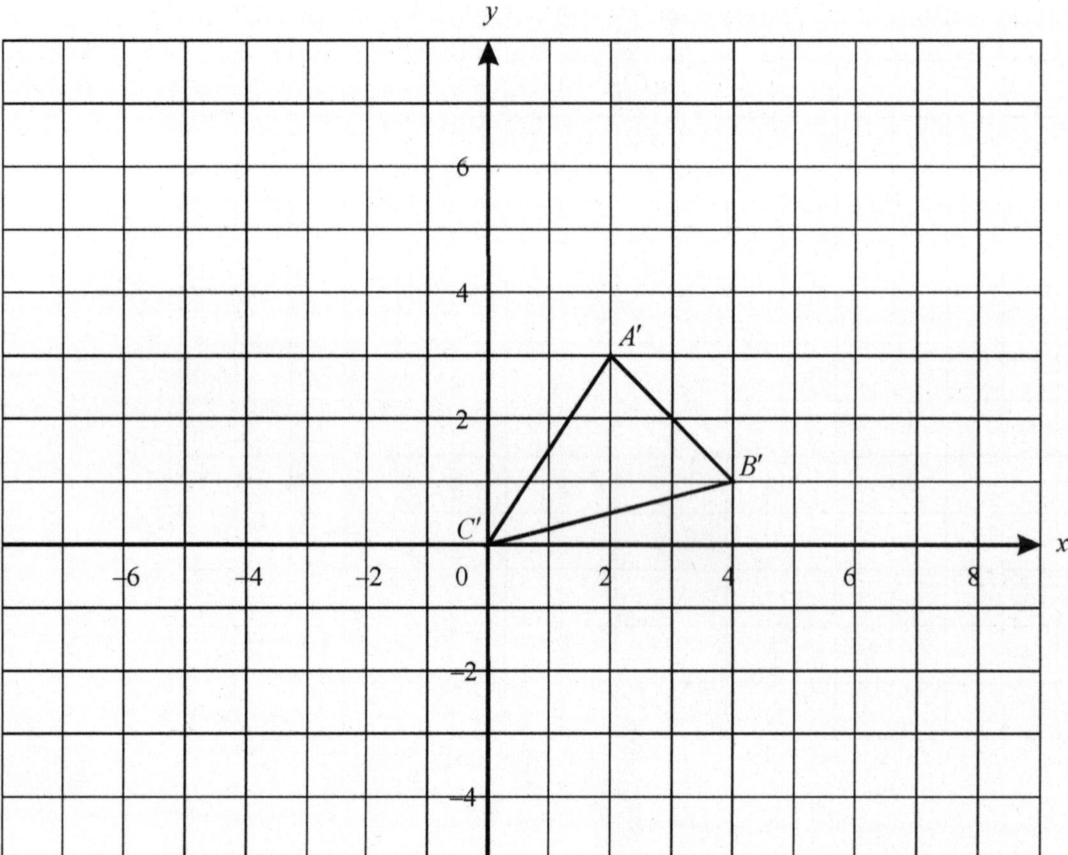

Lesson 13 IDENTIFYING THE TRANSFORMATION

In this lesson, you will identify the transformation when given the original shape and its translation image. In a translation, the sides of the original shape and the image are parallel to each other. In a reflection, the transformation takes on a mirror image of the original shape. In a rotation, the shape turns, with the vertices of the original shape the same distance from the rotation point as the vertices of the rotation image. In a dilation, the shape and its image are similar figures, but one shape is bigger than the other.

NOTES

The four types of transformations are **translation**, **reflection**, **rotation**, and **dilation**.

Example 1

Identify the transformation of triangle *ABC* to triangle $A'B'C'$.

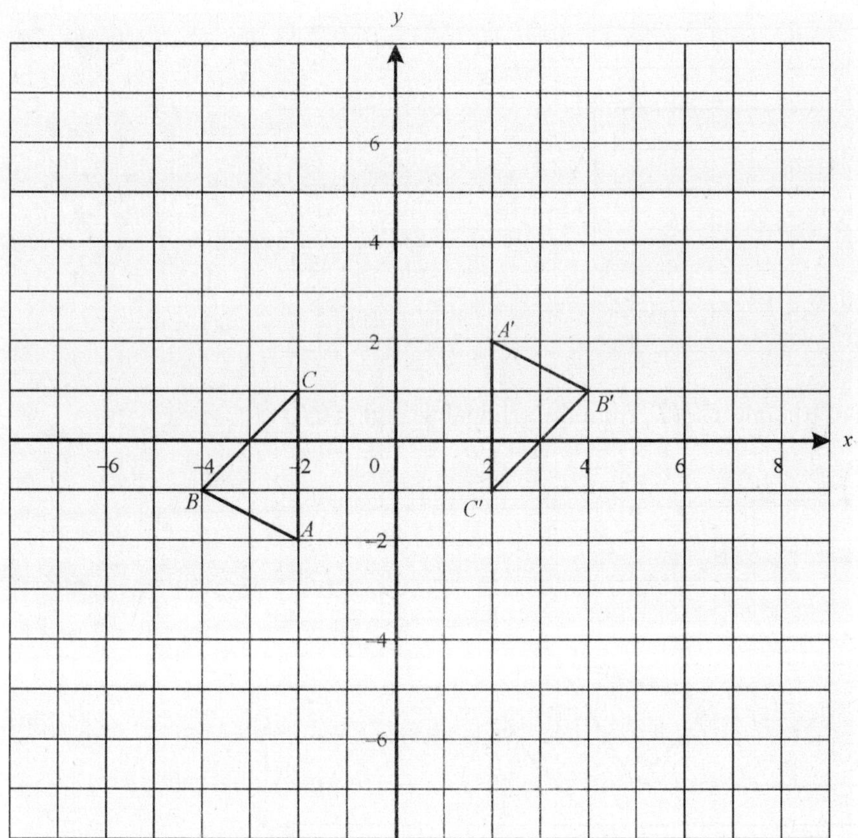

Solution

The image is not a dilation because the size of the triangle is the same. The image is not a translation because the sides are not parallel. The image is not a reflection because the image is not a mirror image of the original. The transformation is a rotation of 180° about the point (0, 0).

PRACTICE EXERCISES

1. Identify the transformation of rectangle *ABCD* below to rectangle $A'B'C'D'$.

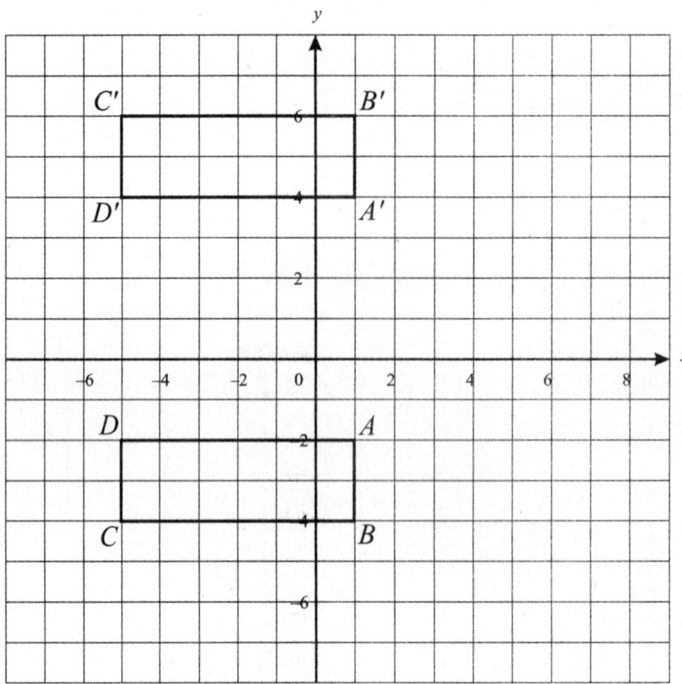

2. Identify the transformation of triangle $G'H'I'$ from the original triangle *GHI*.

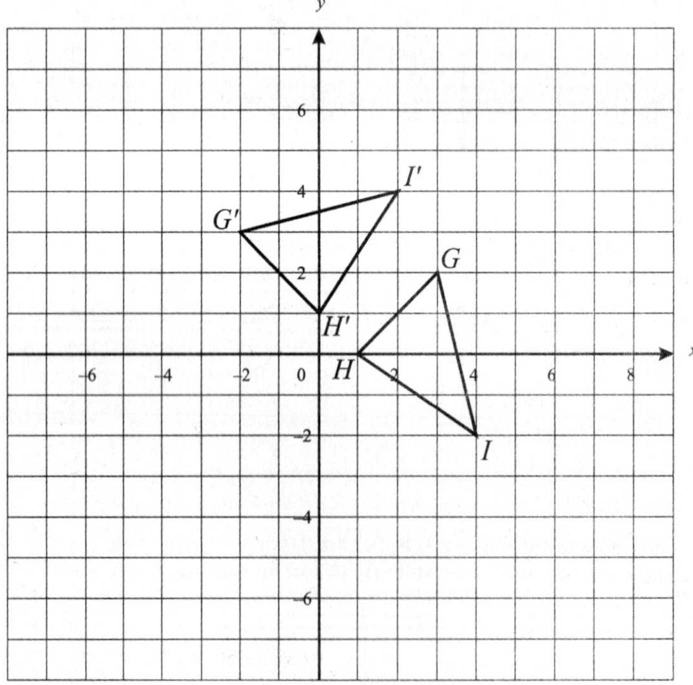

3. Identify the transformation of triangle JKL to triangle $J'K'L'$.

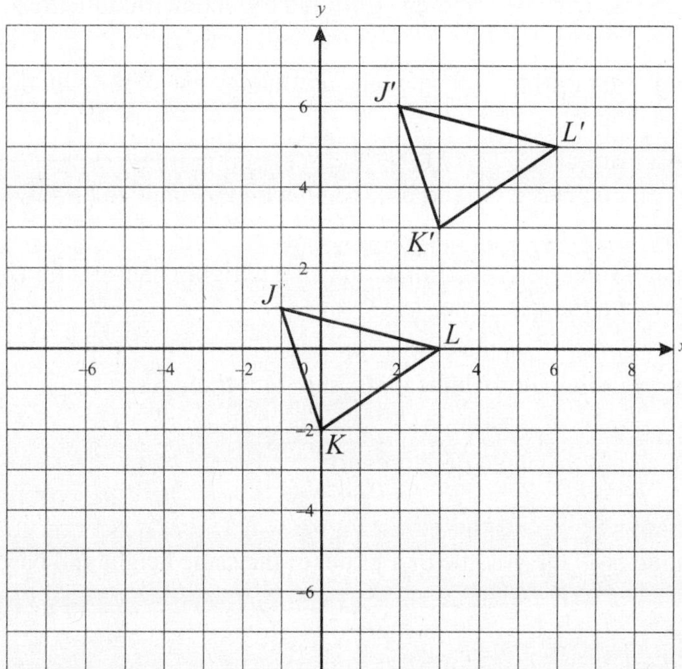

REVIEW SUMMARY

- Use SohCahToa to help you remember the ratios for the trigonometric functions.
- When using a trigonometric ratios to find an angle, use the inverse of the function. For example $\tan^{-1}$ is the inverse value of a tangent ratio.
- When deciding which trigonometric ratio to use, begin with the angle to be solved or a known angle.
- When solving for missing sides, set up an equation using a trigonometric ratio and then use cross-multiplication to solve for a variable.
- Draw diagrams to assist in solving problems involving right triangles.
- The angle of elevation equals the angle of depression.
- The volume of a pyramid is $\frac{1}{3}$ the volume of a prism of the same height and base.
- The volume of a cone is $\frac{1}{3}$ the volume of a cylinder of the same height and base.
- When dealing with different rectangular prisms that have the same volume, the prism with dimensions closest to a cube will have the smallest surface area.
- When working with different rectangles that have the same perimeter, the rectangle with the maximum area possible is the one closest in shape to a square. The closer the values of the rectangle's length and width are to one another, the larger the area of the rectangle.
- Similar triangles have equal corresponding angles and proportional corresponding sides.
- When solving problems involving similar triangles, form an equation using two of the ratios of the corresponding sides. Cross-multiply to solve.
- To prove that two triangles are congruent, use one of the three conditions of congruence: SSS, SAS, and ASA.
- Congruent triangles are similar triangles; however, similar triangles are not congruent triangles.
- When drawing two-dimensional plans of three-dimensional objects, consider the angle you are looking from the top view, front view, and right view.
- Build from a two-dimensional plan when drawing a three-dimensional diagram.
- Triangles and their images are congruent after a translation, rotation, or reflection.

- To make rotation of a figure easier, you can use rotation sticks to connect to points you are moving.
- When doing successive reflections or translations, the order in which you do them does not affect the resulting image.
- When combining reflections and translation, the order **does** affect the resulting image.
- A triangle and its dilation image are similar triangles because the angles are equal and the sides are proportional.
- To identify a single transformation, look at the orientation of the image.

PRACTICE TEST

1. For the following triangle, identify the ratio for sin *B*.

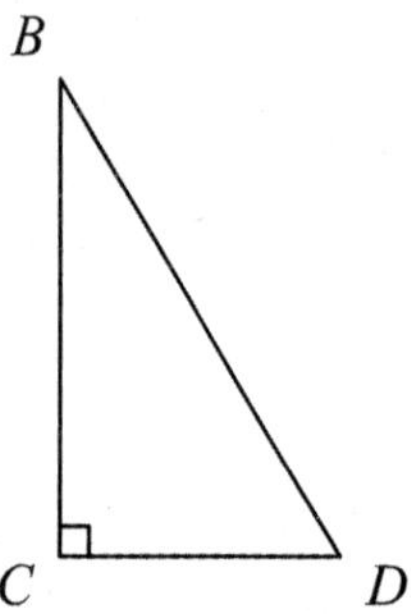

2. For the following triangle, determine the measure of angle *C* to the nearest degree.

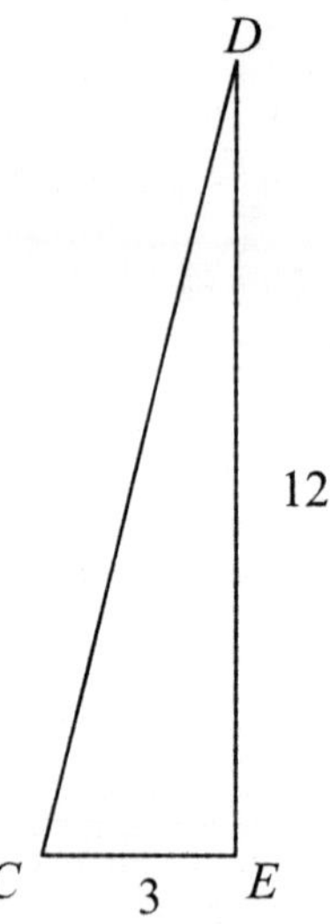

3. For the following triangle, determine the length of x to the nearest tenth of a centimetre.

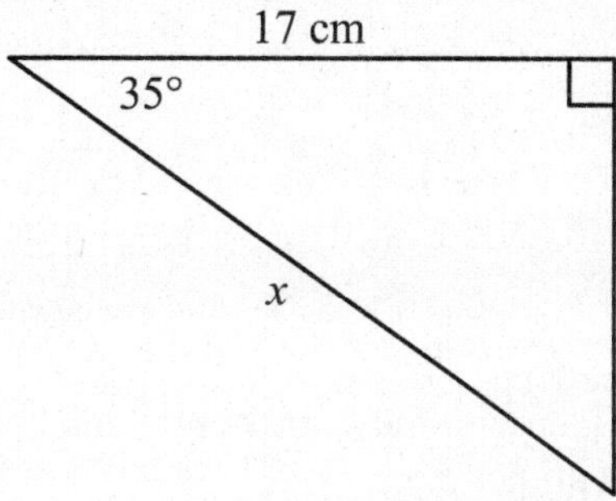

4. A kite is flying at the end of a 15 m string. The string is being held 1.5 m above the ground. The angle of elevation from the end of the string to the kite is 70°. What is the vertical height of the kite from the ground, to the nearest tenth of a metre?

5. A 6 m ladder is leaning against a wall. The base of the ladder is 2 m from the wall. To the nearest degree, what is the measure of the angle formed by the ladder and the ground?

6. a) Calculate the volume of a cone that has a height of 10 cm and a base radius of 4.2 cm.

b) What is the volume of a cylinder with the same height and base radius? (Round your answer to the nearest tenth of a cubic centimetre.)

7. Ramir is building a warehouse in which to store his car collection. The warehouse is in the shape of a rectangular prism and must have a volume of at least 320 m^3. If his main concern is the cost of the materials to build the warehouse, which of the following dimensions should Ramir choose?

A. 1 m by 1 m by 320 m

B. 2 m by 16 m by 10 m

C. 6 m by 7 m by 7 m

D. 8 m by 5 m by 8 m

8. Cathy wants to rope off a rectangular swimming area at her lake front cottage. She has 100 m of cord to rope off three sides. The forth side is formed by the beach. Which of the following dimensions will give Cathy the largest swimming area?

A. 50 m by 50 m

B. 50 m by 25 m

C. 34 m by 32 m

D. 20 m by 60 m

9. Which of the following acronyms does not represent a condition of congruence for triangles?

A. SSS **B.** AAA **C.** ASA **D.** SAS

10. Which of the following statements accurately describes the congruence of the triangles below?

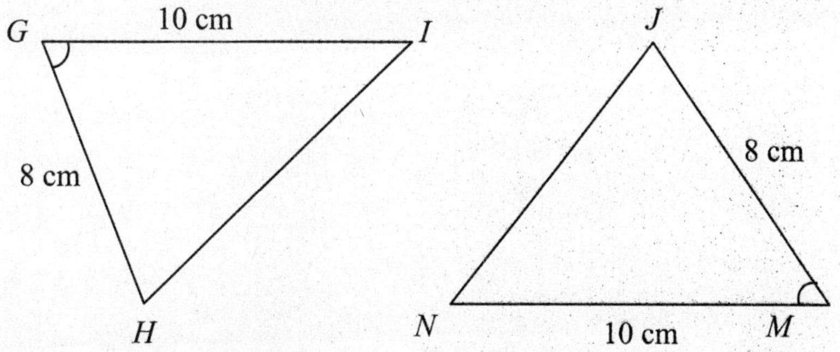

A. triangle *GHI* is congruent to triangle *MJN*
B. triangle *GHI* is congruent to triangle *JNM*
C. triangle *GHI* is congruent to triangle *NJM*
D. triangle *GHI* is congruent to triangle *MNJ*

11. For the triangle below, calculate the value of x, to the nearest tenth of a metre.

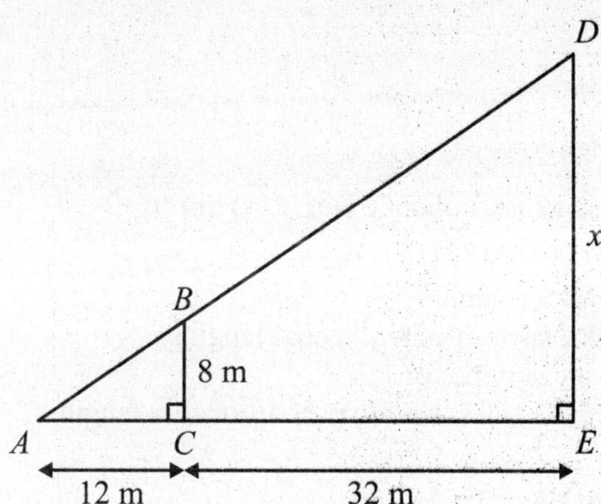

12. Two trees are 100 m apart. From a point exactly 50 m from each tree, the angle of elevation to the top of one tree is 30° and to the top of the other is 55°. How much taller, to the nearest tenth of a metre, is one tree than the other?

13. Which of the following statements about triangles is **not** true?

A. All congruent triangles are similar.
B. All congruent triangles have sides with equal lengths.
C. All similar triangles are congruent.
D. All similar triangles have sides that are proportional in length.

14. For the following three-dimensional diagram, draw the plan (top view), front view, and right view of the object.

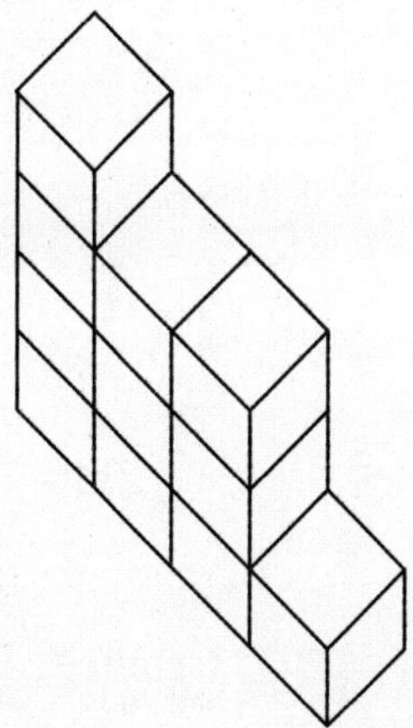

15. Using the following views, draw a three-dimensional diagram of the object.

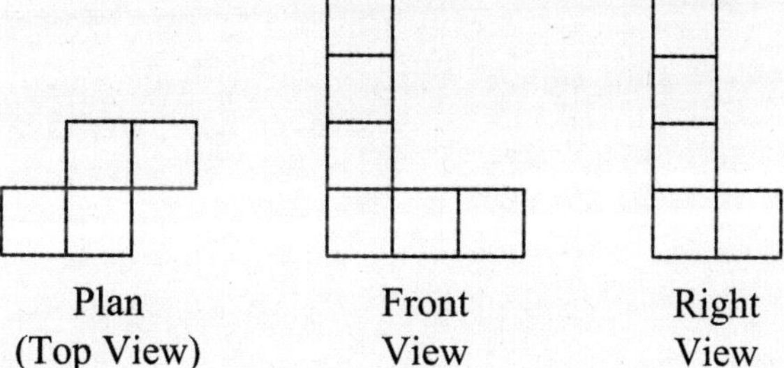

16. Draw triangle *ABC* with vertices *A*(0, 1), *B*(2, 2), *C*(2, 0). Perform a dilation by a scale factor of 3 about the origin (0, 0). Label the dilation image with primes. Explain why the original triangle and the dilation image are similar triangles.

17. Draw triangle *DEF* with vertices *D*(–1, 3), *E*(– 4, 1), *F*(–2, –2). Rotate the triangle 90° clockwise about the point *P*(1, 1) and draw the image. Label the image with primes. Is the rotated image congruent to the original triangle *DEF*?

18. Find the final image of quadrilateral $ABCD$ below after a reflection in a line 1 unit to the right of the of the y-axis followed by a translation 2 left and 3 down. Label the final image with primes.

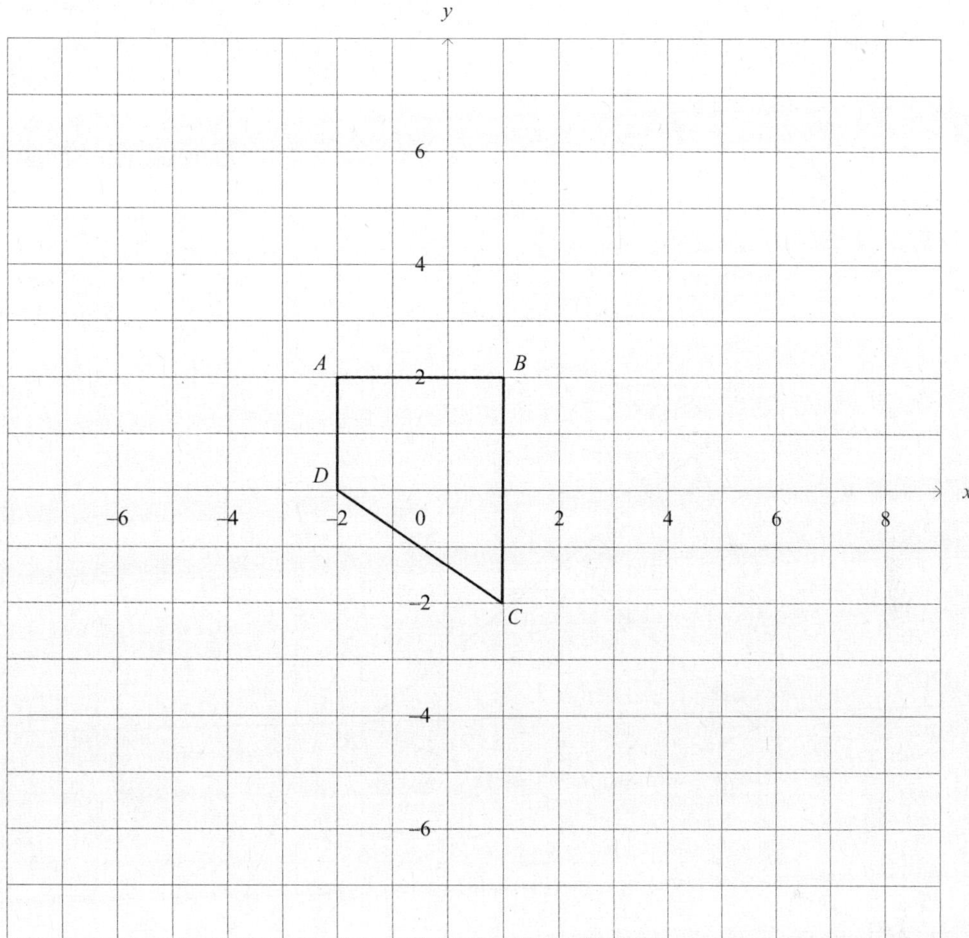

19. For the following diagram, identify the transformation that was performed onto triangle ABC to get triangle $A'B'C'$.

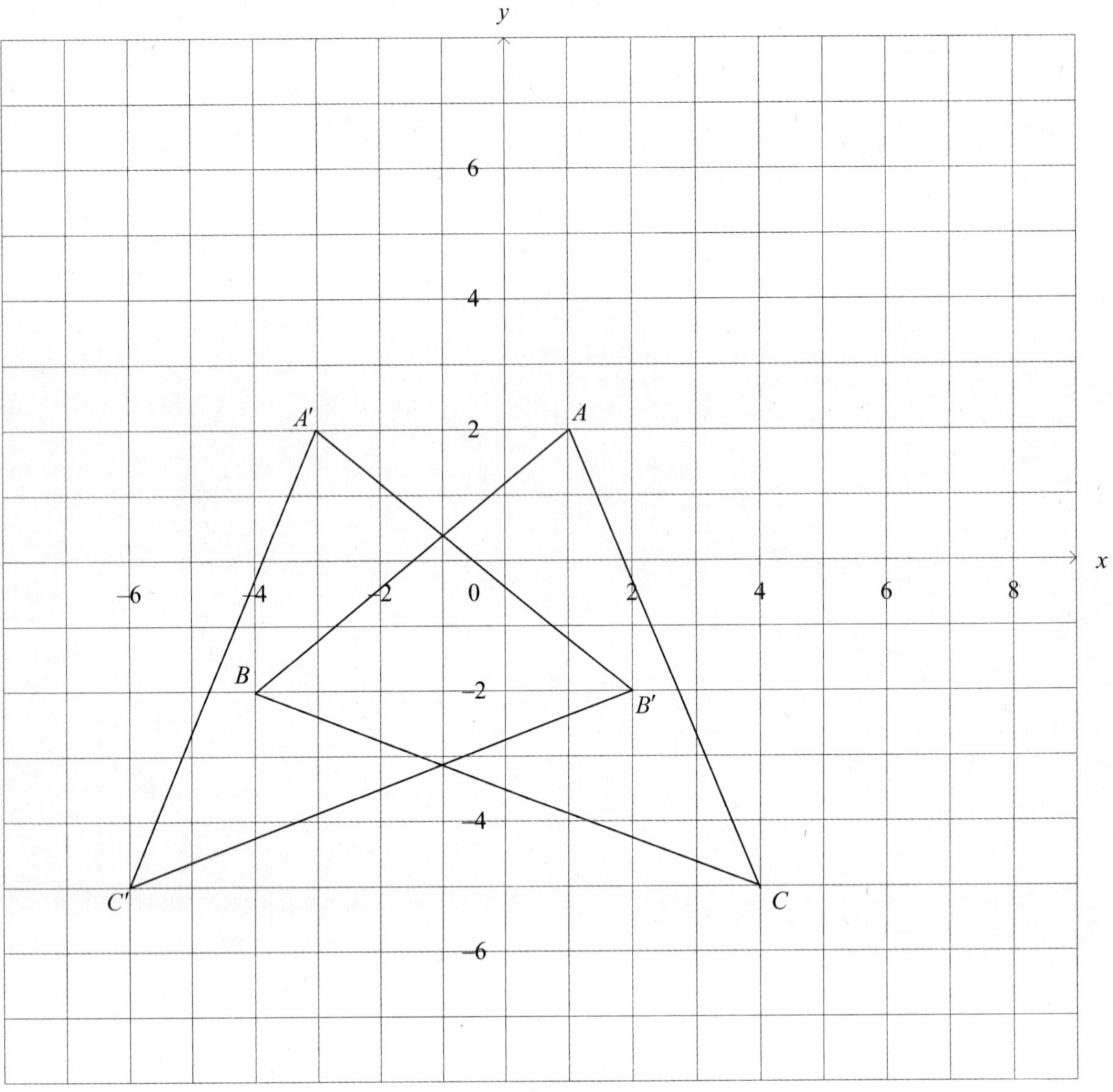

20. The triangle $D''E''F''$ is the result of a reflection of a triangle about a line 2 units above the x-axis, followed by a translation 2 units left and 3 units down. Find the coordinates of the original triangle.

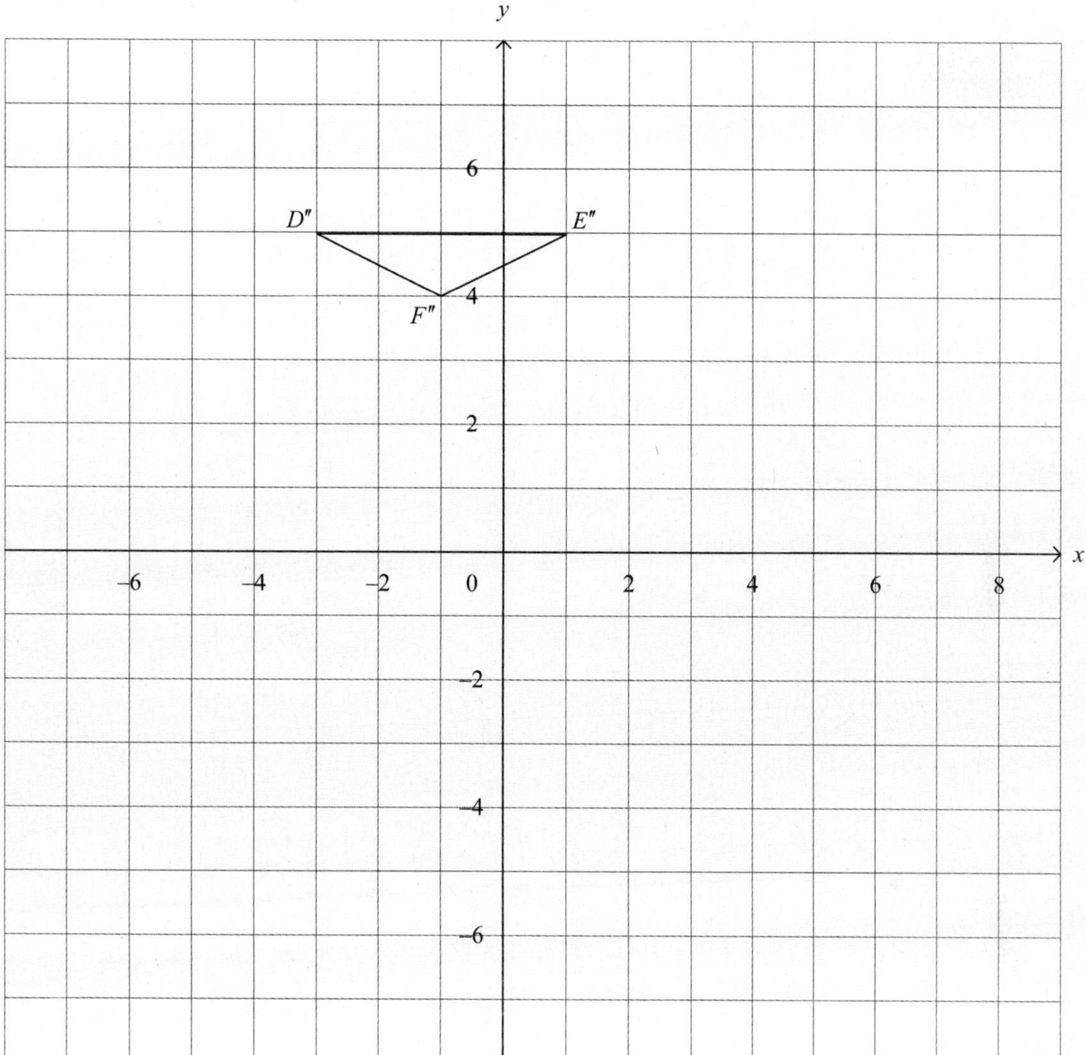

NOTES

DATA ANALYSIS

When you are finished this unit, you should be able to …

- design an experiment or investigation with two variables (SO 1)
- conduct an experiment or investigation between two variables (SO 1)
- analyze and make predictions about an experiment or investigation between two variables (SO 1)
- draw scatter plots for data that is continuous (SO 2)
- draw scatter plots for data that is discrete (SO 2)
- identify relationships from information presented in a scatter plot (SO 3)
- determine the line of best fit for a scatter plot (SO 4)
- draw a line of best fit from a given set of data (SO 5)
- make critical analysis of statistics presented by the media and the other sources (SO 7)
- assess the strengths and weaknesses of methods of data collection (SO 6)
- calculate the theoretical probability of events (SO 8)
- calculate the experimental probability of events (SO 8)
- show how probability and statistics are used in everyday life (SO 9)
- solve problems involving the probability of independent events (SO 10)

PREREQUISITE SKILLS AND KNOWLEDGE

Prior to beginning this unit, you should be able to. . .

- determine how to collect data
- design and use a survey for the collection of data
- evaluate the mean, median, mode, and range for a set of data
- plot points on the coordinate grid
- solve simple probability questions
- determine the probability of independent events in a limited sample space
- use sample data to make predictions about a population

Lesson 1 INVESTIGATING RELATIONSHIPS BETWEEN DATA

NOTES

In order to compare two variables and draw conclusions about what, if any, relationship they have, you can collect data through an experiment or analyze existing research data.

You can compare such things as the amount of time spent studying for a test with the mark received on the test. By collecting data and then graphing it on a grid, you might conclude that the more time spent studying for a test, the higher the mark. However, you might find this is a general trend, but not true in all cases.

Example 1

Compare the number of shots on goal that a hockey player takes with the actual number of goals scored.

Solution

You could collect this data by watching several hockey games and keeping your own statistics. Alternatively, you might be able to get the statistics from a team's coaching staff if they are keeping this particular statistic. If you are researching a professional team like the Edmonton Oilers, you might be able to find the statistics on the Internet or in the newspaper. The following data represents the shots taken versus goals scored by six Edmonton Oilers forwards during a preseason.

Data can be displayed in table format.

Players	**1**	**2**	**3**	**4**	**5**	**6**
Shots	10	8	7	13	15	12
Goals	3	2	1	5	5	4

Look for a relationship between the two variables. Is a variable increasing or decreasing? What about the other variable?

It appears that the more shots one of these players takes, the more goals he is likely to score.

PRACTICE EXERCISES

1. For each of the following tables of data, describe the relationship between the variables.

a)

Outside Temperature on a Spring Day					
Time of day	8:00	10:00	12:00	14:00	16:00
Temperature	–1°C	1°C	6°C	10°C	11°C

b)

Temperature of a Cup of Hot Chocolate Over Time					
Time (min)	Start	2	4	6	8
Temperature	50°C	40°C	27°C	22°C	20°C

2. Use the relationship in the table to answer the questions that follow.

Mass of Loonies					
Number of Loonies	5	7	10	13	15
Mass (g)	75	105	150	195	225

a) What is the mass of one loonie?

b) What is the mass of 20 loonies?

3. Use the relationship in the table to answer the questions that follow.

Volume of a Cube Relative to Length of its Sides				
Length of sides (cm)	3	5	7	9
Volume of cube (cm^3)	27	125	343	729

a) What is the volume of a cube with side length of 4 cm?

b) What is the length of a side of a cube with a volume of 216 cm^3?

Lesson 2 GRAPHING SCATTER PLOTS

NOTES

On a graph, the horizontal axis is referred to as the ***x*-axis** and the vertical axis is referred to as the ***y*-axis**.

The **origin** is the point on a coordinate grid with an *x*- and *y*-value of 0. It is described as the point (0, 0)

A **scatter plot** is a graphical method of displaying the relationship between two variables. In a scatter plot, two sets of data are plotted as ordered pairs on a coordinate plane. The ordered pairs are identified as (x, y) according to where they fall along each axis. For example, when graphing the point (4, 3), you would start at the origin (0, 0) and move along the *x*-axis to 4. Next, you would move up the *y*-axis to 3 and place your point as in the graph below.

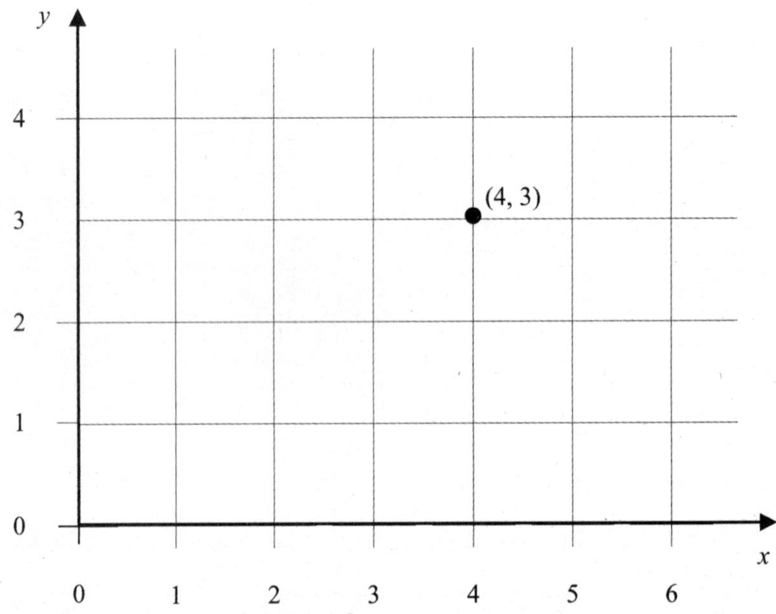

You may be given a scatter plot and asked to describe the relationship between the two variables. The *x*- and *y*-axis are labelled with the two variables that are being compared. For example, the *x*-axis might be labelled "Shots on Goal" and the *y*-axis "Goals Scored."

There are three main patterns to look for in relation to the point on a graph.

1. As one variable increases, so does the other.
2. As one variable increases, the other decreases.
3. The points are scattered everywhere, and there appears to be no relationship between the variables.

Example 1

Describe the relationship between the variables of each scatter plot below.

NOTES

Are the graphed points increasing together, decreasing together, or following no pattern?

a)

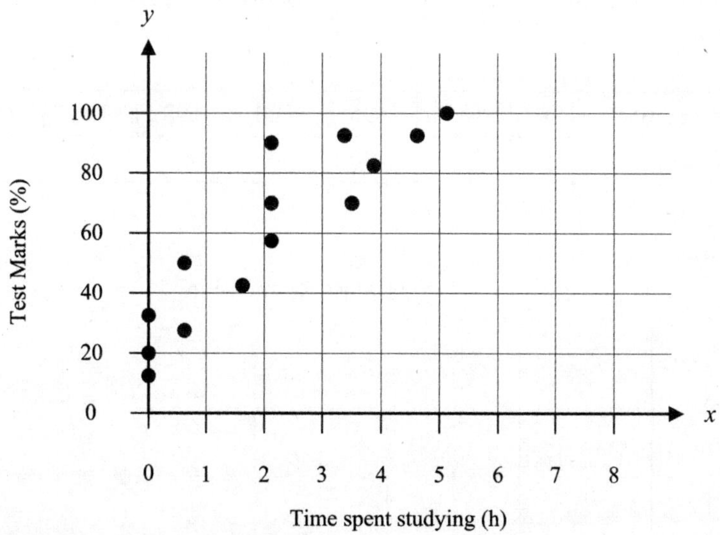

Solution

The test mark generally increases as the number of hours of study increases.

b)

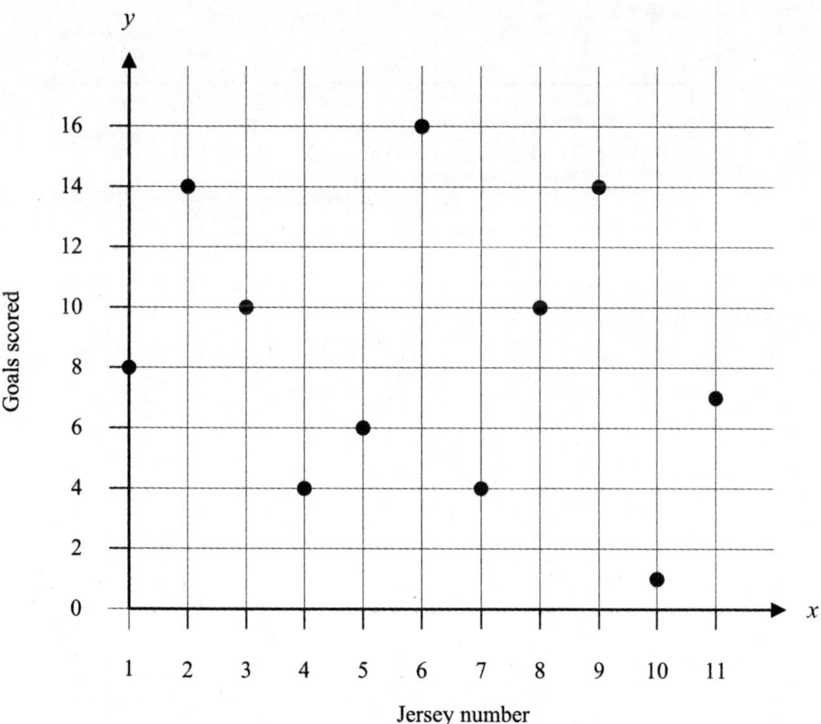

Solution

There is no relationship between the jersey number and the number of goals scored.

NOTES

Example 2

The table below gives the height and weight of each of seven players on a basketball team. Plot the data in a scatter plot. Label the axes. Choose a suitable increment for numbering the axes. All points should be plotted. Give the scatter plot a title. Describe the relationship between the two variables.

Height (cm)	180	185	195	190	193	188	194
Mass (kg)	75	80	100	90	88	90	95

Solution

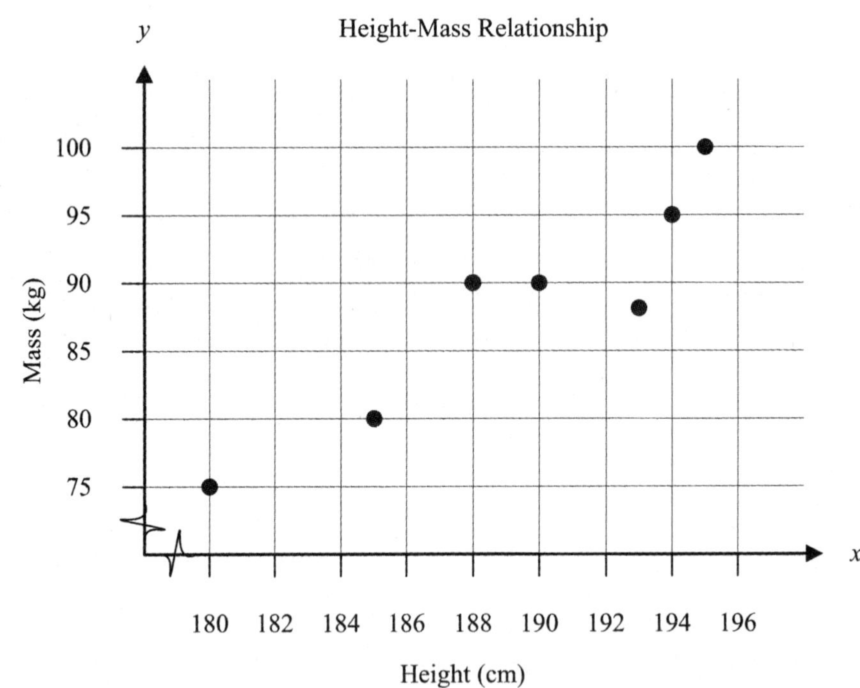

Put a break in the graph to show that numbers not needed in your graph have been left out. Here, along the x-axis, the symbol  indicates that the heights from 0 to 179 cm have been left off the grid.

When numbering the axes, use equal increments. Here, the height increases in increments of 2 cm, while the mass increases in increments of 5 kg.

The scatter plot shows that as the height of these players increases, mass also increases.

PRACTICE EXERCISES

1. For each of the following tables of data, draw a scatter plot. Be sure to address each of the following points.
- Draw and label the axes.
- Choose a scale that allows you to plot all the data.
- Plot a point to represent each piece of data.
- Give the graph a title.
- Describe the relationship between the variables.

a) The table below represents winning times in a 100 m race in seven specified years.

Year	1950	1960	1970	1980	1990	2000	2005
Time (s)	13	12.5	12	11.5	11	10.5	10

b) The table below represents the population in Canada in 7 specific years.

Year	1971	1976	1981	1986	1991	1996	2001
Population (million)	21.6	23.0	24.3	25.3	27.3	28.8	30.0

c) The table below represents, for seven particular people, the relationship between each person's mass and his or her IQ.

Mass (kg)	65	70	75	80	85	90	100
IQ	125	85	140	95	100	130	95

d) The table represents the relationship between the temperature of a cup of hot chocolate and the time that it spends on a counter.

Time (min)	0	2	4	6	8
Temperature	50°	40°	27°	22°	20°

Lesson 3 LINE OF BEST FIT

NOTES

A **line of best fit** is a line that is drawn on a scatter plot to help a person make predictions about the graphed data. If the plot shows a relationship between the variables, the line can be used to estimate one variable when the value of the other variable is given. A line of best fit is of little use when the variables have no apparent relationship. When drawing a line of best fit, you should line up your ruler so that it goes through the middle of the pattern formed by the points on the scatter plot. Try to follow the angle of the pattern as best as you can and then draw the line along your ruler. Some dots will be above the line and some will be below. The line represents an average of the values as you follow the pattern.

If the relationship indicates that one variable increases as the other increases, the slope of the line is said to be positive. A positive slope will rise from left to right on the graph. In a relationship where a variable decreases as the other variable increases, the slope will be negative, and the line will slope downward from left to right.

Example 1

Plot the data below on a scatter plot and draw the line of best fit.

This table represents the population of Canada in eight specific years.

Year	1950	1960	1970	1980	1985	1990	1995	2005
Population (millions)	13.8	18	24	27	29.5	31	32	35

Solution

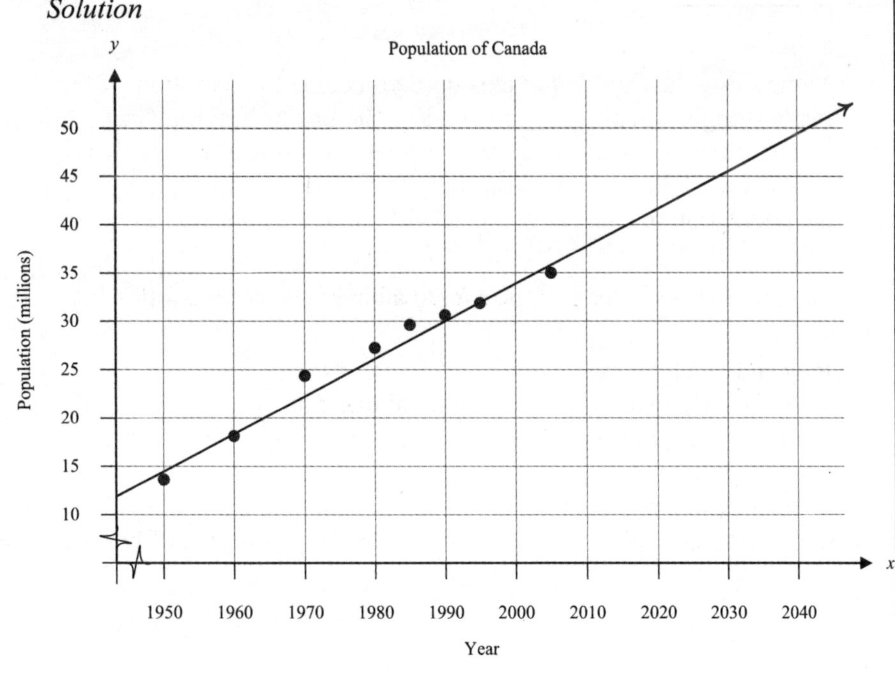

The line should go through the middle of the points, with some falling above and some below.

The line should be as close as possible to the angle created by the points.

NOTES

Extend the axes for both year and population and mark additional values along each. In doing so, you can make prediction about the future of Canada. Your line of best fit may not be exactly the same as the example, but the values should be close.

Example 2

Using the line of best fit created in Example 1, answer the following questions.

a) What was the population of Canada in 1975?

Solution

Move along the *Year* axis (x) until you come to 1975; that is halfway between 1970 and 1980. Then, move straight up to the line of best fit. Next, move straight left to the *Population* axis (y). The population for 1975 is approximately 24 million.

b) What would you estimate the population of Canada to be in 2020?

Solution

Make sure that your line is long enough to go past the year 2020. Then follow the same procedure as you did to find the solution to the last question. According to the line of best fit, the population of Canada in 2020 will be approximately 42 million.

c) According to the trend shown in this graph, in what year will the population of Canada reach approximately 40 million?

Solution

Move along the *Population* axis until you come to 40 million. Then, move straight across until you intersect the line of best fit. Go straight down from this point to see what year corresponds with a population of 40 million. According to the line of best fit, the year that the population of Canada will reach 40 million is approximately 2016.

When you draw a scatter plot, be sure to address each of the following points.

- Draw and label the axes.
- Choose a scale that allows you to plot all the data.
- Plot a point to represent each piece of data.
- Give the graph a title.
- Draw a line of best fit.
- Answer any questions that follow the table using your line of best fit.

PRACTICE EXERCISES

1. The table below shows the price of one litre of gasoline over time at a particular gas station.

Year	1970	1980	1990	2000	2005
Price per litre of gasoline (CAN)	\$0.10	\$0.27	\$0.35	\$0.56	\$0.73

a) Draw a scatter plot to represent the data.

b) How much will one litre of gasoline cost in 2015? Will this answer be reasonable if the price of gasoline continues to increase at the same rate as it has from 2000 to 2005?

c) What is the most probable price that one litre of gasoline cost in 1985?

2. The table below compares the time it takes for nine students to walk to a certain school with the distance they must walk.

a) Draw a scatter plot to represent the data.

Student	**1**	**2**	**3**	**4**	**5**	**6**	**7**	**8**	**9**
Distance (km)	1.2	2	0.9	0.7	1.5	1.9	0.6	1.8	1.1
Time (min)	23	30	15	14	18	25	10	26	15

b) If a student took 20 minutes to get to school, approximately how far was he or she away from school?

c) If a student had to walk 2.4 km to school, approximately how long did it for him or her to get there?

Lesson 4 SAMPLING METHODS

Sampling is a method of collecting data from a portion of a population.

NOTES

In this context, a population can be defined as all the items, objects, or people being considered in a statistical investigation. If you were discussing the Grade 9 math class, the entire class would be the population. If you took a sample from the class, you might just be talking about one person selected from each row.

A **sample** represents a small portion of the population. If you were discussing the population of Canada and wanted to take a sample, you might choose 10 people from each province as the sample.

There are many different methods of collecting data by sampling. Some sampling methods provide more reliable information than others. If a television station wanted to determine how many Canadians liked to watch hockey, they might collect data by taking a sample of the Canadian population. If the television station sampled only people at a hockey game, the results would most likely show that almost all Canadians like to watch hockey. This is not a reliable sample of all Canadians, as most people who attend hockey games probably have some interest in watching hockey on television. In the general population of Canada, many people will have no interest in hockey.

This sample is said to have a **bias** because only people at a hockey game were sampled.

Bias is a "slanted" or unequal presentation of information.

Samples are used because they are less time-consuming and less costly than trying to collect data from an entire population.

Bias produces an **unreliable** sample.

A popular method of sampling is **random sampling**. In random sampling, all members of the population have an equal chance of being selected. An example of a random sample would be a situation where each student in your school has his or her name written on a slip of paper and all the papers are then put in a box. Then, 10 names are drawn and the students are asked if math is their favourite subject in school. This would represent a random sample because everyone in the population has an equal chance of being selected. This would be a reliable sample that should reflect the feelings of the population of the school.

In **random sampling**, everyone in the population has an equal opportunity of being selected.

NOTES

A **sample** represents a small portion of the population.

Bias makes samples unreliable.

Random sampling gives everyone in the population an equal chance of being selected.

Example 1

The executives at a Canadian television station are trying to decide if they should broadcast the movie *Shrek*. They decide to conduct a telephone survey to ask people if they would like to see this movie on television. To get a sample of the Canadian population, they decide to randomly pick names out of phone books. They sample people in all provinces, and they sample more people in the provinces that have a greater population. Answer the following questions about this sample.

a) How was the sample selected?
b) Why do you think it was selected this way?
c) Is the data collected biased?
d) Was the data collection method appropriate for the data and the issue?

Solution

a) The samples were selected from phone books across Canada with more people selected in the more populated provinces.
b) It was probably selected in this fashion to get a valid representation across the country.
c) No. The method is not biased. No single group was chosen to provide responses. The sampling was random.
d) The collection method was appropriate for the data and the issue.

Example 2

To determine how many people in Edmonton liked pizza, 100 people eating at a local Boston Pizza restaurant were sampled. Answer the following questions about this sample.

a) How was the sample selected?
b) Why do you think it was selected this way?
c) Was the data collected biased?
d) Was the data collection method appropriate for the data and the issue?
e) How could the sample be improved?

Solution

a) One hundred customers at a Boston Pizza restaurant were sampled.
b) It was a quick way to get a sample.
c) Yes. The method is biased because the only people selected were at a restaurant that specializes in pizza.
d) The data collection method was not appropriate.
e) Use a random sample of 100 people from all different parts of Edmonton by choosing people from the phone book. This would give a more reliable representation of the number of people in Edmonton who like pizza.

PRACTICE EXERCISES

Answer the following questions about each of the samples below.

a) How was the sample selected?
b) Why do you think it was selected this way?
c) Was the data collected biased?
d) Was the data collection method appropriate for the data and the issue?
e) How could the sample be improved?

1. Researchers wanted to determine the number of hours of homework done by Alberta students each week. To find out, they sampled 100 students in Calgary malls on a Monday night.

2. Researchers wanted to determine how many students in a high school were vegetarians. Each grade level in the school was represented by a box containing the name of every student in that grade along with his or her dietary preference.

3. A Canadian insurance company is trying to discover how many 16 year-olds in Canada have a car accident in their first year of driving. They decide to sample all the girls from one high school in each province.

PRACTICE QUIZ

1. Describe the relationship between the quantities in the table.

Time (min)	0	20	40	60	80
Height of a snowman on a sunny spring day (cm)	150	140	125	110	100

2. a) Draw a scatter plot, including a line of best fit, for the data below.

Day	**1**	**2**	**3**	**4**	**5**	**6**	**7**
Attendance at Disneyland in a day (thousands)	**150**	**185**	**140**	**133**	**190**	**160**	**165**

b) Describe the relationship of the variables plotted.

c) How many people would you predict would enter Disneyland on day 9?

d) What factors might cause a day at Disneyland to have a reduced attendance?

3. A sample of 40 people was taken at a veterinary clinic to determine how many pets are owned by families in Alberta.

a) What is the population that the survey intends to represent?

b) Describe the sample.

c) Is the sample random? Explain.

d) Does the sample reflect the population?

Lesson 5 STATISTICAL INFORMATION AND THE MEDIA

NOTES

The media often reports statistical data in a way that may be misleading. Sometimes this is unintentional. Sometimes, in advertising, for example, the statistical data is made to reflect only what the advertiser wants. Many car manufacturers advertise 0% financing for their cars, although the price at which they sell the car is higher with 0% financing than it would be if you chose some other promotion they offer.

Example 1

Identify whether or not the information in the following statements is misleading. Explain how.

It is important to read and think carefully about what given statistics represent. Some statistical data may be misleading.

a) In Edmonton in 1995, there were 500 accidents involving cars and 30 involving bicycles. It is safer to ride a bicycle than to drive a car.

b) At Marmot ski hill in 2003, 60% of the snowboarding accidents happened to people who had taken snowboarding lessons. It is safer to go snowboarding without taking lessons.

Solution

a) This is misleading because there are more people driving cars than riding bikes, so more car accidents than bike accidents would be expected.

b) This is misleading because most people who snowboard probably took lessons at one time or another. The population of snowboarders who took lessons includes almost all snowboarders. It is definitely not safer to snowboard without taking lessons.

PRACTICE EXERCISES

1. Identify whether or not the information in the following statements is misleading. If misleading, explain how.

a) In 2004, there were 80 house fires in Calgary. Of the 80 families who had house fires, 65 of them had pets. Having a pet increases the chance of having a house fire.

b) About 600 000 people in China die of lung cancer each year. In Chinese cities, approximately 34% of people who die of lung cancer deaths are female. More Chinese men are dying of lung cancer than women.

Lesson 6 THEORETICAL AND EXPERIMENTAL PROBABILITY

NOTES

In a situation in which each event is equally likely, probability can be calculated as follows.

The **theoretical probability** of an event

$$=\frac{\text{number of favourable outcomes}}{\text{total number of outcomes}}.$$

The probability of rolling a 3 with a regular six-sided die is calculated as follows:

$$P(3)=\frac{1}{6}$$

Theoretical probability is based on the number of favourable outcomes divided by the total number of outcomes.

The outcomes for rolling the die are 1, 2, 3, 4, 5, and 6. Each of these outcomes is equally likely. In calculating the probability of rolling a 3, there is 1 favourable outcome divided by 6 possible outcomes. This would represent theoretical probability.

In **experimental probability**, an experiment is conducted and the results of the experiment are used to calculate the probability of a particular outcome.

Example 1

A die was rolled 25 times and the outcomes were recorded in the table below.

Frequency represents how often a certain outcome occurs.

Experimental probability is based on the results from an experiment.

Outcome (Number rolled)	1	2	3	4	5	6
Frequency (Number of times rolled)	4	5	6	2	4	4

Solution

According to this data, the experimental probability of rolling a 3 would be $\frac{6}{25}$.

This probability is based on the fact that there were 6 favourable outcomes of rolling a 3, divided by the total number of times the experiment was performed, 25.

NOTES

Example 2

Based on the experimental data above, if a die were rolled 150 times, how many times would you expect the favourable outcome of rolling a 4?

Solution

According to the data, the probability of rolling a 4 is $\frac{2}{25}$.

To make a prediction on the desired outcome, take the probability and multiply it by the desired number of rolls.

Thus, the expected number of fours is calculated as

$\frac{2}{25} \times \frac{150}{1} = \frac{300}{25} = 12$.

So, when the die is rolled 150 times, the expected number of times that a 4 will be rolled is 12.

In making predictions, the experimental probability is multiplied by the number of trials.

Experimental probabilities are often different than theoretical probabilities. The larger the number of trials in a probability experiment, the closer the probability will be to the theoretical probabilities. The results from rolling a die 1 000 times will be closer to the theoretical probability than the results from rolling a die 50 times would be.

A larger data set reduces the statistical significance of random results that do not fit the theoretical probability. One unusual result in 50 trails will effect the experimental probability more than one unusual result in 1 000 trails.

Example 3

A bag contains 4 red marbles, 5 green marbles, and 6 blue marbles. A person reaches into the bag and, without looking, draws out one marble. Calculate the probability of the following outcomes:

a) A green marble is selected on the first draw
b) A blue marble is selected on the first draw
c) A green or red marble is selected on the first draw

Solution

a) There are 5 favourable outcomes out of 15 possible outcomes.

$$P(\text{Green}) = \frac{5}{15}$$

$$P(\text{Green}) = \frac{1}{3}$$

b) $P(\text{Blue}) = \frac{6}{15}$

$$P(\text{Blue}) = \frac{2}{5}$$

c) $P(\text{Green or Red}) = \frac{11}{15}$

PRACTICE EXERCISES

1. Each letter in the word "mathematics" is written on a separate card and the cards are then placed in a box. A person reaches into the box and, without looking, selects one card. Find the probability of the following events.

a) Reaching into the box and selecting a *t*

b) Reaching into the box and selecting a *c*

c) Reaching into the box and selecting a letter that is **not** an *a*.

2. In an experiment, a die was rolled 120 times. The results are recorded in the table below.

Outcome	1	2	3	4	5	6
Frequency	12	18	25	20	25	20

Use the outcomes from the experiment to answer the following questions.

a) What is the probability of rolling a 2?

b) What is the probability of rolling a 5?

c) If the die is rolled 300 times, how many times should the outcome 3 occur?

d) If the die is rolled 250 times, how many times should the outcome 1 occur?

3. In the lottery game Lotto 6/49, a person must choose 6 of the numbers from 1 to 49. If someone correctly chooses the 6 numbers that are drawn, he or she wins the lottery. All numbers are equally likely to occur. Trevor researched which numbers had been selected most often over the last year. He decided to select 6 numbers that had been drawn least often in the last year because he thought the probability of these numbers being drawn now would be higher. Will Trevor's method increase his probability of winning? Why or why not?

4. The weather forecast indicates that the probability of precipitation tomorrow is 60%. What does this mean?

5. In a card game called "In Between," two cards are initially dealt. In order to win the game, the third card dealt must have a value between those of the first two. What is the probability of winning in each of the following situations if each situation starts with a full deck of 52 cards?

a) The first two cards are a 2 and a 7

b) The first two cards are a king and a 10

c) The first two cards are a 4 and a 4

Lesson 7 INDEPENDENT EVENTS

NOTES

Independent events are events in which one outcome has no effect on the next. An example of independent events would be the tossing of two coins. The first coin could have the outcomes of heads or tails, and the second coin could have the same two outcomes of heads or tails. The outcome of the first event has no effect on the second event. Thus, the events are independent.

Independent events are events in which the outcome of the first event has no effect on the outcome of the second event.

Consider the event of selecting two 4s from a deck of cards. On the first selection, the probability is $P(4) = \frac{4}{52}$. Now imagine that the first card selected was a 5 of hearts and that the card was not put back in the deck. The second selection now has the probability $P(4) = \frac{4}{51}$. These events are not independent because the outcome of the first event has an effect on the outcome of the second event. In the second event, there is one less card to choose from.

Example 1

In a coin toss of two coins, what is the probability of tossing heads on the first coin and heads on the second coin.

Solution

The probability of tossing heads on the first coin is $P(\text{H}_1) = \frac{1}{2}$.

The probability of tossing heads on the second coin is $P(\text{H}_2) = \frac{1}{2}$.

To find the probability of two independent events such as $P(\text{H}_1)$ and $P(\text{H}_2)$, multiply the two probabilities together.

The key word "and" tells you to multiply when working with probability questions.

$$P(\text{H}_1 \text{ and } \text{H}_2) = \frac{1}{2} \times \frac{1}{2}$$

$$P(\text{H}_1 \text{ and } \text{H}_2) = \frac{1}{4}$$

Thus, the probability of tossing two heads is $\frac{1}{4}$.

When finding the probability of independent events, multiply the separate probabilities together to get the probability of the combined events.

Example 2

Find the probability of rolling 6 with a die, followed by tossing a coin and getting tails, and finally rolling another die and getting a 3, thus producing the sequence of a 6, a tail, and a 3.

Solution

$P(6) = \frac{1}{6}$

$P(\text{T}) = \frac{1}{2}$

$P(3) = \frac{1}{6}$

$P(6, \text{T}, 3) = \frac{1}{6} \times \frac{1}{2} \times \frac{1}{6}$

$P(6, \text{T}, 3) = \frac{1}{72}$

The probability of rolling a 6, tossing a tail, and then rolling a 3 is $\frac{1}{72}$.

NOTES

When finding the probability of one event "and" a second event, multiply the two probabilities together.

NOTES

Example 3

Use a tree diagram to show all the possible outcomes of tossing three pennies. Then identify the probability of all three pennies landing heads.

Solution

When using a tree diagram, list the possible outcomes for the first event. Draw branches from each outcome to represent the number of possible outcomes for the second event. Continue until all of the events are completed.

Tree Diagram

Coin 1	Coin 2	Coin 3	Outcomes
H	H	H	H H H
		T	H H T
	T	H	H T H
		T	H T T
T	H	H	T H H
		T	T H T
	T	H	T T H
		T	T T T

There are 8 different possible outcomes. Only one outcome has 3 heads. Thus, the probability of tossing 3 heads is $\frac{1}{8}$. This probability can also be arrived by multiplying the independent events:

$\frac{1}{2}\times\frac{1}{2}\times\frac{1}{2}=\frac{1}{8}$.

1st Coin $P(\mathrm{H}_1)=\frac{1}{2}$

2nd Coin $P(\mathrm{H}_2)=\frac{1}{2}$

3rd Coin $P(\mathrm{H}_3)=\frac{1}{2}$

$P(\mathrm{H}_1\mathrm{H}_2\mathrm{H}_3)=\frac{1}{2}\times\frac{1}{2}\times\frac{1}{2}=\frac{1}{8}$

PRACTICE EXERCISES

1. **a)** Find the probability of rolling a 4 on a green die and a 6 on a red die.

   b) Find the probability of rolling an even number on a green die and a 3 on a red die.

   c) Find the probability of rolling a number greater than 4 on a red die and a number less than 2 on a green die.

   d) Find the probability of rolling a prime number on a green die and a number greater than 6 on a red die.

2. To open his combination lock, John dials three digits, each digit a number from 0 to 9. What is the probability that someone could guess his combination?

3. For the following questions, imagine that you select one card from a deck of 52 cards, then replace the card, and select a second card.

a) What is the probability of selecting a queen on your first draw and a 10 on your second draw?

b) What is the probability of selecting a diamond on your first draw and a 6 on your second draw?

c) What is the probability of selecting a face card on your first draw and the queen of hearts on your second draw?

4. Pat and Kathy are starting a family and hope to have four children. What is the probability that they will have 4 boys?

5. John has a three-dial combination lock with the numbers 0 to 40 on each dial. Given that the same number can be used more than once, what is the probability that someone will guess his three-number combination?

REVIEW SUMMARY

- To identify the relationship between two variables, look for a pattern in the data.
- Label the axes of scatter plots clearly and mark them off in equal increments.
- Put a break in your graph when the increments marked on either axis do not start from zero.
- To identify a relationship between the two variables in a scatter plat, look for a clustering of points.
- When drawing a line of best fit, draw it through the middle of the clustering of the points.
- A line of best fit is only useful when the variables appear to have a relationship.
- You can extend a line of best fit to make predictions about the variables.
- Proper sampling methods must be used if the sample is to be representative of the population studied.
- Bias in a sample makes the results unreliable.
- Statistics can sometimes be presented in ways that are misleading.
- Experimental probability is a prediction based on actual results from an experiment.
- Theoretical probability of an event $= \dfrac{\text{number of favourable outcomes}}{\text{total number of outcomes}}$.
- To find the combined probability of independent events, multiply the probability of each event or use a tree diagram.
- In probability questions dealing with combined events, the key word "and" means to multiply.

PRACTICE TEST

1. Which of the following scatter plots will produce the line of best fit with the most reliable results?

A.

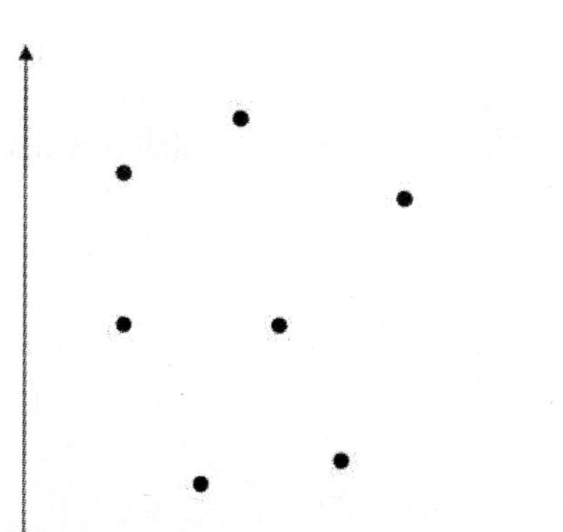

B.

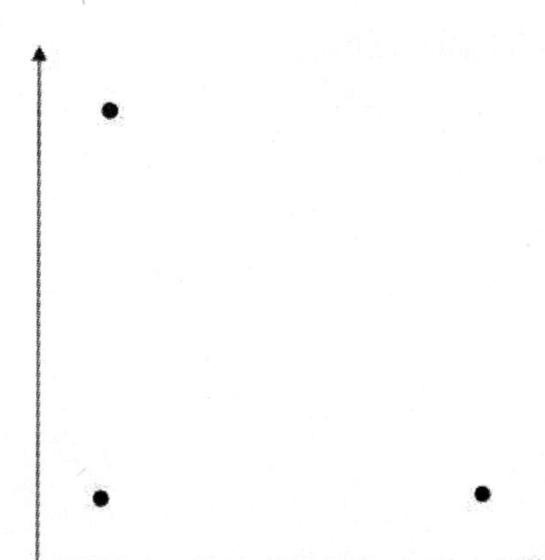

C.

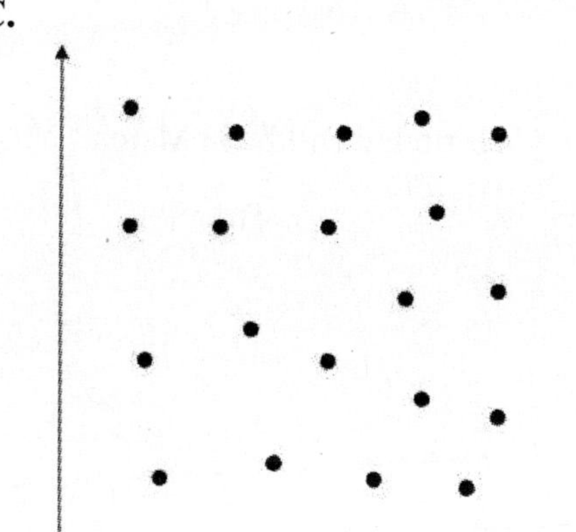

D.

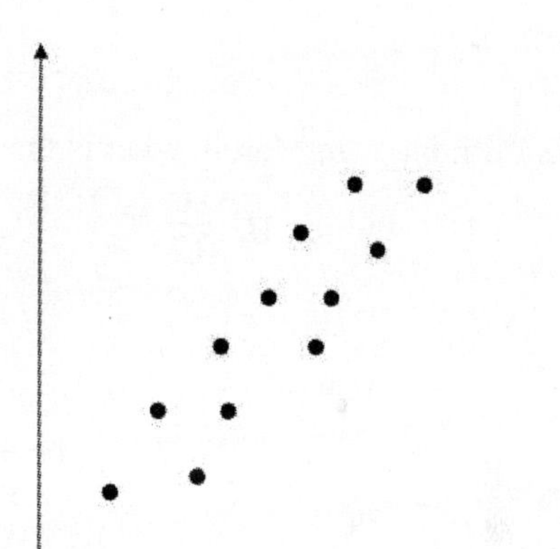

2. The probability of rolling a 2 with a die and tossing a head with a coin is

A. $\frac{2}{3}$ **B.** $\frac{1}{6}$ **C.** $\frac{5}{12}$ **D.** $\frac{1}{12}$

3. A sampling method in which everyone has an equal chance of being selected is called a

A. random sample
B. clustered sample
C. varied sample
D. population sample

4. If 100 tickets were sold for a raffle and Stan bought 3 tickets, what would be the probability that he would win the raffle?

A. $\frac{1}{100}$ **B.** $\frac{2}{100}$ **C.** $\frac{3}{100}$ **D.** 0

5. If Jenna's birthday is in March, what is the probability that Amy's birthday will be in March?

A. 1 **B.** $\frac{1}{12}$ **C.** $\frac{1}{144}$ **D.** $\frac{1}{11}$

6. a) The first two positions in a postal code are occupied by a letter and a digit. Kent and Win Lee have just met at summer camp. If it is assumed that Kent does not know where Win Lee lives, what is an expression that will allow Kent to determine the probability that he can correctly guess the first letter and number of his new friend's postal code?

A. $\frac{1}{26} \times \frac{1}{10}$ **B.** $\frac{1}{26}$ **C.** $\frac{1}{26} \times \frac{1}{9}$ **D.** $\frac{1}{25} \times \frac{1}{9}$

b) What is the probability that Kent will correctly guess the first letter and number of Win Lee's postal code?

A. $\frac{1}{260}$ **B.** $\frac{1}{234}$ **C.** $\frac{1}{225}$ **D.** $\frac{1}{26}$

7. a) A tetrahedral die has 4 sides numbered 1, 2, 3, 4. A tetrahedral die was rolled 50 times. The results are shown in the table below. Which outcome has an experimental probability of $\frac{6}{25}$?

Outcome	1	2	3	4
Frequency	12	18	6	14

A. 1 **B.** 2 **C.** 3 **D.** 4

b) How many times would you expect the outcome 2 to occur if the tetrahedral die were rolled 180 times?

A. 18 **B.** 60 **C.** 65 **D.** 68

8. Imagine that a scatter plot is drawn for each set of data described below. For which of the following scatter plots would a line of best fit have limited use?

A. The amount of money earned and the amount of money spent each month
B. Hours spent listening to music and shoe size of listeners
C. Years of driving experience and number of accidents
D. Speed of a car and how long it takes to stop the car

9. The data below compares the length of various ducks found in Canada with their mass. Construct a scatter plot for the data and then draw a line of best fit.

Length (cm)	45	50	35	60	63	40	45	47	35	46
Mass (g)	630	670	305	1 030	1 100	400	700	755	360	700

a) Describe any relationship that exists.
b) Use the line of best fit to find the approximate mass of a duck measuring 55 cm long?
c) Use the line of best fit to find the approximate length of a duck weighing 1 200 g?

10. A bag contains 5 orange marbles, 2 blue marbles, and 3 white marbles. Without looking, a person draws one marble from the bag. Each marble is replaced before the next one is drawn. What is the value of each of the following probabilities?

a) *P*(white, then blue)
b) *P*(orange, then blue, then white)
c) *P*(orange, then another orange)
d) *P*(3 white marbles in a row)

NOTES

Student Notes and Problems

Answers and Solutions

NOTES

NUMBER CONCEPTS AND OPERATIONS

Lesson 1—Number Systems

PRACTICE EXERCISES
Answers and Solutions

1. **a)** rational
   b) integer, rational
   c) rational
   d) natural, whole, integer, rational
   e) rational, integer
   f) irrational
   g) rational
   h) irrational
   i) rational

2. 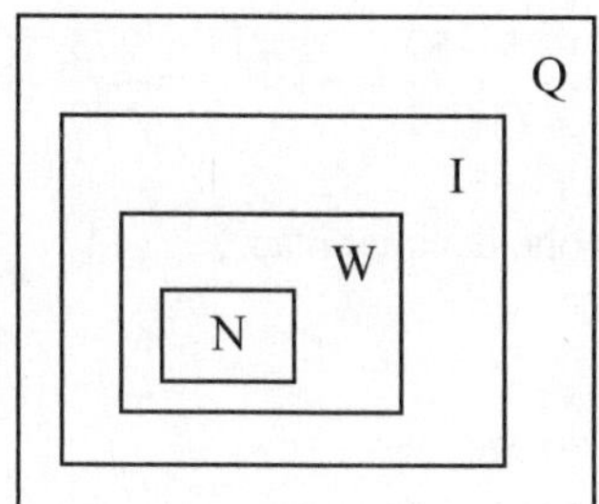

3. The number – 8 is a rational number because it can be written as a fraction $\frac{-8}{1}$ and because it can be expressed as a terminating decimal (–8.0). It is not a whole number because there are no negative numbers in the set of whole numbers.

4. The numbers $0.\overline{8}$, 2.34, 2.151 515. . ., 3.14, and –15.679 54 are all rational.

   The number 8.359 087 . . . is irrational because it is a non-terminating decimal with no set pattern.

5. The fraction $\frac{1}{3}$ belongs to the set of rational numbers because it can be written as a fraction.

Lesson 2—Square Roots

PRACTICE EXERCISES
Answers and Solutions

1. **a)** 12 and –12
   b) 110 and –110
   c) 0.011 and –0.011
   d) 0.25 and –0.25
   e) $\frac{5}{7}$ and $-\frac{5}{7}$

2. **a)** 5.5 or –5.5

   The radical $\sqrt{30}$ falls between $\sqrt{25}$ and $\sqrt{36}$.

   Therefore, the number is between 52 and 62.

   52 = 25, 62 = 36

   $36 - 25 = 11$

   $30 - 25 = 5$

   Therefore, the square root of 30 is approximately $\frac{5}{11}$ more than 5.

   $\frac{5}{11} = 0.\overline{45}$

   Rounded to one decimal place, $0.\overline{45} = 0.5$.

   So, $\sqrt{30} \approx 5.5$ or -5.5

   b) 11.2 or –11.2

   The radical $\sqrt{125}$ falls between $\sqrt{121}$ and $\sqrt{144}$.

   The number is between 11^2 and 12^2.

   $11^2 = 121$ and $12^2 = 144$

   $144 - 121 = 23$

   $125 - 121 = 4$

   Therefore, the square root of 125 is approximately $\frac{4}{23}$ more than 11.

   $\frac{4}{23} = 0.1739$

   Rounded to one decimal place 0.173 9 = 0.2.

   So, $\sqrt{125} \approx 11.2$ or -11.2

c) 6.7 or –6.7

The radical $\sqrt{45}$ falls between $\sqrt{36}$ and $\sqrt{49}$

The number is between 6^2 and 7^2.

$6^2 = 36$ and $7^2 = 49$

$49 - 36 = 13$

$45 - 36 = 9$

Therefore, the square root of 45 is approximately $\frac{9}{13}$ more than 6.

$\frac{9}{13} = 0.6923$

Rounded to one decimal place, 0.692 3 = 0.7.

So, $\sqrt{45} \approx 6.7$ or -6.7

d) 1.3 or –1.3

The radical $\sqrt{1.57}$ can be written $\sqrt{\frac{157}{100}}$ to make it easier to work with, which can also be written as $\frac{\sqrt{157}}{\sqrt{100}}$.

The radical $\sqrt{100}$ is equal to 10; 100 is a perfect square.

The radical $\sqrt{157}$ falls between $\sqrt{144}$ and $\sqrt{169}$.

The number is between 12^2 and 13^2.

$12^2 = 144$ and $13^2 = 169$

$169 - 144 = 25$

$157 - 144 = 13$

Therefore, the square root of 157 is approximately $\frac{13}{25}$ more than 12.

$\frac{13}{25} = 0.52$

Therefore, $\frac{\sqrt{157}}{\sqrt{100}} \approx \frac{12.52}{10} = 1.252$

Rounded to one decimal place, $1.252 = 1.3$.

So, $\sqrt{1.57} \approx 1.3$ or -1.3

e) 0.7 or –0.7

The radical $\sqrt{\frac{13}{27}}$ can be written as $\frac{\sqrt{13}}{\sqrt{27}}$.

The radical $\sqrt{13}$ falls between $\sqrt{9}$ and $\sqrt{16}$.

The number is between 3^2 and 4^2.

$3^2 = 9$ and $4^2 = 16$

$16 - 9 = 7$

$13 - 9 = 4$

Therefore, the square root of 13 is approximately $\frac{4}{7}$ more than 3.

$3\frac{4}{7} = \frac{25}{7}$

The radical $\sqrt{27}$ falls between $\sqrt{25}$ and $\sqrt{36}$.

The number is between 5^2 and 6^2.

$5^2 = 25$ and $6^2 = 36$

$36 - 25 = 11$

$27 - 25 = 2$

Therefore, the square root of 27 is approximately $\frac{2}{11}$ more than 5.

$5\frac{2}{11} = \frac{57}{11}$

Therefore,

$$\frac{\sqrt{13}}{\sqrt{27}} \approx \frac{\frac{25}{7}}{\frac{57}{11}} = \frac{25}{7} \div \frac{57}{11} = \frac{25}{7} \times \frac{11}{57} = \frac{275}{399} \approx 0.689\,223\ldots$$

Rounded to one decimal place, 0.689 223… = 0.7.

So, $\sqrt{\frac{13}{27}} \approx 0.7$ or -0.7

f) 3

The radical $\sqrt{9}$ is equal to 3; 9 is a perfect square.

3. a) 9.5 cm

The area is 90 cm^2, which falls between the perfect squares of 81 and 100.

Therefore, this number will be between 9^2 and 10^2 cm^2.

$9^2 = 81$, $10^2 = 100$

$100 - 81 = 19$

$90 - 81 = 9$

Therefore, the square root of 90 is approximately $\frac{9}{19}$ more than 9.

$\frac{9}{19} \approx 0.4737$

Rounded to the nearest tenth, 0.473 7 = 0.5.

So, $\sqrt{90} \approx 9.5$ cm

b) 12.8 cm

The area is 165 cm^2, which falls between the perfect squares of 144 and 169.

Therefore, the number will be between 12^2 and 13^2 cm^2.

$12^2 = 144$, $13^2 = 169$

$169 - 144 = 25$

$165 - 144 = 21$

Therefore, the square root of 165 is approximately $\frac{21}{25}$ more than 9.

$\frac{21}{25} = 0.84$

Rounded to the nearest tenth, 0.84 = 0.8.

So, $\sqrt{165} \approx 12.8$ cm

c) 0.6 cm

The area is $0.36\ cm^2$. The number 0.36 can also be written as $\frac{36}{100}$ and 36 and 100 are both perfect squares.

$6^2 = 36$ and $10^2 = 100$

$$\sqrt{\frac{36}{100}} = \frac{\sqrt{36}}{\sqrt{100}} = \frac{6}{10} = 0.6$$

Therefore, the square root of $0.36\ cm^2$ is 0.6 cm.

d) 89.4 cm

The area is $8\ 000\ cm^2$, which falls between the perfect squares of 7 921 and 8 100.

Therefore, the number will be between 89^2 and 90^2 cm^2.

$89^2 = 7\ 921$ and $90^2 = 8\ 100$

$8\ 100 - 7\ 921 = 179$

$8\ 000 - 7\ 921 = 79$

Therefore, the square root of 8 000 is approximately $\frac{79}{179}$ more than 89.

$\frac{79}{179} = 0.441\ 340\ldots$

Rounded to the nearest tenth, $0.441\ 340\ldots = 0.4$.

So, $\sqrt{8\ 000} \approx 89.4$ cm

4. **a)** 13 and –13
b) 2.2 and –2.2
c) 10.6 and –10.6
d) 0.6 and –0.6
e) 6.7 and –6.7

5. **a)** 14.1 m

$200 = s^2$

$\sqrt{200} = \sqrt{s^2}$

$s = 14.1$ m

Each side of the garden is 14.1 m.

b) 56.4 m of fence

Find the perimeter of the garden. Since all 4 sides have a length of 14.1 m, you can multiply 14.1 by 4 to get 56.4 m.

So, Ben will need 56.4 m of fence to enclose the garden.

Lesson 3—Exponent Terminology

PRACTICE EXERCISES
Answers and Solutions

1. **a)** 2
b) -4
c) $\frac{7}{8}$
d) -0.4
e) 336
f) $\left(\frac{\sqrt{5}}{2}\right)$

Lesson 4—Multiplying and Dividing Exponents

PRACTICE EXERCISES
Answers and Solutions

1. a) $4^4 \times 4^3 = 4^{4+3}$
$= 4^7$

b) $5^3 \times 5^6 \times 5^4 = 5^{3+6+4}$
$= 5^{13}$

c) $7^5 \times 7^{-3} = 7^{5-3}$
$= 7^2$

d) $x^4 \times x^8 = x^{4+8}$
$= x^{12}$

e) $f^3 \times f^{-5} \times f^{-4} = f^{3-5-4}$
$= f^{-6}$

f) $(8)(-8)^3(-8)^4 = (-8)^{1+3+4}$
$= (-8)^8$

2. a) x

b) 10^2

c) n^{-2}

d) $(-4)^2$

e) $\left(\frac{3}{7}\right)^{21}$

3. a) 6^9

b) a^{-4}

c) 1.2^7

d) n^{-1}

e) $y^2 \times y^5 = y^7$

4. There are 10^{24} stars in the universe.
$10^{13} \times 10^{11} = 10^{(11+13)} = 10^{24}$

Lesson 5—Power of Products, Quotients, and Powers

PRACTICE EXERCISES
Answers and Solutions

1. a) $\left(x^2y^3\right)^4 = x^{2\times4}y^{3\times4}$
$= x^8y^{12}$

b) $\left(\frac{r^3}{p^{-2}}\right)^5 = \left(\frac{r^{3\times5}}{p^{-2\times5}}\right)$
$= \frac{r^{15}}{p^{-10}}$ or $r^{15}p^{10}$

c) $\left(\frac{5}{8^2}\right)^3 = \frac{5^3}{8^{2\times3}}$
$= \frac{5^3}{8^6}$ or $5^3 8^{-6}$

d) $\left(\frac{3}{7}\right)^2 = \frac{3^2}{7^2}$
$= \frac{9}{49}$

e) $\left(3^4\right)^6 = 3^{4\times6}$
$= 3^{24}$

2. a) $\left(2^{-3}\right)^4 = 2^{(-3)\times4}$
$= 2^{-12}$ or $\frac{1}{2^{12}}$

b) $\left(v^4\right)^6 = v^{4\times6}$
$= v^{24}$

c) $\left(v^{-4}\right)^{-6} = v^{-4\times-6}$
$= v^{24}$

d) $\left[(-2)^3\right]^4 = (-2)^{3\times4}$
$= (-2)^{12}$

e) $\left[(-5)^3\right]^4 = (-5)^{3\times4}$
$= (-5)^{12}$

3. a) $\left(7^5 \times 7^2\right)^8 = \left(7^{8\times5} \times 7^{8\times2}\right)$

$= 7^{40} \times 7^{16}$

$= 7^{40+16}$

$= 7^{56}$

or

$\left(7^5 \times 7^2\right)^8 = \left(7^{5+2}\right)^8$

$= 7^{7\times8}$

$= 7^{56}$

b) $\left(3^5 \times 3^{-2}\right)^{-3} = 3^{(5)\times(-3)} \times 3^{(-2)\times(-3)}$

$= 3^{-15} \times 3^6$

$= 3^{-15+6}$

$= 3^{-9}$ or $\dfrac{1}{3^9}$

or

$\left(3^5 \times 3^{-2}\right)^{-3} = \left(3^{5-2}\right)^{-3}$

$= \left(3^3\right)^{-3}$

$= 3^{-9}$ or $\dfrac{1}{3^9}$

c) $\left(5^{11} \div 5^6\right)^4 = 5^{(11\times4)} \div 5^{(6\times4)}$

$= 5^{44} \div 5^{24}$

$= 5^{(44-24)}$

$= 5^{20}$

or

$\left(5^{11} \div 5^6\right)^4 = \left(5^{(11-6)}\right)^4$

$= \left(5^5\right)^4$

$= 5^{(5\times4)}$

$= 5^{20}$

d) $\left[(-2)^4 \div (-2)^8\right]^2 = (-2)^{4\times2} \div (-2)^{8\times2}$

$= (-2)^8 \div (-2)^{16}$

$= (-2)^{8-16}$

$= (-2)^{-8}$ or $\dfrac{1}{(-2)^8}$

or

$\left[(-2)^4 \div (-2)^8\right]^2 = \left[(-2)^{4-8}\right]^2$

$= \left[(-2)^{-4}\right]^2$

$= (-2)^{-4\times2}$

$= (-2)^{-8}$ or $\dfrac{1}{(-2)^8}$

e) $\left(\dfrac{1.3^4}{1.3^{-2}}\right)^3 = \dfrac{1.3^{4\times3}}{1.3^{(-2)\times3}}$

$= \dfrac{1.3^{12}}{1.3^{-6}}$

$= (1.3)^{12-(-6)}$

$= 1.3^{18}$

or

$\left(\dfrac{1.3^4}{1.3^{-2}}\right)^3 = \left(1.3^{(4)-(-2)}\right)^3$

$= \left(1.3^6\right)^3$

$= (1.3)^{6\times3}$

$= 1.3^{18}$

f) $\left(g^4 \div g\right)^6 = g^{4\times6} \div g^{1\times6}$

$= g^{24} \div g^6$

$= g^{24-6}$

$= g^{18}$

or

$\left(g^4 \div g\right)^6 = \left(g^{4-1}\right)^6$

$= \left(g^3\right)^6$

$= g^{3\times6}$

$= g^{18}$

g) $\left(mn^4\right)^6 = m^{1\times6}n^{4\times6}$

$= m^6n^{24}$

h) $\left(m^5 \times m^{-3}\right)^4 = m^{5\times4} \times m^{(-3)\times(4)}$

$= m^{20} \times m^{-12}$

$= m^{20-12}$

$= m^8$

or $\left(m^5 \times m^{-3}\right)^4 = \left(m^{5-3}\right)^4$

$= \left(m^2\right)^4$

$= m^{2\times4}$

$= m^8$

i) $(t^4)^3 \div (t^7)^2 = t^{4\times3} \div t^{7\times2}$
$= t^{12} \div t^{14}$
$= t^{12-14}$
$= t^{-2}$ or $\frac{1}{t^2}$

j) $(3^{-2})^{-1} \times (3^4)^{-2} = 3^{(-2)\times(-1)} \times 3^{(4)\times(-2)}$
$= 3^2 \times 3^{-8}$
$= 3^{(2-8)}$
$= 3^{-6}$ or $\frac{1}{3^6}$

Lesson 6—Zero and Negative Exponents

PRACTICE EXERCISES
Answers and Solutions

1. **a)** Any base to the exponent 0 is equal to 1.
$(-3)^0 = 1$

b) A negative exponent inverts the base.
$4^{-1} = \frac{1}{4}$

c) Any signs outside of the brackets are applied after the exponent is applied.
$-(6)^0 = -(1) = -1$

d) The lack of brackets means that the negative sign acts as a coefficient of (–1).
$-7^{-3} = -1\times\left(\frac{1}{7}\right)^3$
$= -\frac{1}{343}$

e) $-5^0 = 1$

f) $-(-8)^0 = -(1)$
$= -1$

g) $-(-4)^2 = -(16)$
$= -16$

h) $-(-4)^{-2} = -\left(\frac{1}{4}\right)^2$
$= -\frac{1}{16}$

i) $3^{-4} = \left(\frac{1}{3}\right)^4$
$= \frac{1}{3^4}$
$= \frac{1}{81}$

j) $\left(\frac{3}{4}\right)^{-3} = \left(\frac{4}{3}\right)^3$
$= \frac{4^3}{3^3}$
$= \frac{64}{27}$

k) $6^{-2} = \left(\frac{1}{6}\right)^2$
$= \frac{1}{36}$

l) $\frac{1}{10^{-3}} = 10^3$
$= 1\,000$

m) $-\left(\frac{-2}{3}\right)^{-3} = -\left(\frac{3}{-2}\right)^3$
$= -\left(-\frac{27}{8}\right)$
$= \frac{27}{8}$

n) $\left(-\frac{4}{5}\right)^{-2} = \left(-\frac{5}{4}\right)^2$
$= \left(-\frac{5}{4}\right)\times\left(-\frac{5}{4}\right)$
$= \frac{25}{16}$

o) $-\left(\frac{7}{3}\right)^{-2} = -\left(\frac{3}{7}\right)^2$
$= -\left(\frac{3^2}{7^2}\right)$
$= -\frac{9}{49}$

2. **a)** $3^3 \times 3^{-1} = 3^{(3-1)}$
$= 3^2$
$= 9$

b) $4^2 \times 4^{-3} \times 4^4 = 4^{(2-3+4)}$
$= 4^3$
$= 64$

c) $\frac{8^{-2}}{8^1} = 8^{(-2-1)}$
$= 8^{-3}$
$= \frac{1}{8^3}$
$= \frac{1}{512}$

d) $\frac{2^5}{2^{-1}} \times \frac{2^{-2}}{2} = 2^{(5+1)} \times 2^{(-2-1)}$
$= 2^6 \times 2^{-3}$
$= 2^3$
$= 8$

e) $\frac{5^{-3}}{5^{-5} \times 5^2} = 5^{(-3+5-2)}$
$= 5^0$
$= 1$

3. a) $n^6 \times n^{-2} = n^{(6-2)}$
$= n^4$

b) $\left(a^{-3}\right)^{-3} = a^{(-3\times-3)}$
$= a^9$

c) $\left(\frac{m^3}{n^2}\right)^{-4} = \left(\frac{m^{(3\times-4)}}{n^{(2\times-4)}}\right)$
$= \frac{m^{-12}}{n^{-8}}$
$= m^{-12} \div n^{-8}$
$= \frac{1}{m^{12}} \div \frac{1}{n^8}$
$= \frac{1}{m^{12}} \times \frac{n^8}{1}$
$= \frac{n^8}{m^{12}}$

or

$\left(\frac{m^3}{n^2}\right)^{-4} = \left(\frac{n^2}{m^3}\right)^4$
$= \frac{n^{(2\times4)}}{m^{(3\times4)}}$
$= \frac{n^8}{m^{12}}$

d) $\frac{r^{-2}}{r^{-2}} = 1$

e) $\frac{a^5 \times a^{-3}}{a^6} = a^{(5-3-6)}$
$= a^{-4}$ or $\frac{1}{a^4}$

Practice Quiz

Answers and Solutions

1. A −7
As a non-terminating decimal, π is an irrational number. Since both $\frac{1}{4}$ and 0.75 can be written as fractions, they are rational numbers.

2. C $\sqrt{8}$
When written as a decimal, this number is a non-terminating decimal with no set pattern.

3. C 9 and −9
You need to give both the negative and positive square root solutions unless the problem deals with a practical application.

4. D 12.2 cm
$\sqrt{150} = 12.2$

5. D − 2
The coefficient is the number multiplying the variables.

6. A 2^{-2}
When multiplying powers with the same base, add the exponents.

7. A 7^{-4}
When dividing powers with the same base, subtract the exponent of the denominator from the exponent of the numerator.

8. C x^6y^{12}
When simplifying the power of a product, multiply the exponents.

9. A 5
Any number with the exponent zero is equal to 1. Thus, $5 \times 1 = 5$.

10 C $\frac{1}{6}$

To make a negative exponent positive, take the reciprocal of the base.

11. B 1

$$\frac{3^2}{3^{-1}} \times \frac{3^{-4}}{3^{-1}} = 3^3 \times 3^{-3}$$
$$= 3^{3-3}$$
$$= 3^0$$
$$= 1$$

12. D $\frac{x^4}{y^{12}}$

When simplifying a power of a quotient, multiply the exponents.

Lesson 7—Using Exponent Laws to Simplify, Evaluate, and Identify Patterns

PRACTICE EXERCISES
Answers and Solutions

1. **a)** Each subsequent number in a pattern is the product of the previous term and $\frac{1}{4}$ or 4^{-1}.

   So, to the next term in the sequence is 4^{-3} or $\frac{1}{64}$.

   b) $4^{-3} = \frac{1}{4^3}$

   $4^{-3} = \frac{1}{64}$

2. **a)** 1

   b) –1

   c) 27

   d) –27

   e) $\frac{1}{(-4)^3} = \frac{1}{-64}$

   f) $-\frac{1}{6^2} = -\frac{1}{36}$

3. $1.5 \times 3^{\left(\frac{60}{6}\right)} = 88\ 573.5$

   The hot dog will cost \$88 573.50 in 60 years.

4. **a)** $n^1 = (-3) = -3$

   b) $n^4 = (-3)^4 = 81$

   c) $n^2 = (-3)^2 = 9$

   d) $n^{-1} = (-3)^{-1} = \frac{1}{-3}$

5. **a)** $n^5 \div n^3 = 25$

   $n^{(5-3)} = 25$

   $n^2 = 25$

   $n = \sqrt{25}$

   $n = 5 \text{ or } -5$

   b) $(n^3)^2 = 729$

   $n^{(3\times2)} = 729$

   $n^6 = 729$

   $\sqrt{n^6} = \sqrt{729}$

   $\sqrt{n^3 \times n^3} = \sqrt{27 \times 27}$

   $n^3 = 27$

   $n = \sqrt[3]{27}$

   $n = 3$

   c) $n^8 \times n^{-12} = \frac{1}{256}$

   $n^{(8-12)} = \frac{1}{2^8}$

   $\frac{1}{n^4} = \frac{1}{2^8}$

   $n^4 = 2^8$

   $\sqrt[4]{n} = \sqrt[4]{2^8}$

   $n = 2^2$

   $n = 4$

6. Set up a table to help you see the pattern.

Power	Last Two Digits	Exponent	2nd Last Digit
6^0	01	0	0
6^1	06	1	0
6^2	36	2	3
6^3	16	3	1
6^4	96	4	9
6^5	76	5	7
6^6	56	6	5
6^7	36	7	3
6^8	16	8	1
6^9	96	9	9

Notice how the last digit is always a 6, and the second-last digit is formed by a repeating pattern of odd numbers: 9, 7, 5, 3, 1.

Because the pattern repeats every five numbers, every exponent that ends in a 4 or a 9 will have the second last digit of 9. Every exponent that ends in a 5 or a 0 will have a second-last digit of 7. The power 6^{200}, therefore, will end in the digits 76.

Lesson 8—Using Exponent Laws to Simplify Questions Involving Coefficients and Variables and to Evaluate Complex Numerical Questions

PRACTICE EXERCISES
Answers and Solutions

1. a) $\left(x^{-3}\right)^2 = x^{(-3\times 2)}$
$= x^{-6}$

b) $\left(\dfrac{m^2n^3}{mn^{-2}}\right) = m^{(2-1)}n^{(3+2)}$
$= mn^5$

c) $\dfrac{x^4y^7z^{-3}}{x^2y^{-5}z^2} = x^{(4-2)}y^{(7+5)}z^{(-3-2)}$
$= x^2y^{12}z^{-5}$

d) $(4g^3h^5)(-5g^{-4}h^3) = (4\times -5)g^{(3-4)}h^{(5+3)}$
$= -20g^{-1}h^8$

e) $(3g^{-5}h^5)(5g^{-4}h^3) = (3\times 5)g^{(-5-4)}h^{(5+3)}$
$= 15g^{-9}h^8$

f) $(ab^{-3})^{-5} = a^{(1\times -5)}b^{(-3\times -5)}$
$= a^{-5}b^{15}$

g) $\dfrac{-36a^5b^{-3}}{-12a^6b^{-5}} = (-36 \div -12)a^{(5-6)}b^{(-3+5)}$
$= 3a^{-1}b^2$

h) $\left(\dfrac{m^2n^{-3}}{m^4n}\right)^2 = (m^{(2-4)}n^{(-3-1)})^2$
$= (m^{-2}n^{-4})^2$
$= m^{-4}n^{-8}$

i) $\left(6x^2y^{-4}\right)\left(-12y^5\right) = \left(6\times -12\right)x^2y^{(-4-5)}$
$= -72x^2y^{-9}$

j) $\dfrac{12a^3b^{-3}}{-18a^5b^2} = \left(12 \div -18\right)a^{(3-5)}b^{(-3-2)}$
$= -\dfrac{2}{3}a^{-2}b^{-5}$ or $\dfrac{-2}{3a^2b^5}$

2. a) $\dfrac{2^5}{2^{-2}} \times \dfrac{2^{-4}}{2^2} = 2^7 \times 2^{-6} = 2^1 = 2$

b) $\dfrac{(-3)^9 \times (-3)^{-6}}{(-3)^2} = \dfrac{(-3)^3}{(-3)^2} = (-3)^1 = -3$

c) $\dfrac{3^7}{3^3} \times \dfrac{9^2 \times 9^0}{9^2 \times 9^{-3}} = 3^4 \times \dfrac{9^{-2}}{9^{-1}} = 3^4 \times 9^{-1}$
$= 81 \times \dfrac{1}{9}$
$= \dfrac{81}{9}$
$= 9$

Lesson 9—Using the Calculator to Key In and Solve BEDMAS Questions

PRACTICE EXERCISES
Answers and Solutions

Answers may vary for key stroking.

1. a) 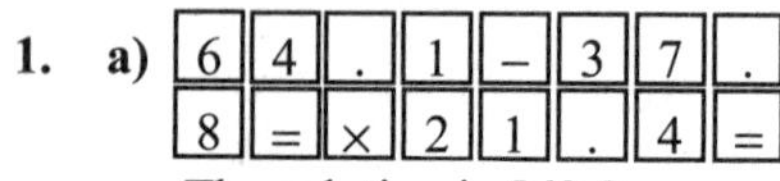

The solution is 562.8.

b) 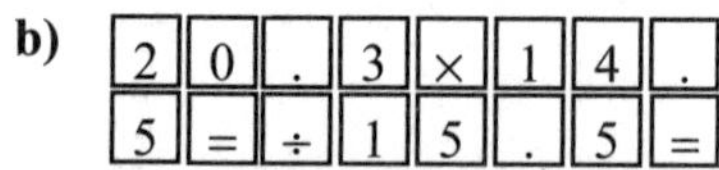

The solution is 19.0.

c) 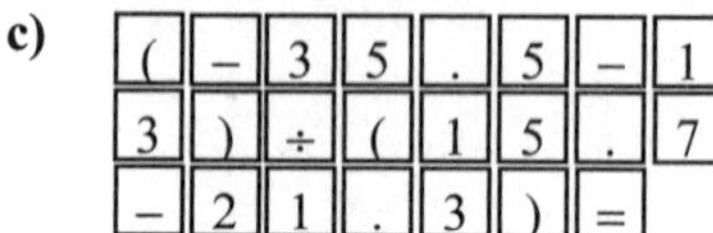

The solution is 8.7.

d) 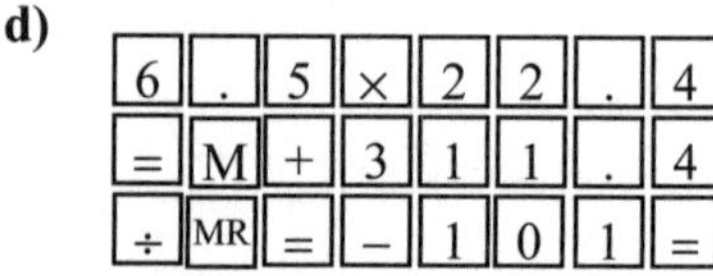

The solution is – 98.9.

e) 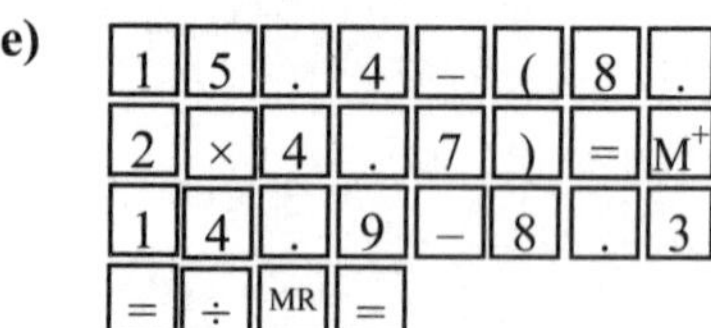

The solution is 0.3.

Lesson 10—Scientific Notation Calculations

PRACTICE EXERCISES
Answers and Solutions

1. a) [4] [.] [3] [Exp] [4] [×] [3] [.] [8] [Exp] [−2] [=]

$1.634 = 1.634 \times 10^3$

b) -2.418×10^{-8}

c) $3.674\,8 \times 10^{10}$

2. a) [7] [.] [8] [9] [Exp] [5] [÷] [2]
[.] [6] [Exp] [2] [=] = –3 034.61

b) 0.03

c) 822 580.65

3. The spacecraft travels at 60 000 km/h. A year is made up of 365 days of 24 hours each. So, the distance travelled in one year will be
60 000 × 24 × 365.

This number is multiplied by the total number of years to reach the star, 296 000.

The distance to the star is $1.555\,776 \times 10^{14}$ km.

Practice Test

Answers and Solutions

1. **D** irrational

$\sqrt{2} = 1.414\,213\,562\ldots$

$\sqrt{2}$ is an irrational number because it resolves into a non-terminating, non-repeating decimal. It cannot be expressed as a fraction that uses an integer for both the numerator and the denominator.

2. **A** 0.536 872
This number terminates, so it is rational.

3. **C** 8 cm

$\sqrt{441} = 21$ cm

$\sqrt{25} = 5$ cm

$21 - 5 = 16$

$16 \div 2 = 8$

The edge of the small square is 8 cm from the edge of the target.

4. **C** 17 and –17

$\sqrt{289} = 17$ and -17

5. **D** $\frac{2}{3}$

The coefficient is the number that is multiplied by the variables.

6. A $(-2)^{18}$

When dealing with the power of a power, multiply the exponents.

7. A 2^7

$$\frac{2^3\times 2^8}{2^4}=\frac{2^{11}}{2^4}$$
$$=2^{11-4}$$
$$=2^7$$

8. D $(2^2)^3\times(-2)^2$

$$=2^6\times 4$$
$$=64\times 4$$
$$=256$$

9. C $30y^8$

$$(5y^2)(6y^6)=5\times 6\times y^{2+6}=30y^8$$

10. C $(-2)^{-4}=\frac{1}{16}$

$$=\frac{1}{(-2)^4}$$
$$=\frac{1}{16}$$

11. B $8x^5y^4$

$$\frac{(4x^3y^2)(4x^5y^6)}{2x^3y^4}=\frac{16x^{3+5}y^{2+6}}{2x^3y^4}$$
$$=\frac{16x^8y^8}{2x^3y^4}$$
$$=8x^{8-3}y^{8-4}=8x^5y^4$$

12. C $2^7\times 2^{-3}\div 2^4$

$$=2^{7+(-3)-4}$$
$$=2^0$$
$$=1$$

13. D 6.7 cm

$\sqrt{44.5}=6.7$

Use only the positive value since it is a length.

14. B 4

$$\frac{(x^3)^2}{x^4}=\frac{x^6}{x^4}$$
$$=x^{6-4}$$
$$=x^2$$
$$=(-2)^2$$
$$=4$$

15. D 2.4×10^9

[3] [.] [6] [Exp] [6] [÷] [1] [.] [5] [Exp] [−3] [=]

$$\frac{3.6\times 10^6}{1.5\times 10^{-3}}=\left(\frac{3.6}{1.5}\right)\times 10^6\div 10^{-3}$$
$$=\left(\frac{7.2}{3}\right)\times 10^{(6+3)}$$
$$=2.4\times 10^9$$

16. A 9

Power	3^2	3^3	3^4	3^5	3^6	3^7
Last digit	9	7	1	3	9	7

Notice that the pattern repeats every four exponents. When the number 3 is raised to an even exponent, the result will either have a last digit of 9 or 1. If the value of the exponent is divisible by 4, the number will end with a 1, and if the value of the exponent is not divisible by 4, the number will end in a 9. Since 30 is not divisible by 4, you can conclude that 3^{30} will end in a 9.

17. A 10^4

$$\frac{1\times 10^{-10}}{1\times 10^{-14}}=10^{-10-(-14)}$$
$$=10^4$$

18. A 1.239×10^4

19. D 154.175

$$\frac{(0.095\times 2550+0.125\times 4229)}{5}$$

20. D $3x^2$

$9x^3y^2 \div 3xy^2 = 3x^{3-1}y^{2-2}$

$= 3x^2y^0$

$= 3x^2$

PATTERNS AND RELATIONS

Lesson 1—Word Problems to Equations

PRACTICE EXERCISES
Answers and Solutions

1. **a)** $10x + 5 = 65$

b) $x - 34 = 6$

c) $3x - 7 = 29$

d) $x^2 = 36$

e) Let x = the amount in Bill's pocket and x + \$45 = amount in his bank account.

$x + (x + 45) = 105$

$2x + 45 = 105$

f) Let x = the first integer and $x + 1$ = the second integer.

$x + (x + 1) = 37$

$2x + 1 = 37$

g) Let x = distance from Edmonton to Calgary and $4x$ = distance from Edmonton to Winnipeg.

$x + 4x = 1\,550$

$5x = 1\,550$

h) Let x = the original number of computers

$x - 3 = 18$

Lesson 2—Manipulating Equations

PRACTICE EXERCISES
Answers and Solutions

1. **a)** $\frac{A}{w} = \frac{l\cancel{w}}{\cancel{w}}$, $\frac{A}{w} = l$

b) $\cancel{3a} - \cancel{3a} - 2b = -8 - 3a$, $\frac{-\cancel{2}b}{-\cancel{2}} = \frac{-8-3a}{-2}$,

$b = \frac{8+3a}{2}$

c) $\frac{I}{pt} = \frac{\cancel{p}r\cancel{t}}{\cancel{pt}}$, $\frac{I}{pt} = r$

d) $\frac{A}{\pi} = \frac{\cancel{\pi}r^2}{\cancel{\pi}}$, $\frac{A}{\pi} = r^2$, $\sqrt{\frac{A}{\pi}} = \sqrt{r^2}$,

$\sqrt{\frac{A}{\pi}} = r$

e) $y - b = mx + \cancel{b} - \cancel{b}$, $\frac{y-b}{x} = \frac{m\cancel{x}}{\cancel{x}}$

$\frac{y-b}{x} = m$

f) $2A = \frac{\cancel{2}bh}{\cancel{2}}$

Multiply both sides by 2 to eliminate the 2 in the denominator.

$2A = bh$, $\frac{2A}{b} = \frac{\cancel{b}h}{\cancel{b}}$, $\frac{2A}{b} = h$

Lesson 3—Using Algebra Tiles to Solve Equations

PRACTICE EXERCISES
Answers and Solutions

1. a) $3x - 2 = x + 4$

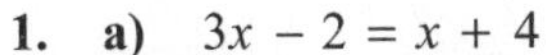

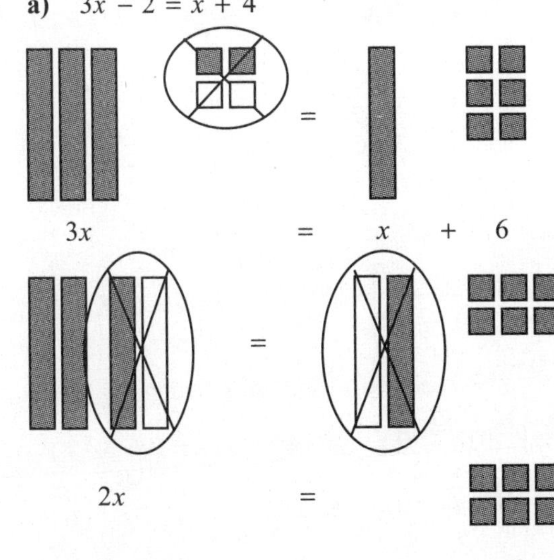

$3x = x + 6$

$2x = $

$2x = 6$

The solution is $x = 3$.

b) $3x - 5 = 2x - 7$

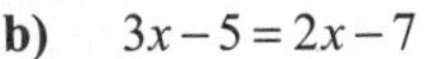

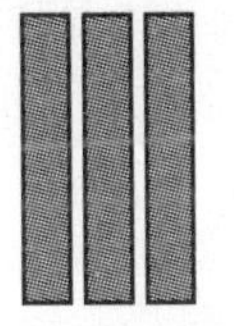

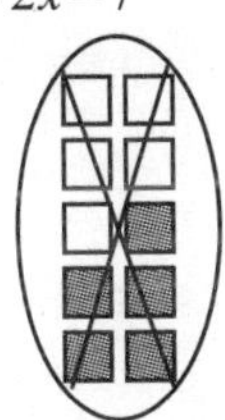

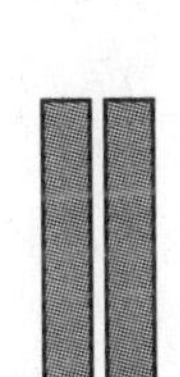

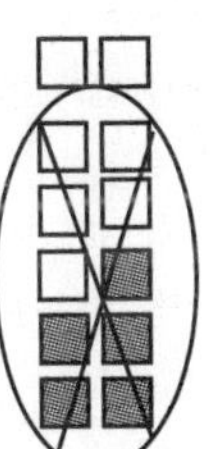

$3x = 2x - 2$

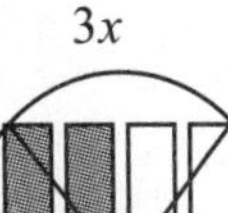

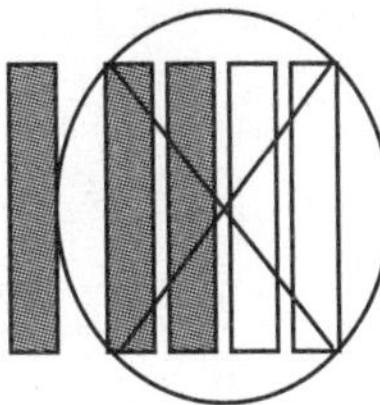

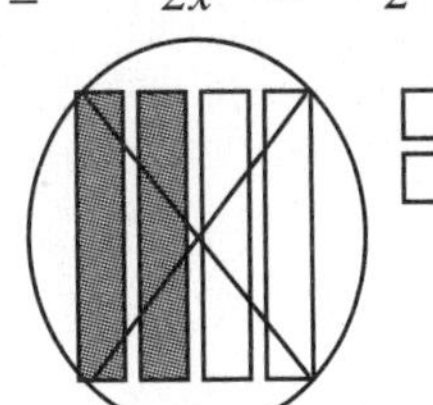

The solution is $x = -2$.

c) $3 + 4x = 9 - 2x$

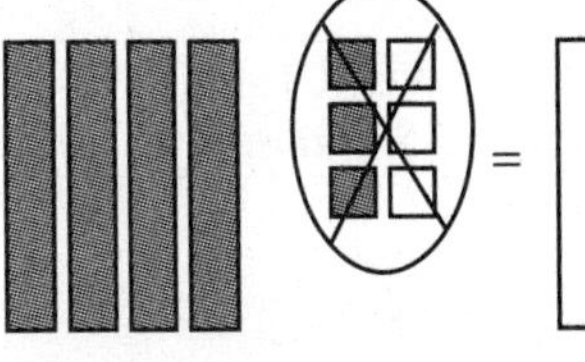

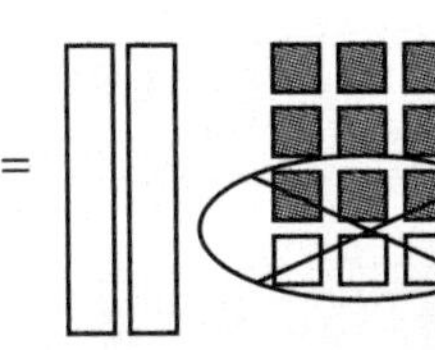

$4x = -2x + 6$

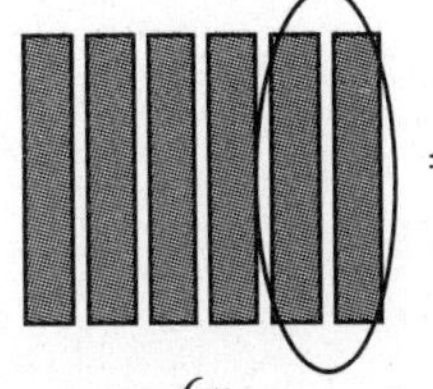

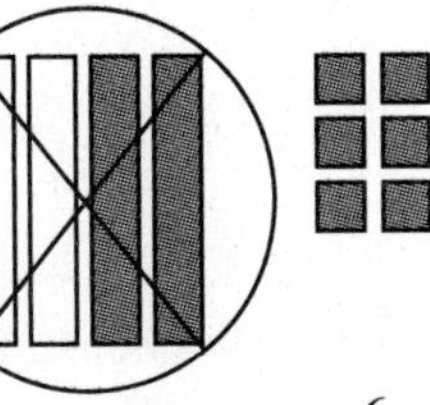

$6x = 6$

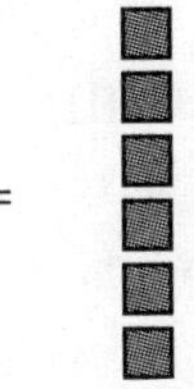

The solution is $x = 1$.

d) $-3x - 2 = 7 - 6x$

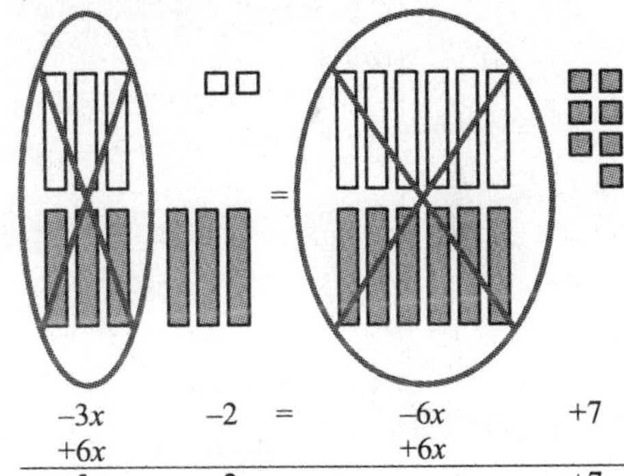

$$\begin{array}{rrcrr} -3x & -2 & = & -6x & +7 \\ +6x & & & +6x & \\ \hline +3x & -2 & = & & +7 \end{array}$$

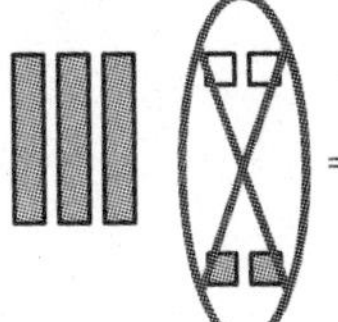

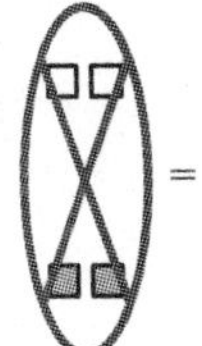

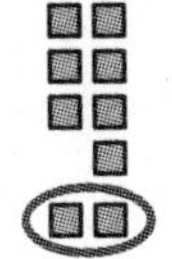

$$\begin{array}{rrcr} +3x & -2 & = & +7 \\ & +2 & & +2 \\ \hline +3x & & = & +9 \end{array}$$

$$\frac{+3x}{+3} = \frac{+9}{+3}$$

$$x = 3$$

The solution is $x = 3$.

Lesson 4—Solving Equations

PRACTICE EXERCISES
Answers and Solutions

1. **a)** $4x-5x=\cancel{5x}-\cancel{5x}-6$

$-1x=-6$

$x=6$

Verify

LS = RS

$3(6)+(6)=5(6)-6$

$24 = 24$

b) $9=9x$

$x=1$

Verify

LS = RS

$-6(1)+9=3(1)$

$3 = 3$

c) $\cancel{5}-\cancel{5}-6x-2x=-\cancel{2x}+\cancel{2x}+5-5$

$-8x=0$

$x=0$

Verify

LS = RS

$5-6(0)=2(0)+5$

$0=0$

d) $2x+2=3x-3$

$2x-3x+\cancel{2}-\cancel{2}=\cancel{3x}-\cancel{3x}-3-2$

$-x=-5$

$x=5$

Verify

LS = RS

$2(5+1)=3(5-1)$

$12 = 12$

e) $41=1.2x-7$

$41+7=1.2x-\cancel{7}+\cancel{7}$

$48=1.2x$

$x=40$

Verify

LS = RS

$41 = 0.5(40)+0.7(40)-7$

$41 = 41$

2. **a)** $2.5x-4+1.3x=3$

$3.8x=7$

$x=1.8$

b) $1.2x+3.5(2.5-x)=41$

$1.2x+8.75-3.5x=41$

$-2.3x=32.25$

$x=-14.0$

c) $5.9-(3x-2.5)=0.5x$

$5.9-3x-2.5=0.5x$

$3.4=3.5x$

$x=1.0$

3. **a)** $14x=\dfrac{-3}{x}$

$14x=-3$

$x=\dfrac{-3}{14}$

b) $\dfrac{x}{4}-\dfrac{2}{3}=3$

$3x-8=36$

$3x=44$

$x=\dfrac{44}{3}=14\dfrac{2}{3}$

c) $\dfrac{5x}{3}-3=8+\dfrac{x}{2}$

$10x-18=48+3x$

$7x=66$

$x=\dfrac{66}{7}=9\dfrac{3}{7}$

d) $-2(3x-1)=2(-4x+3)$

$-6x+2=-8x+6$

$2x=4$

$x=2$

Lesson 5—Solving Word Problems by Creating Equations

PRACTICE EXERCISES
Answers and Solutions

1. The numbers are 73, 74, 75, and 76.

Let x = 1st number
$x + 1$ = 2nd number
$x + 2$ = 3rd number
$x + 3$ = 4th number

$$\begin{aligned} x+x+1+x+2+x+3&=298 \\ 4x+6&=298 \\ 4x&=292 \\ x&=73 \end{aligned}$$

2. The numbers are 64 and 65.

Let x = the 1st number, and
$x + 1$ = the 2nd number

$$\begin{aligned} x+3(x+1)&=259 \\ x+3x+3&=259 \\ 4x+3&=259 \\ 4x&=256 \\ x&=64 \end{aligned}$$

3. Raymond is 10.

Let x = Bob's age
$2x + 4$ = Ellen's age
$\frac{1}{3}x + 6$ = Raymond's age

$$x+2x+4+\frac{1}{3}x+6=50$$

Multiply all terms by 3 to eliminate the fraction.

$$\begin{aligned} 3x+6x+12+x+18&=150 \\ 10x+30&=150 \\ 10x&=120 \\ x&=12 \end{aligned}$$

Now, substitute the value for x back into the expressions for the unknown ages.

Bob's age $= x$ Raymond's age $= \frac{1}{3}x+6$

$= 2(12) + 4$ $= \frac{1}{3}(12)+6$

$= 24 + 4$ $= 4 + 6$

$= 26$ $= 10$

4. The length of the base is 9 cm and the two equal sides are each 13 cm.

Let x = the length of one equal side
$x - 4$ = the base length

$$\begin{aligned} x+x+x-4&=35 \\ 3x-4&=35 \\ 3x&=39 \\ x&=13 \end{aligned}$$

5. The two numbers are 23 and 30.

Let x = the 1st number
$x + 7$ = the 2nd number

$$\begin{aligned} x+7+x&=53 \\ 2x+7&=53 \\ 2x&=46 \\ x&=23 \end{aligned}$$

1st number $= x$
$= 23$
2nd number $= x + 7$
$= 23 + 7$
$= 30$

6. There are 7 loonies, 11 quarters, and 21 dimes.

Let x = the number of loonies
$x + 4$ = the number of quarters
$3x$ = the number of dimes

$$100x + 25(x+4) + 10(3x) = 1185$$
$$155x + 100 = 1185$$
$$155x = 1085$$
$$x = 7$$

The number of loonies $= x$
$= 7$
The number of quarters $= x + 4$
$= (7) + 4$
$= 11$
The number of dimes $= 3x$
$= 3(7)$
$= 21$

7. The length of the rectangle is 25 m and the width is 13 m.

Let x = width
$2x - 1$ = length

$$P = 2l + 2w$$
$$76 = 2(2x-1) + 2(x)$$
$$76 = 4x - 2 + 2x$$
$$76 = 6x - 2$$
$$78 = 6x$$
$$13 = x$$

Width $= x$
$= 13$
Length $= 2x - 1$
$= 2(13) - 1$
$= 26 - 1$
$= 25$

Lesson 6—Solve and Graph Inequalities

PRACTICE EXERCISES
Answers and Solutions

1. a) $\frac{\not{4}x}{\not{4}} > \frac{4}{-4}$

$x < -1$

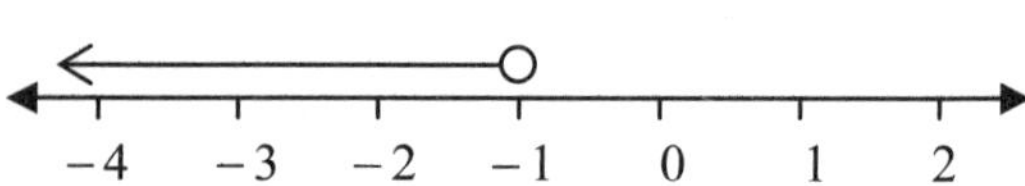

b)

$-6 \geq 3 - x$
$\underline{-3 \quad -3}$
$-9 \geq -x$
$\frac{-9}{-1} \leq \frac{-\not{x}}{-\not{1}}$
$9 \leq x$ or $x \geq 9$

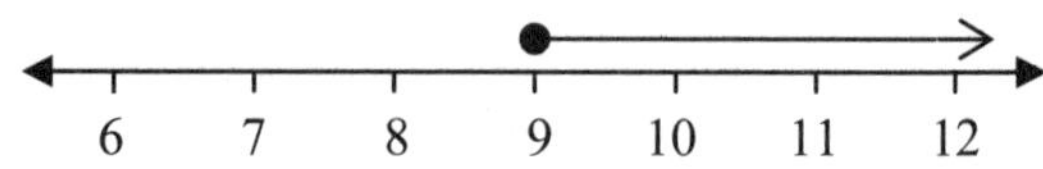

c) $2x - x + \not{2} - \not{2} > \not{x} - \not{x} + 4 - 2$

$x > 2$

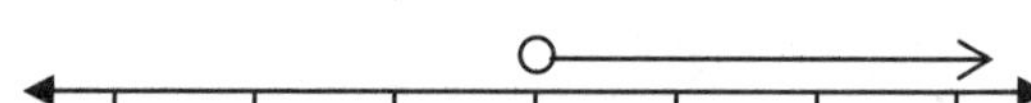

2. a) $4x - 2x + \not{2} - \not{2} \geq \not{2x} - \not{2x} - 2 - 2$

$2x \geq -4$
$x \geq -2$

b) $2x - 2 < 3x + 6$

$-x < 8$
$x > -8$

c) $12 - 6x > 2x + 2 - 2$

$12 - 6x > 2x$
$\not{12} - \not{12} - 6x - 2x > \not{2x} - \not{2x} - 12$
$-8x > -12$
$x < \frac{12}{8}$
$x < \frac{3}{2}$ or $1\frac{1}{2}$

3. $x > -5$

Thus, 0 and 2 are part of the solution to the inequality.

Practice Quiz

Answers and Solutions

1. Let x = the number of dimes

$x + 8$ = the number of quarters

$10x + 25(x+8) = 445¢$ or

$0.10x + 0.25(x+8) = 4.45$

$0.10x + 0.25x + 2.00 = 4.45$

$0.35x + \cancel{2.00} - \cancel{2.00} = 4.45 - 2.00$

$0.35x = 4.45$

$x = 7$

$x + 8 = 15$

There are 7 dimes and 15 quarters.

2. **B** $a = \frac{V}{bc}$ or $\frac{V}{bc} = a$

The given equation can be manipulated to be solved for the value of a.

$$\frac{V}{bc} = \frac{a\cancel{b}\cancel{c}}{\cancel{b}\cancel{c}}$$

3.

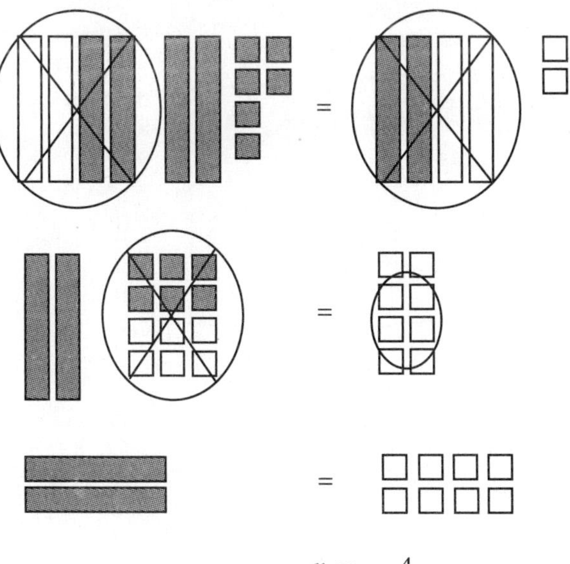

$x = -4$

4. **A** $x = -6$

$6x - 2x + \cancel{10} - \cancel{10} = \cancel{2x} - \cancel{2x} - 14 - 10$

$4x = -24$

$x = -6$

5. **B** $x = 3.5$

$12x - 32 = 10$

$12x - \cancel{32} + \cancel{32} = 10 + 32$

$12x = 42$

6. **B** $x = \frac{-4}{3}$

$6x - 14 = 12x - 6$

$6x - 12x - \cancel{14} + \cancel{14} = \cancel{12x} - \cancel{12x} - 6 + 14$

$-6x = 8$

$x = \frac{-4}{3}$

7. The first installment was \$40, the second was \$65, and the third was \$80.

Let x = the first installment

$x + 25$ = the second installment

$2x$ = the third installment

$x + (x+25) + 2x = 185$

$4x + 25 = 185$

$4x + \cancel{25} - \cancel{25} = 185 - 25$

$4x = 160$

$x = 40$

The first installment $= x$

$= \$40$

The second installment $= x + 25$

$= 40 + 25$

$= \$65$

The third installment $= 2x$

$= 2(40)$

$= \$80$

8. 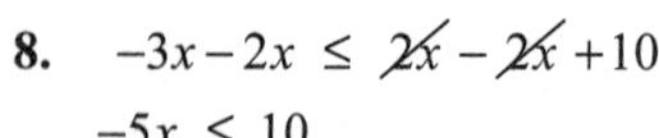

$-3x - 2x \leq \cancel{2x} - \cancel{2x} + 10$

$-5x \leq 10$

Since you are dividing by a negative, reverse the sign.

$\frac{-\cancel{5}x}{-\cancel{5}} \leq \frac{10}{-5}$

$x \geq -2$

−5 −4 −3 −2 −1 0 1

Lesson 7—Polynomials Terminology

PRACTICE EXERCISES
Answers and Solutions

1. a) The coefficients are 6 and –4.
The variable is t.
There is no constant. (The constant is 0.)
The polynomial is a binomial.

b) The coefficients are –2 and 1
The variables are a and t.
The constant is –6.
The polynomial is a trinomial.

c) The coefficients are –1 and 2.
The variables are x and y.
There is no constant. (The constant is 0.)
The polynomial is a binomial.

d) The coefficients are –1, 3, and –1.
The variables are d, c, and p.
The constant is 5.
The polynomial is a polynomial.

e) The coefficient is $\frac{7}{8}$.
The variable is x.
There is no constant. (The constant is 0.)
The polynomial is a monomial.

f) The coefficient is 1.
The variable is x.
The constant is $-\frac{3}{5}$.
The polynomial is a binomial.

Lesson 8—Evaluating Polynomials by Substitution

PRACTICE EXERCISES
Answers and Solutions

1. a) $2(13)+2(10)$

46

b) $3.14(15)^2$

$= 706.5$

c) $(12)(9)(15)$

$1\,620$

d) $2(-4)^2 - 7(-4) + 12$

$2(16) - 7(-4) + 12$

72

e) $(-5)^2 - (-6)^3$

$25 - (-216)$

241

f) $(-3)^{-2} + 2(-1)^{-3}$

To evaluate, enter the equation into your calculator rather than changing negative exponents to positive exponents.

$-1.\overline{8}$

or

$(-3)^{-2} + 2(-1)^{-3}$

$\frac{1}{(-3)^2} + 2\left(\frac{1}{-1}\right)^3$

$\frac{1}{9} + 2(-1)$

$\frac{1}{9} - 2 = \frac{-17}{9}$

Lesson 9—Using Algebra Tiles and Diagrams to Add and Subtract Polynomials

PRACTICE EXERCISES
Answers and Solutions

1. a)

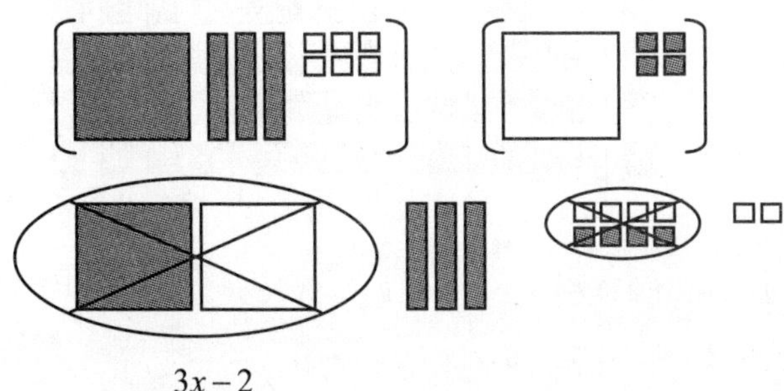

$3x-2$

b)

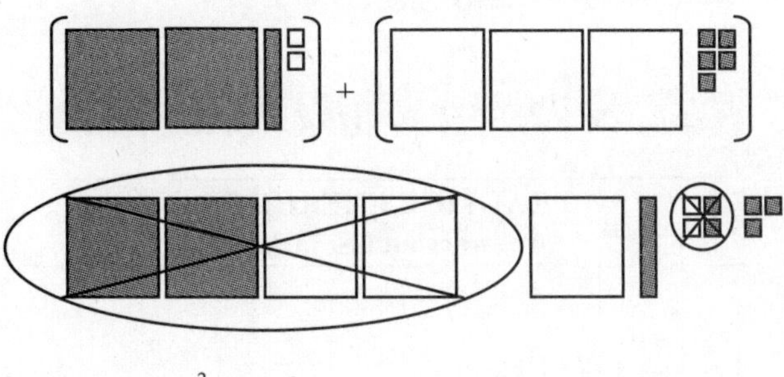

$-x^2+x+3$

c)

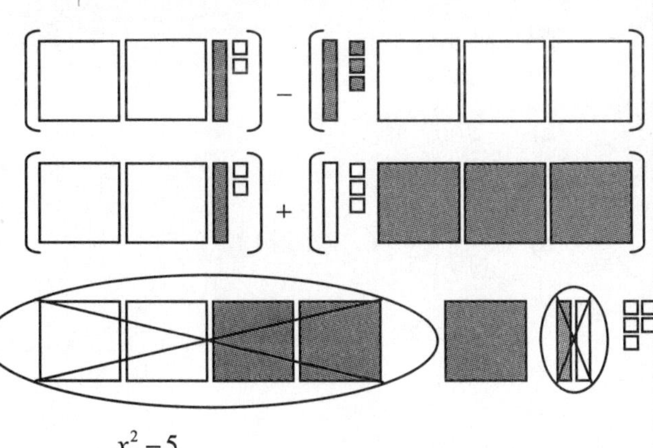

x^2-5

d)

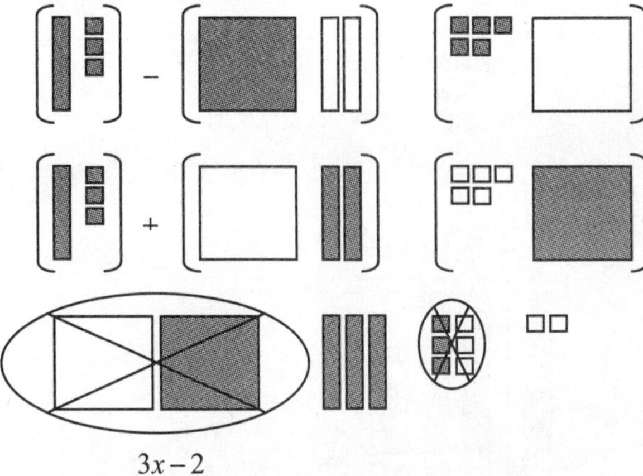

$3x-2$

Lesson 10—Adding and Subtracting Polynomials

PRACTICE EXERCISES
Answers and Solutions

1. a) $3x^2+4x-8-2x^2+8x-9$

$3x^2-2x^2+4x+8x-8-9$

$x^2+12x-17$

b) $x^2-7x-3-2x+11$

$x^2-7x-2x-3+11$

x^2-9x+8

c) $3x-4x^2-5-3x^2$

$-4x^2-3x^2+3x-5$

$-7x^2+3x-5$

d) $-5x^2-6x+1+2x^2-7+8x$

$-5x^2+2x^2-6x+8x+1-7$

$-3x^2+2x-6$

e) $3x-5-3+6x+8x-7$

$3x+6x+8x-5-3-7$

$17x-15$

f) $6x^2-5x+7+2x^2+4x+6-x+5$

$6x^2+2x^2-5x+4x-x+7+6+5$

$8x^2-2x+18$

Lesson 11—Multiplying, Dividing, and Factoring Polynomials Using Algebra Tiles

PRACTICE EXERCISES
Answers and Solutions

1. a) $3x+12$

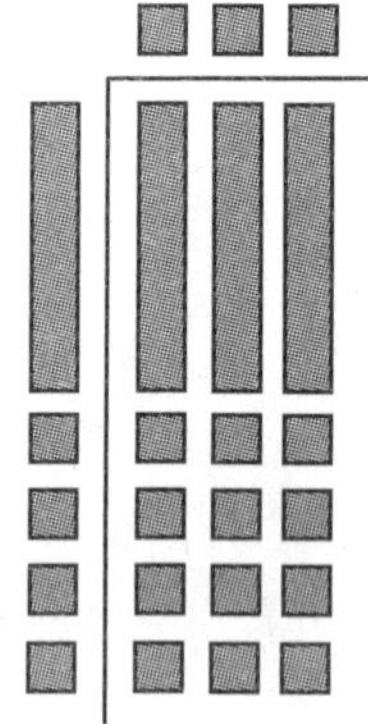

b) $2x^2+12x$

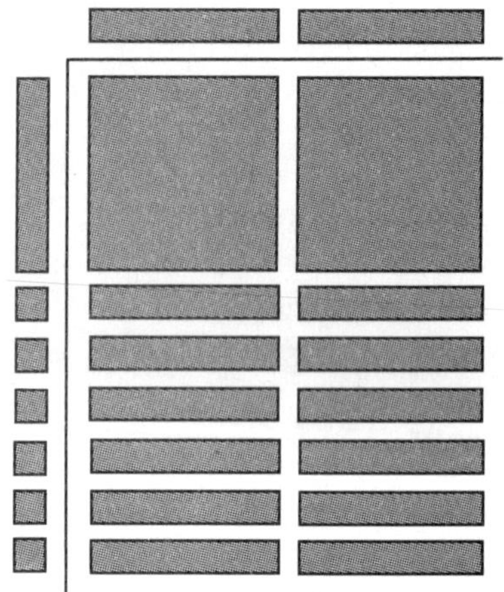

c) x^2+4x+3

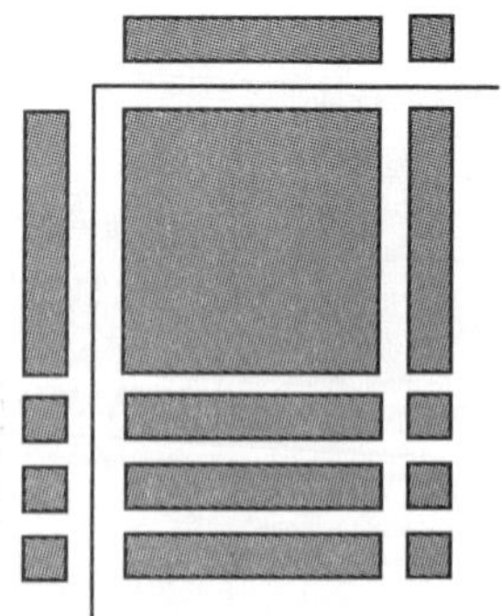

d) $2x^2+11x+12$

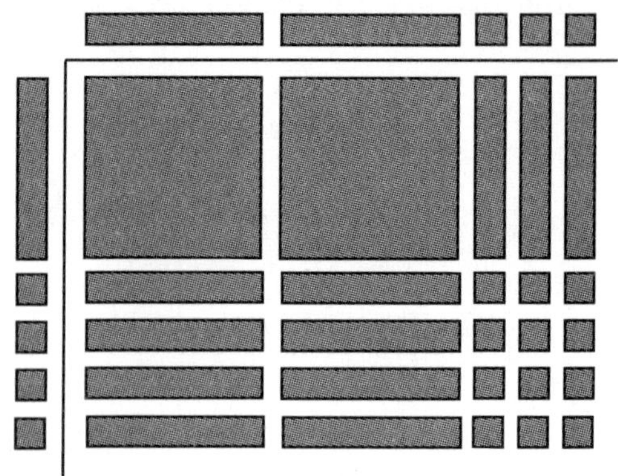

2. a) $x^2+6x+5=(x+1)(x+5)$

b) $x^2+5x+6=(x+2)(x+3)$

c) $3x^2+3x=(3x)(x+1)$

d) $6x^2+7x+2=(3x+2)(2x+1)$

Lesson 12—Multiplying Polynomials

PRACTICE EXERCISES
Answers and Solutions

1. a) $(3)(-4)\left(x^2\right)\left(x^3\right)$

$=-12x^{2+3}$

$=-12x^5$

b) $4x^{2+3}y^{1+2}$

$=4x^5y^3$

c) $-27m^{1+4}n^3$

$=-27m^5n^3$

d) $\left(\frac{2}{\cancel{3}}\right)\left(\frac{\cancel{3}}{5}\right)(a^3)(a^2)(b^4)(b^5)$

$=\frac{2}{5}a^5b^9$

2. a) $-2x^2+2x+12$

b) $(3x)(4x^2)+(3x)(-2x)+(3x)(-3)$

$=12x^3-6x^2-9x$

c) $(3xy)(-5x^2)+(3xy)(2xy)+(3xy)(-3y^2)$

$=-15x^3y+6x^2y^2-9xy^3$

d) $-14ab^4+42a^2b^3-28a^6b$

3. **a)** $(x)(x)+(x)(6)+(5)(x)+(5)(6)$
$=x^2+6x+5x+30$
$=x^2+11x+30$
b) $(2x)(x)+(2x)(-3)+(5)(x)+(5)(-3)$
$=2x^2-6x+5x-15$
$=2x^2-x-15$
c) $(2x)(x)+(2x)(-4)+(-3)(x)+(-3)(-4)$
$=2x^2-8x-3x+12$
$=2x^2-11x+12$
d) $(3x)(-x)+(3x)(8)+(-7)(-x)+(-7)(8)$
$=-3x^2+24x+7x-56$
$=-3x^2+31x-56$
e) $(2x+8)(3x+2)$
$(2x)(3x)+(2x)(2)+(8)(3x)+(8)(2)$
$=6x^2+4x+24x+16$
$6x^2+28x+16$

Lesson 13—Factoring Polynomials

PRACTICE EXERCISES
Answers and Solutions

1. **a)** $10x + 15$
$=5(2x+3)$
b) $12x^2 - 4x$
$=4x(3x-1)$
c) $18x^3+12x^2-6x$
$6x(3x^2+2x-1)$
d) $21x^2y-14x^2+28x^3y^3$
$7xy(3x-2y+4x^2y^2)$
e) $2m^3n^4-8m^2n$
$2m^2n^3(mn-4)$

2. **a)** $18x-33$
$=3(6x-11)$
b) $7n^2-21n+7$
$=7(n^2-3n+1)$
c) $7m^2+7m+14$
$7(m^2+m+2)$

3. **a)** sum $=8$
product $=15$
1×15 -1×-15
3×5 -3×-5
$(x+3)(x+5)$
b) sum $=15$
product $=56$
1×56 -1×-56
2×28 -2×-28
4×14 -4×-14
7×8 -7×-8
$(x+7)(x+8)$
c) sum $=-7$
product $=12$
1×12 -1×-12
2×6 -2×-6
3×4 -3×-4
$(x-3)(x-4)$
d) sum $=-5$
product $=-14$
$(x-7)(x+2)$
e) sum $=-10$
product $=-24$
$(a-12)(a+2)$
f) sum $=23$
product $=-24$
$(a-1)(a+24)$
g) sum $=17$
product $=30$
$(n+2)(n+15)$
h) sum $=8$
product $=-20$
$(n+10)(n-2)$
i) sum $=7$
product $=10$
$(n+2)(n+5)$

4. a) $=2(x^2-5x+4)$

Factor x^2-5x+4

sum $=-5$

product $=4$

$(x-4)(x-1)$.

Thus, the completely factored solution is $2(x-4)(x-1)$.

b) $m(m^2-2m-48)$

$=m(m-8)(m+6)$

c) $5(c^2-11c+30)$

$=5(c-6)(c-5)$

Lesson 14—Dividing a Polynomial by a Monomial

PRACTICE EXERCISES
Answers and Solutions

1. a) $\frac{12x^2}{4x}-\frac{8x}{4x}$

$=3x-2$

b) $\frac{12x^3}{-2x^2}-\frac{20x^2}{-2x^2}$

$=-6x+10$

c) $\frac{-28}{-7}+\frac{14x}{-7}$

$=4-2x$

d) $\frac{15x^4}{5x^2}-\frac{30x^3}{5x^2}+\frac{35x^2}{5x^2}$

$=3x^2-6x+7$

e) $\frac{4n^2}{4}-\frac{12n}{4}-\frac{6}{4}$

$=n^2-3n-\frac{3}{2}$

f) $\frac{2a^2}{-3}+\frac{15}{-3}-\frac{3a}{-3}$

$=\frac{-2a^2}{3}-5+a$

Practice Quiz 2

Answers and Solutions

1. a) $-6, 3$

b) x, y

c) -8

2. $2(-2)^3-4(-2)^2+7$

$=2(-8)-4(4)+7$

$=-16-16+7$

$=-25$

3. $\left(4x-3x^2+1\right)-\left(2x^2-4x-3\right)$

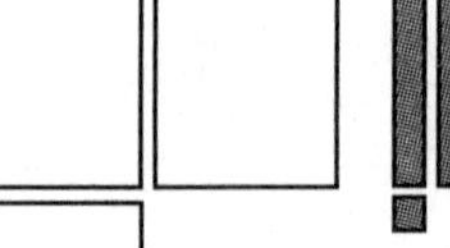
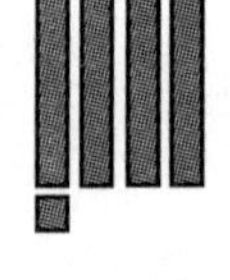
$-$
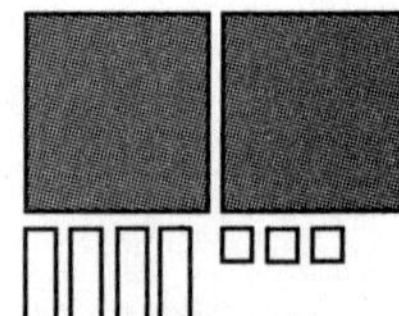

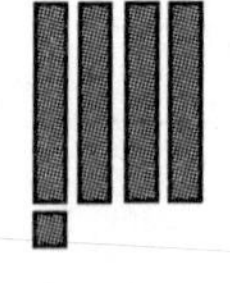
$+$
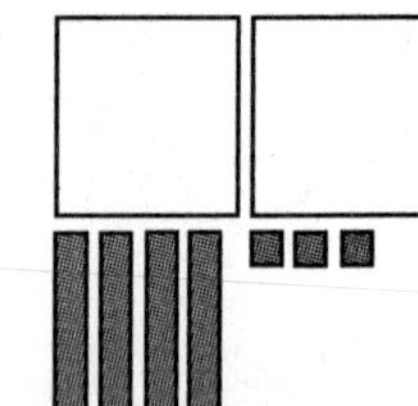

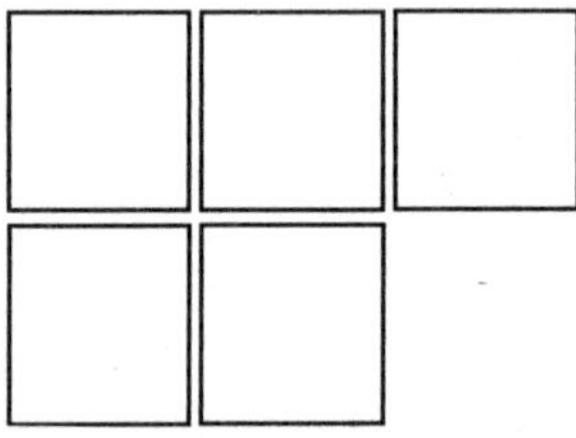
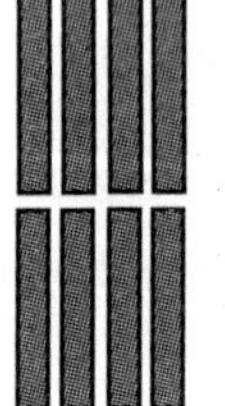

$-5x^2+8x+4$

4. $(8x^2-3x-12)+(6x^2-4x+8)$

$=14x^2-7x-4$

5. a) $-20g^2+36g-3$

b) $8x^2+20x-6x-15$

$8x^2+14x-15$

6. a) sum $=3$

product $=-40$

$(m+8)(m-5)$

b) sum $=-10$

product $=25$

$(n-5)(n-5)$

7. $\dfrac{15x}{-5}-\dfrac{20}{-5}-\dfrac{30x^3}{-5}$

$-3x+4+6x^3$

Lesson 15—Using Equation Skills to Solve Problems

PRACTICE EXERCISES
Answers and Solutions

1. With both conveyor belts working together, it will take $8\frac{4}{7}$ min or 8 min, 35 s to fill the truck.

Let x = the time for both conveyors to fill the truck.

$$\frac{x}{15}+\frac{x}{20}=1$$

$$\left(\frac{\overset{4}{\cancel{60}}}{1}\right)\left(\frac{x}{\cancel{15}}\right)+\left(\frac{\overset{3}{\cancel{60}}}{1}\right)\left(\frac{x}{\cancel{20}}\right)=\left(\frac{60}{1}\right)1$$

$$4x+3x=60$$

$$7x=60$$

$$x=\frac{60}{7}=8\frac{4}{7}$$

$$\frac{4}{7}\times\frac{60\text{ sec}}{1}\text{ min}=34.286\text{ s}$$

Since it will take longer than 34 s, round the answer up to 8 min, 35 s.

2. Colleen will need a mark of 90% on her fourth test to achieve an average of 85%.

Let $x=$ her mark on the fourth test

$$\frac{74+90+86+x}{4}=85$$

$$\frac{250+x}{4}=85$$

$$\left(\frac{\cancel{4}}{1}\right)\frac{(250+x)}{\cancel{4}}=85\left(\frac{4}{1}\right)$$

$$250+x=340$$

$$x=90$$

3. It will take 4 hours to fill the pool if all the pipes are used at the same time.

Let $x=$ the total amount of time for all three pipes to fill the pool together.

$$\frac{x}{8}+\frac{x}{12}+\frac{x}{24}=1$$

$$\left(\frac{\overset{3}{\cancel{24}}}{1}\right)\left(\frac{x}{\cancel{8}}\right)+\left(\frac{\overset{2}{\cancel{24}}}{1}\right)\left(\frac{x}{\cancel{12}}\right)+\left(\frac{\overset{1}{\cancel{24}}}{1}\right)\left(\frac{x}{\cancel{24}}\right)=\left(\frac{24}{1}\right)\left(\frac{1}{1}\right)$$

$$3x+2x+x=24$$

$$6x=24$$

$$x=4\text{ hr}$$

Practice Test

Answers and Solutions

1. B When you double the value of n and add 1, you get the value for the math expression in each column of the table.

2. C Using the distributive property, you get $2(n-4)=2n-8$.

3. D $8x-4$

You can find the perimeter of a rectangle by using the formula $P=2l+2w$.

Inserting the given values, you get

$2(2x+1)+2(2x-3)=8x-4$

or

$P=2(l+x)$

$P=2[(2x+1)+(2x-3)]$

$P=2(4x-2)$

$P=8x-4$

4. B $-2x+3=4x-4$

5. A 9 cm

$864=(12)(8)(h)$

$864=96(h)$

$\frac{864}{96}=\frac{\cancel{96}(h)}{\cancel{96}}$

$9\text{ cm}=h$

6. C $6x-42=-12$

$6x-\cancel{42}+\cancel{42}=-12+42$

$6x=30$

$x=5$

7. B $4x-5x-\cancel{7}+\cancel{7}\geq\cancel{5x}-\cancel{5x}-9+7$

$-x\geq-2$

$x\leq 2$

8. D $x=0.75$

$\left(\frac{\overset{2}{\cancel{8}}}{1}\right)\frac{-1}{\cancel{4}}=\left(\frac{\overset{1}{\cancel{8}}}{1}\right)\frac{1}{\cancel{8}}-\left(\frac{\overset{4}{\cancel{8}}}{1}\right)\frac{x}{\cancel{2}}$

$-2=1-4x$

$-2-1=\cancel{1}-\cancel{1}-4x$

$-3=-4x$

$x=\frac{3}{4}=0.75$

9. B 10

Alternative C is incorrect because a negative number is less than a positive one. Alternative D gives a constant. Alternative A does not appear in the polynomial.

10. C $9p-3$

$\text{GCF}=3$

Dividing the equation by the GDF, you get $3P-1$.

Multiplying these together, you have $3(3P-1)$.

11. At the present time, Ed is 15 and Jim is 45.

Ed $=x$

Jim $=3x$

Six years ago:

Ed $=x-6$

Jim $=3x-6$

$(x-6)+(3x-6)=48$

$4x-12=48$

$4x-\cancel{12}+\cancel{12}=48+12$

$4x=60$

$x=15$

Or, since it is six years later and each of them has aged six years, add 12 to the total.

$x+3x=48+12$

$4x=60$

$x=15$

So, Ed $=x$

$=15$

And Jim $=3x$

$=3(15)$

$=45$

12. $(3-7x+5x^2)+(-8x+9x^2+4)$

$14x^2-15x+7$

13. $(2x-7)(4x+5)$

$=8x^2+10x-28x-35$

$8x^2-18x-35$

14. $-5p(4p^3+5p-7p^2)$

$=-20p^4-25p^2+35p^3$

15. $3x^2+3x-36$

GCF $=3$

$3(x^2+x-12)$

Now, factor the trinomial:

sum $=1$

product $=-12$

$(x-3)(x+4)$

Now, multiply the trinomial by the GCF:

$3(x-3)(x+4)$

16. $\dfrac{32x^2y^3-40x^4y^2}{-8xy^2}$

$=\dfrac{32x^2y^3}{-8xy^2}-\dfrac{40x^4y^2}{-8xy^2}$

$=-4xy+5x^3$

17. If both hoses are used at the same time, it will take 10 min to fill the pool.

Let $x=$ the total time to fill the pool

$\dfrac{x}{30}+\dfrac{x}{15}=1$

$\left(\dfrac{\overset{1}{\cancel{30}}}{1}\right)\dfrac{x}{\cancel{30}}+\left(\dfrac{\overset{2}{\cancel{30}}}{1}\right)\dfrac{x}{\cancel{15}}=\left(\dfrac{30}{1}\right)1$

$x+2x=30$

$3x=30$

$x=10$

18. Add the two previous numbers to get the next number in the sequence.

$8+13=21$

$21+13=34$

The next two numbers are 21 and 34.

This sequence, known as the **Fibonacci Sequence**, is used to describe such things as the increasing radius of a spiral sea shells.

19. Let $x=$ the first number

$x+1=$ the second number

$x+2=$ the third number

$x+x+1+x+2=33$

$3x+3=33$

20.

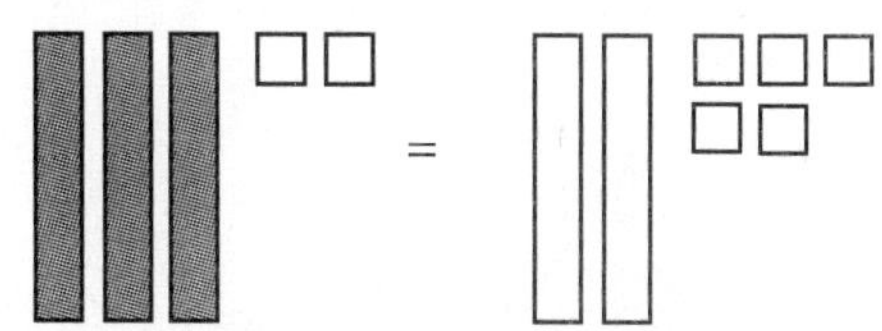

SHAPE AND SPACE

Lesson 1—The Tangent Ratio and Right Triangles

PRACTICE EXERCISES
Answers and Solutions

1. **a)** **i)** $\overline{DF}$

ii) $\overline{DE}$

iii) $\overline{EF}$

b) **i)** $\overline{GH}$

ii) $\overline{IH}$

iii) $\overline{IH}$

iv) GH

2. In a right triangle, the tangent of an angle refers to the relationship between the side opposite the angle divided by the side adjacent to the angle. In this case, the tangent of 60° will always reduce to the ratio 1.732 divided by 1. The opposite side will always be 1.732 times larger than the adjacent side.

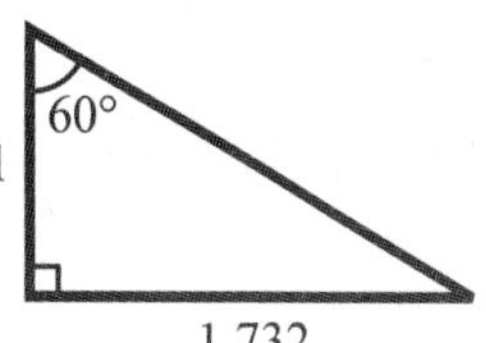

3. **a)**

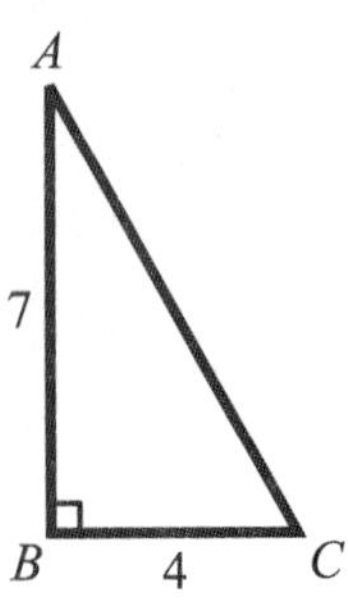

b)

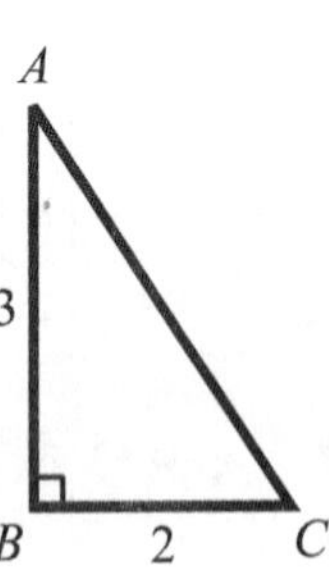

c)

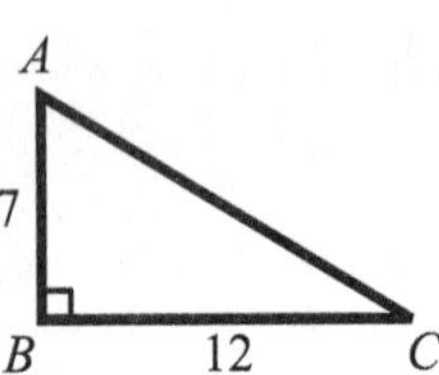

d)

4. **a)** tan 27° = 0.510
b) tan 63° = 1.963
c) tan 80° = 5.671
d) tan 45° = 1.000

5. **a)** $\tan A = \frac{5}{12}$

$\tan B = \frac{12}{5}$

b) $\tan A = \frac{9}{18} = \frac{1}{2}$

$\tan B = \frac{18}{9} = \frac{2}{1} = 2$

6. **a)** $\tan 40° = \frac{x}{6}$

$\frac{0.839}{1} = \frac{x}{6}$

$x = 5.0 \text{ cm}$

b) $\tan 35° = \frac{x}{23}$

$\frac{0.700}{1} = \frac{x}{23}$

$x = 23 \times 0.700$

$x = 16.1 \text{ cm}$

c) $\tan 56° = \frac{10}{x}$

$\frac{1.483}{1} = \frac{10}{x}$

$x = \frac{10}{1.483}$

$1.483x = 10$

$x = 6.7 \text{ cm}$

d) $\tan 9° = \frac{5}{x}$

$\frac{0.158}{1} = \frac{5}{x}$

$0.158x = 5$

$x = \frac{5}{0.158}$

$x = 31.6 \text{ cm}$

7. **a)** $\angle B = \tan^{-1}(0.876)$

$\angle \text{B} = 41°$

b) $\angle \text{B} = \tan^{-1}(0.236)$

$\angle B = 13°$

c) $\angle \text{B} = \tan^{-1}(23.845)$

$\angle \text{B} = 88°$

d) $\angle B = \tan^{-1}\left(\frac{5}{9}\right)$

$\angle B = 29°$

e) $\angle B = 65°$

$\angle B = \tan^{-1}\left(\frac{15}{7}\right)$

f) $\angle B = 69°$

$\angle B = = \tan^{-1}\left(\frac{8}{3}\right)$

8. a) $\tan B = \frac{7}{8}$

$\tan^{-1}\left(\frac{7}{8}\right) = 41°$

$\angle B = 41°$

b) $\tan B = \frac{10}{8}$

$\angle B = 51°$

c) $\tan B = \frac{20}{25}$

$\angle B = 39°$

Lesson 2—The Sine and Cosine Ratio and Right Triangles

PRACTICE EXERCISES
Answers and Solutions

1. a) $\sin J = \frac{\overline{KL}}{\overline{JL}}$

b) $\cos J = \frac{\overline{JK}}{\overline{JL}}$

c) $\sin L = \frac{\overline{JK}}{\overline{JL}}$

d) $\cos L = \frac{\overline{KL}}{\overline{JL}}$

2.

0.174 | 80° | 1

In the right triangle, the ratio of the adjacent side of an 80° angle divided by the hypotenuse will always reduce to 0.174 divided by 1. This means that the side adjacent to an 80° angle is always 0.174 times the length of the hypotenuse.

3. a) $\sin 25° = \frac{x}{20}$

$\frac{0.423}{1} = \frac{x}{20}$

$x = 8.5$ cm

b) $\cos 70° = \frac{x}{12}$

$\angle x = 12 \cos 70°$

$\frac{0.342}{1} = \frac{x}{12}$

$x = 4.1$ cm

c) $\cos 30° = \frac{8.2}{x}$

$\frac{0.866}{1} = \frac{8.2}{x}$

$x = \frac{8.2}{\cos 30°}$

$0.866x = 8.2$

$x = 9.5$ cm

d) $\sin 9° = \frac{4}{x}$

$\angle x = \frac{4}{\sin 9°}$

$x = 25.6$ cm

e) $\sin 39° = \frac{x}{8.5}$

$\angle x = 8.5 \sin 39°$

$x = 5.3$ cm

4. **a)** $\sin D = \dfrac{8}{12}$

$\angle D = \sin^{-1}\left(\dfrac{8}{12}\right)$

$\angle D = 42°$

b) $\sin D = \dfrac{7}{14}$

$\angle D = \sin^{-1}\left(\dfrac{7}{14}\right)$

$\angle D = 30°$

c) $\cos D = \dfrac{18}{20}$

$\angle D = 26°$

d) $\cos D = \dfrac{7.2}{8.4}$

$\angle D = 31°$

Lesson 3—Solving Problems Involving Right Triangles

PRACTICE EXERCISES
Answers and Solutions

1. The horizontal length of the shadow is 346.4 m.

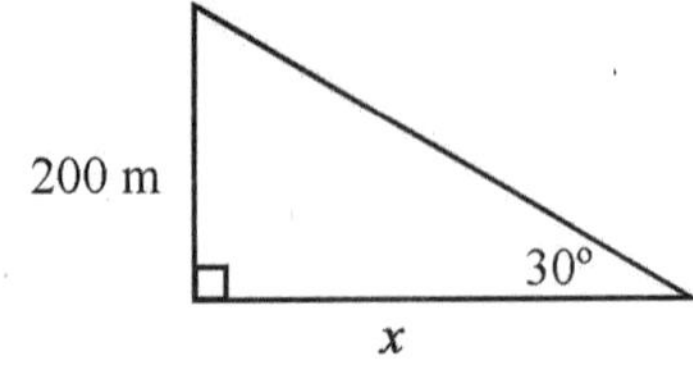

$\tan 30° = \dfrac{200}{x}$

$x = 346.4 \text{ m}$

2. The angle formed between the ladder and the ground is 73°.

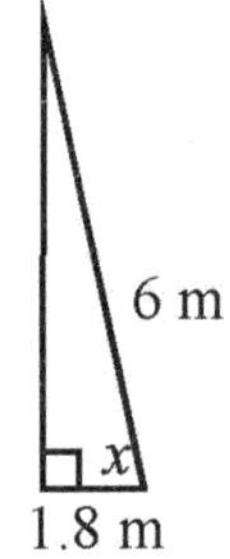

$\cos X = \dfrac{1.8}{6}$

$\angle X = 73°$

3.

a) The width of the rectangle is 13.0 cm.

$\tan 33° = \dfrac{x}{20}$

$\angle\ x = 20 \tan 33°$

$x = 13.0 \text{ cm}$

b) The length of the diagonal is 23.8 cm.

$\cos 33° = \dfrac{20}{y}$

$\angle\ y = \dfrac{20}{\cos 30°}$

$y = 23.8 \text{ cm}$

4. The height of the kite is 15.4 m.

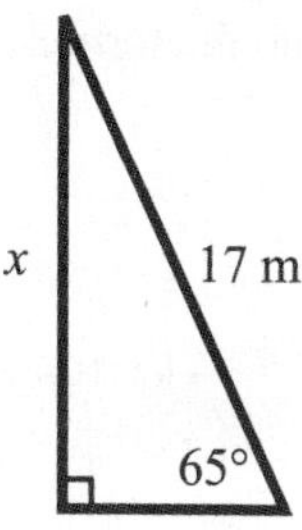

$\sin 65° = \frac{x}{17}$

$\angle x = 17\sin 65°$

$x = 15.4$ m

5. The building is 17.6 m tall.

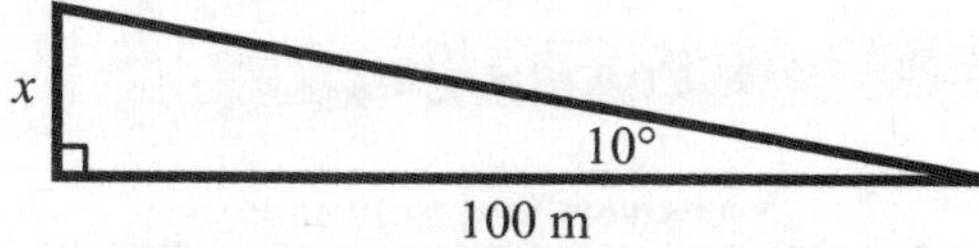

$\tan 10° = \frac{x}{100}$

$< x = 100\tan 10°$

$x = 17.6$ m

6. The jet is climbing at an angle of 7°.

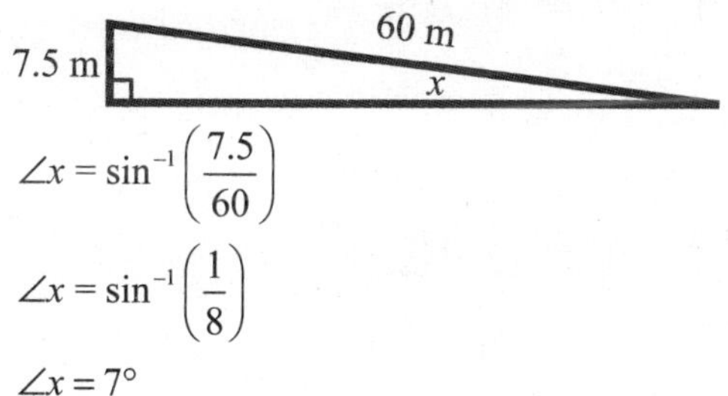

$\angle x = \sin^{-1}\left(\frac{7.5}{60}\right)$

$\angle x = \sin^{-1}\left(\frac{1}{8}\right)$

$\angle x = 7°$

Lesson 4—Volume of Cones and Pyramids

PRACTICE EXERCISES
Answers and Solutions

Remember to use the button for π on your calculator, not 3.14, to get a more accurate solution.

1. a) $V = \frac{\pi r^2 h}{3}$

$V = \frac{\pi(6)^2(4)}{3}$

$V = 150.8 \text{ cm}^3$

b) $V = \frac{\pi(11.5)^2(7.4)}{3}$

$V = 1024.8 \text{ cm}^3$

c) $V = \frac{1}{3}\pi\left(\frac{d}{2}\right)^2(h)$

$V = \frac{1}{3}\pi\left(\frac{16.4}{2}\right)^2(13)$

$V = \frac{\pi(8.2)^2(13)}{3}$

$V = 915.4 \text{ cm}^3$

d) $V = \pi\left(\frac{d}{2}\right)^2 h$

$V = \frac{1}{3}\pi\left(\frac{9.6}{2}\right)^2(9.4)$

$V = \frac{1}{3}\pi(4.8)^2(9.4)$

$V = \frac{\pi(4.8)^2(9.4)}{3}$

$V = 226.8 \text{ cm}^3$

2. The volume of the grain is $2\,303.8 \text{ m}^3$.

$V = \frac{\pi(20)^2(5.5)}{3}$

$V = 2\,303.8 \text{ m}^3$

3. The volume of the cone is 615.8 cm^3.

First, find the volume of the cylinder.

$V = \pi r^2 h$

$V = \pi(7)^2(12)$

$V = 1\,847.3\text{ cm}^3$

Since the volume of the cone is $\frac{1}{3}$ that of the cylinder, multiply the volume of the cylinder by $\frac{1}{3}$.

$V = \frac{1\,847.3\text{ cm}^3}{615.8\text{ cm}^3}$

$V = 615.8\text{ cm}^3$

4. **a)** $V = \frac{lwh}{3}$

$V = \frac{(6)(7)(10)}{3}$

$V = 140\text{ m}^3$

b) $V = \frac{(4)(9)(6.5)}{3}$

$V = 78\text{ m}^3$

c) $V = \frac{(3.5)(8)(9.8)}{3}$

$V = 91.5\text{ m}^3$

5. The dimensions would be the same. The volume of a pyramid is $\frac{1}{3}$ that of a rectangular prism with the same dimensions.

6. The volume of the pyramid is $2\ 278\ 500\text{ m}^3$.

$V = \frac{(210)(210)(155)}{3}$

$V = 2\ 278\ 500\text{ m}^3$

7. The height of the pyramid is 9.3 cm.

Substitute all the given values into the formula.

$V = \frac{lwh}{3}$

$124 = \frac{(5)(8)(h)}{3}$

$124 = \frac{(40)(h)}{3}$

Multiply both sides by 3 to get rid of the denominator.

$(3)124 = \frac{(40)(h)(3)}{3}$

$372 = 40h$

$9.3\text{ cm} = h$

Practice Quiz 1

Answers and Solutions

1. $\text{Sin } 47° = \frac{0.731}{1}$

In a right triangle, the sine ratio is the side opposite the angle divided by the hypotenuse. Therefore, for a 47° angle, the opposite is 0.731 times as long as the hypotenuse.

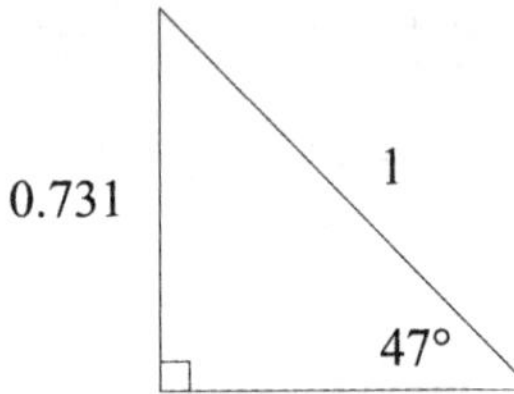

2. **a)** $\angle A = \sin^{-1}\left(\frac{3}{5}\right)$

$\angle A = 37°$

b) $\angle A = \tan^{-1}\left(\frac{7}{3}\right)$

$\angle A = 67°$

c) $\angle A = \cos^{-1}\left(\frac{1}{8}\right)$

$\angle A = 83°$

3. **a)** $\sin 20° = \frac{x}{8}$

$x = 8\sin 20°$

$\frac{0.342}{1} = \frac{x}{8}$

$x = 2.7\text{ cm}$

b) $\cos 63° = \frac{6}{x}$

$x = \frac{6}{\cos 63°}$

$\frac{0.454}{1} = \frac{6}{x}$

$x = 13.2\text{ cm}$

4. **a)** $\tan B = \frac{12}{14}$

$\angle B = \tan^{-1}\left(\frac{12}{14}\right)$

$\angle B = 41°$

b) $\cos B = \frac{17}{19}$

$\angle B = \cos^{-1}\left(\frac{17}{19}\right)$

$\angle B = 27°$

5. The angle of elevation of the ramp is 9°.

$\tan A = \frac{0.5}{3}$

$\angle A = \tan^{-1}\left(\frac{0.5}{3}\right)$

$\angle A = 9°$

6. The height of the building is 8.4 m.

$\tan 40° = \frac{x}{10}$

$x = 10\tan 40°$

$x = 8.4\text{ m}$

7. The volume of the cone is 191.7 cm^3.
Since the volume of a cone with the same height and base as a cylinder is $\frac{1}{3}$ the volume of the cylinder, $\frac{575}{3} = 191.7\text{ cm}^3$.

8. The width of the pyramid is 24 cm.

$216 = \frac{(9)(3)(w)}{3}$

$216 = \frac{27w}{3}$

$648 = 27w$

$24 = w$

Lesson 5—Solving Design Problems Involving Three-Dimensional Objects

PRACTICE EXERCISES
Answers and Solutions

1.

Length	Width	Height	Volume	Surface Area
1	1	40	40	162
1	2	20	40	124
1	4	10	40	108
1	5	8	40	106
2	2	10	40	88
2	4	5	40	76

The dimensions that produce the smallest surface area are 2 cm by 4 cm by 5 cm, which has a surface area of 76 cm^2.

2. For any rectangular prism, the dimensions that are closest to a cube will produce the least surface area. In this case, these dimensions are 10 m by 10 m by 9 m, for a surface area of 560 m^2.

$A = 2(10)(10) + 2(10)(9) + 2(9)(10)$

$A = 560\text{ m}^2$

3. a) First, calculate the volume of the boxes.

$V = (6)(3)(2)$

$V = 36 \text{ cm}^3$

Next, calculate the volume of the shipping crate.

$V = (24)(8)(11)$

$V = 2\,112 \text{ cm}^3$

Then, divide the two answers to see how many small boxes fit in the shipping crate.

$\frac{2112}{36} = 58.7$

Since you cannot have 0.7 of a box, only 58 boxes will fit in the shipping crate.

b) Find the volume of the shipping crate when its dimensions are doubled.

$V = (48)(16)(22)$

$V = 16\,896 \text{ cm}^3$

$\frac{16\,896}{36} = 469.3$

Thus, 469 small boxes will fit in the shipping crate if its dimensions are doubled.

Lesson 6—Solving Two-Dimensional Problems

PRACTICE EXERCISES
Answers and Solutions

1. The largest garden Barrie can make will be 3 m by 3 m with an area of 9 m^2.

Width (m)	Length (m)	Area (m^2)
1	5	5
2	4	8
3	3	9

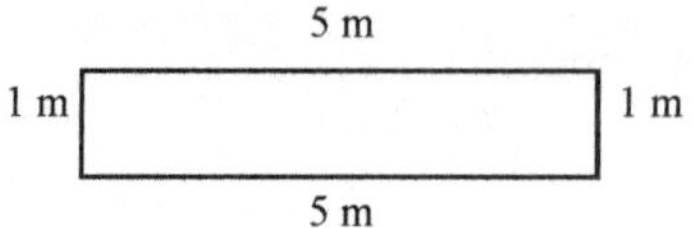

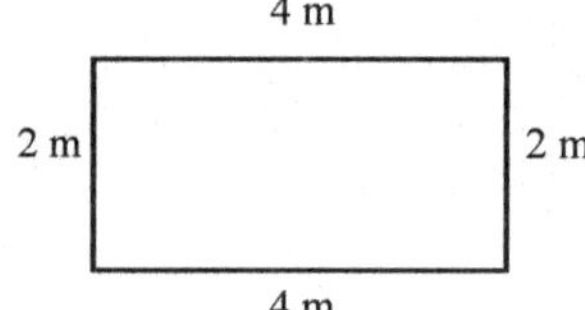

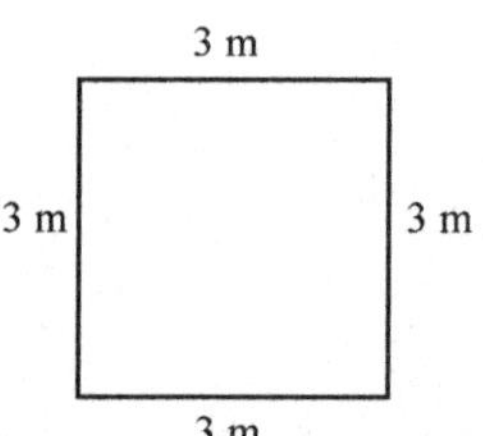

The 3 m by 3 m rectangle has the largest area.

2. The dimensions of the largest area he could rope off are 3 m by 3 m.

If the corner walls are to make up one length and width, the 6 m of rope must be split to make the other length and width. Of the possible divisions shown below, 3 m by 3 m results in the largest area.

Width (m)	Length (m)	Area (m^2)
1	5	5
2	4	8
3	3	9

3. To find the dimensions of the roped-off area, take the side parallel to the beach and subtract it from 300 m. Then, divide the result by 2 to get the lengths of the remaining two sides. Then, find the area.

a)

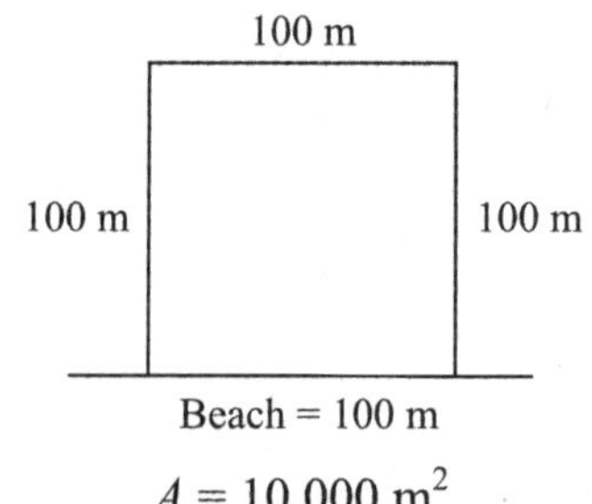

$A = 10\,000 \text{ m}^2$

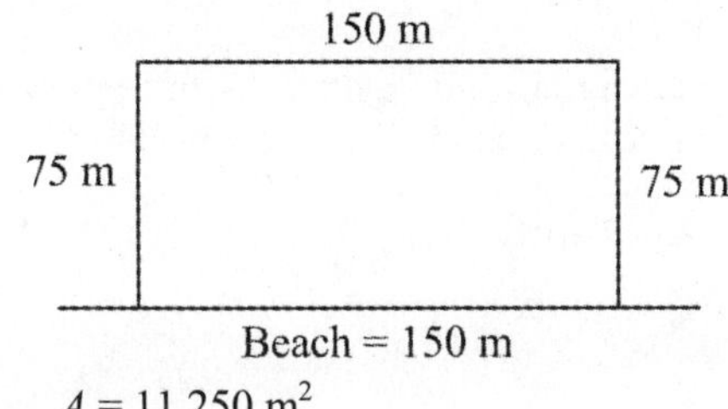

$A = 11\ 250\ \text{m}^2$

c)

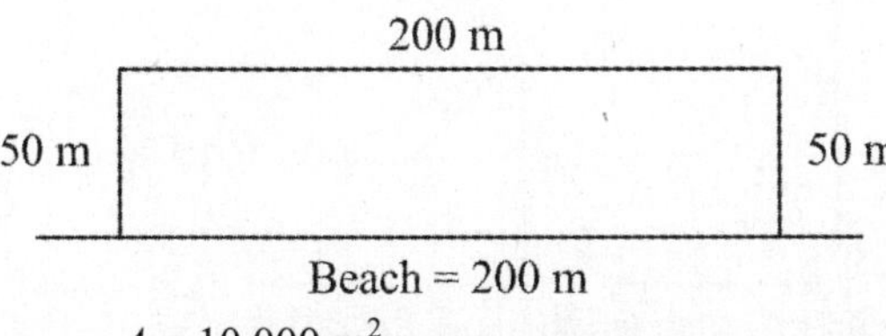

$A = 10\ 000\ \text{m}^2$

d)

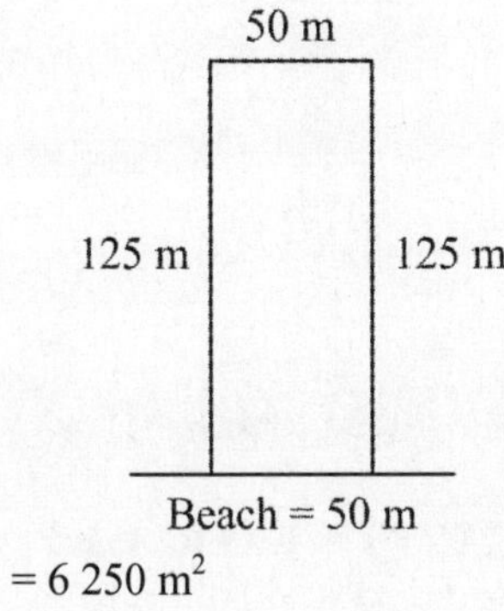

$A = 6\ 250\ \text{m}^2$

4. The dimensions that give the largest area have two roped sides of 75 m and one roped side of 150 m. In this case, where only three sides are enclosed, the square shape will not be the shape with the maximum area. The maximum area is achieved when the longest side is equal to the sum of the two shorter sides.

Lesson 7—Similar Triangles

PRACTICE EXERCISES
Answers and Solutions

1. $\dfrac{\text{big}\Delta}{\text{little}\Delta}$

$\dfrac{5.2}{4} = 1.3$

$\dfrac{6.5}{5} = 1.3$

$\dfrac{3.9}{3} = 1.3$

The triangles are similar triangles because all the angles are equal and the sides are proportional. Therefore, ΔGHI is similar to ΔJLK .

2. **a)** $\dfrac{12}{x} = \dfrac{9}{6}$

$9x = 72$

$x = 8$

b) $\dfrac{5}{2} = \dfrac{x}{3}$

$2x = 15$

$x = 7.5$

c) $\dfrac{11}{6} = \dfrac{x}{4}$

$6x = 44$

$x = \dfrac{44}{6}$

$x = \dfrac{22}{3}$

$x = 7.\overline{3}$

d) $\dfrac{4}{15} = \dfrac{5}{x}$

$4x = 75$

$x = 18.75$

3. The tree is 21.25 m tall.

Draw a diagram. Convert all units to metres.

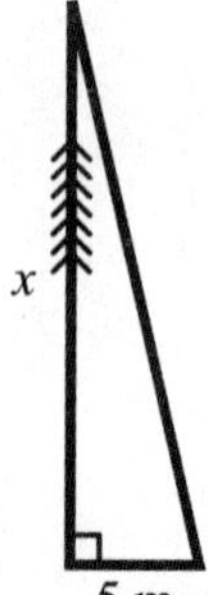

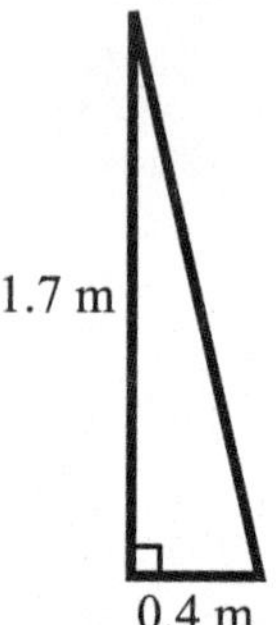

$$\frac{x}{1.7}=\frac{5}{0.4}$$
$$0.4x=8.5$$
$$x=21.25$$

4. The length of the third side of the garden is 9.5 m.

Draw a diagram and identify the side you are solving for.

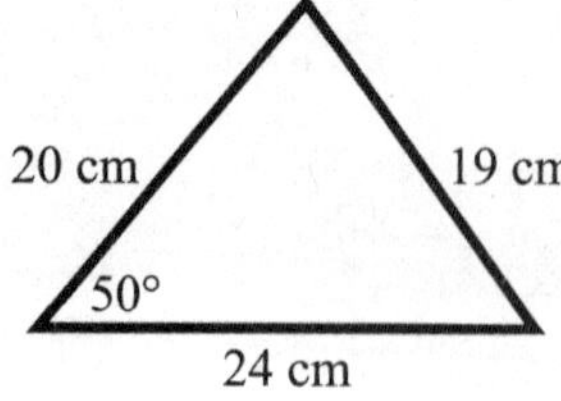

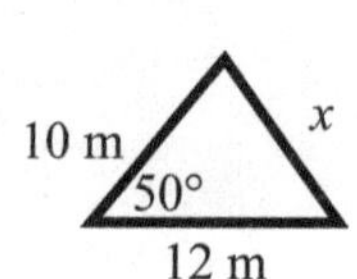

Set up an equation with two of the ratios of corresponding sides, one of which must contain the variable you are solving for.

$$\frac{20}{10}=\frac{19}{x}$$
$$20x=190$$
$$x=9.5$$

or

$$\frac{24}{12}=\frac{19}{x}$$
$$24x=228$$
$$x=9.5$$

5. The ladder reaches 4.8 m up the wall.

Draw a diagram and identify the side you are solving for. Change all units to metres.

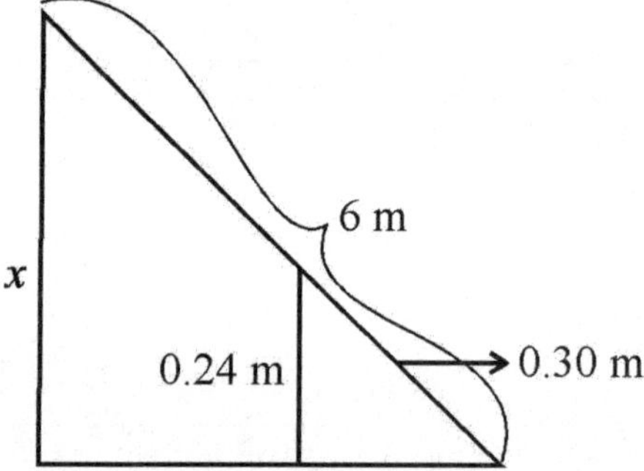

Set up an equation using the ratios of corresponding sides.

$$\frac{x}{0.24}=\frac{6}{0.30}$$
$$0.30x=1.44$$
$$x=4.8$$

Lesson 8—Congruent Triangles

PRACTICE EXERCISES
Answers and Solutions

1. a) These triangles are congruent because they have equal sides and equals angles, so they satisfy the condition SSS, ASA, and SAS.

b) The triangles are congruent because they meet the condition SSS in which all three sides are equal.
Therefore, $\Delta DEF \cong \Delta GIH$

c) The triangles are congruent because they share a common side, $\overline{AC}$, and the corresponding angles that contain this side are also equal, meeting the condition ASA.
Therefore, $\Delta ABC \cong \Delta CEA$.

d) The triangles are congruent because they share angle $\angle L$ and the sides that contain it are also equal, meeting the condition SAS.
Therefore, $\Delta JKL \cong \Delta MNL$

2. $\angle T = \angle R$
$\angle I = \angle O$
$\angle P = \angle W$
$TI = RO$
$TP = RW$
$IP = OW$

3. a) $HJ = MK$
$HI = ML$
$IJ = LK$

Thus, $\Delta HIJ \cong \Delta MLK$ because of condition SSS.

b) $\angle NMO = \angle POM$
$\angle NOM = \angle PMO$
$MO = MO$

Thus, $\Delta MNO \cong \Delta OPM$ because of condition ASA.

4. When two triangles are congruent, their corresponding sides and angles are all equal. Triangles are considered to be similar when their corresponding angles are equal and their corresponding sides are proportionally equal. Therefore, all congruent triangles can also be considered similar triangles.

Lesson 9—Three-Dimensional Sketches and Views of Objects

PRACTICE EXERCISES
Answers and Solutions

1. a)

b)

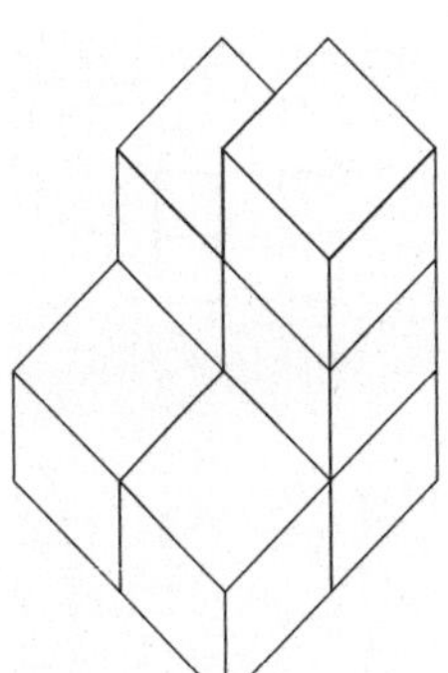

c)

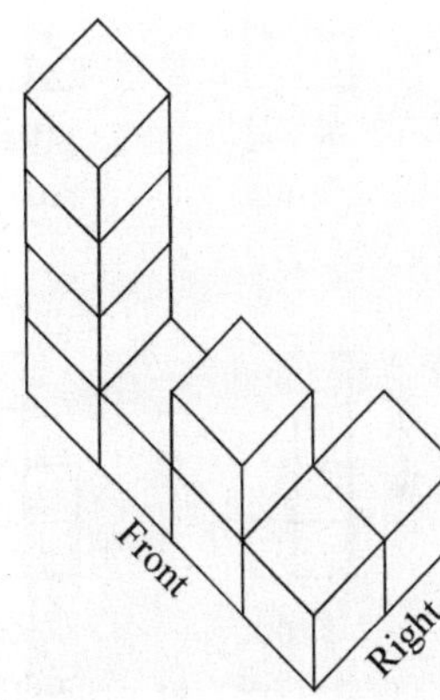

d)

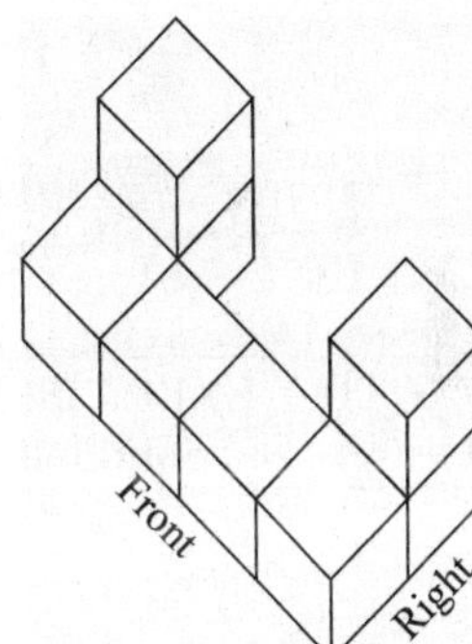

2. a)

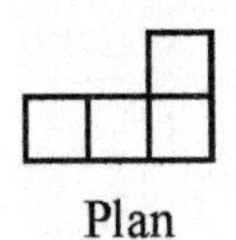

Plan
(Top View)

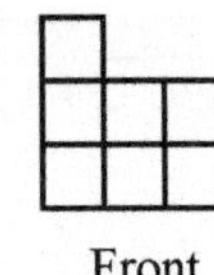

Front
View

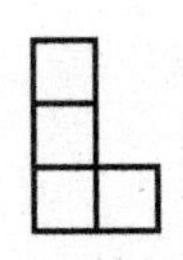

Right
Side View

b)

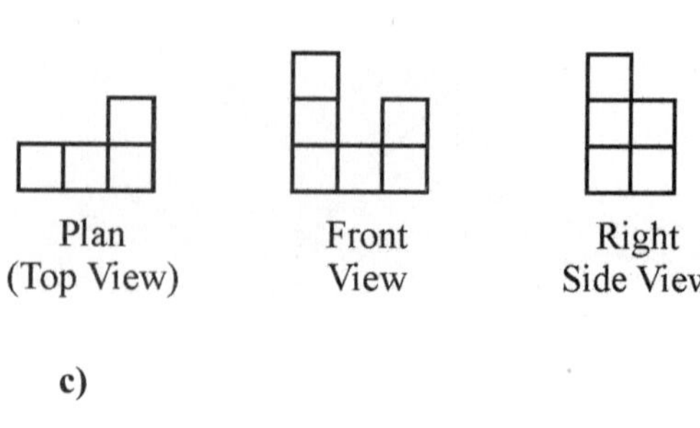

Plan (Top View) | Front View | Right Side View

c)

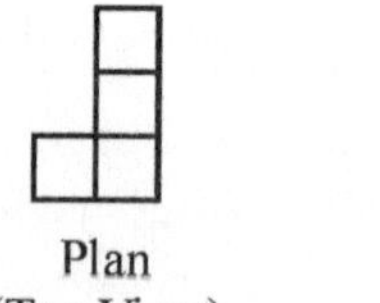

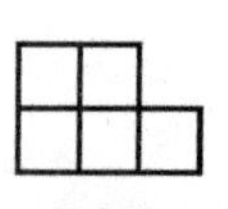

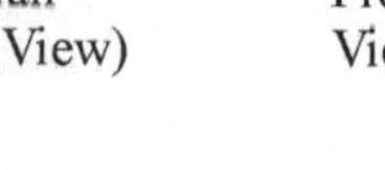

Plan (Top View) | Front View | Right Side View

d)

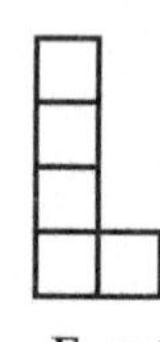

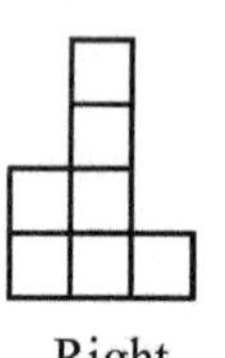

Plan (Top View) | Front View | Right Side View

Lesson 10—Drawing Diagrams to Solve Problems

PRACTICE EXERCISES
Answers and Solutions

1. The scale is 0.5 cm = 20 cm.

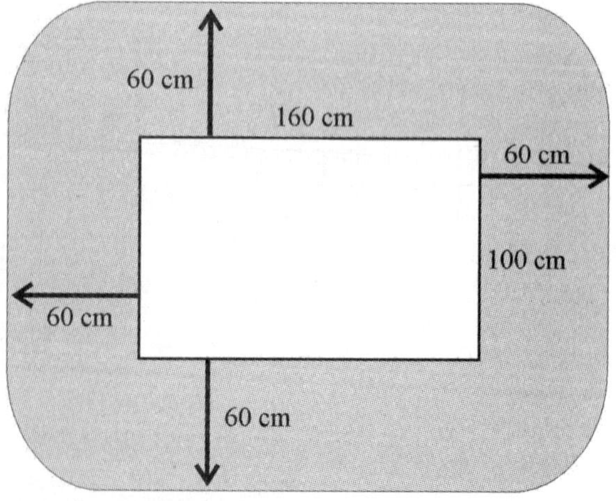

2. Answers will vary depending on the scale chosen.

We are using the scale of 0.5 cm = 10 m. Since the given distance is 80 m, draw a 4 cm line. Make a point on each end of the line and label one *A* and the other *B*. Now, divide this distance by 2. Take the solution and measure from point *A* or *B* and place a dot to locate the washroom.

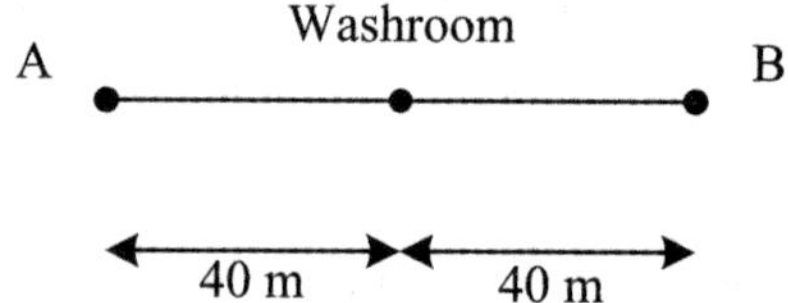

3. Answers will vary depending on the scale chosen.

We are using the scale of 0.5 cm = 1 m.

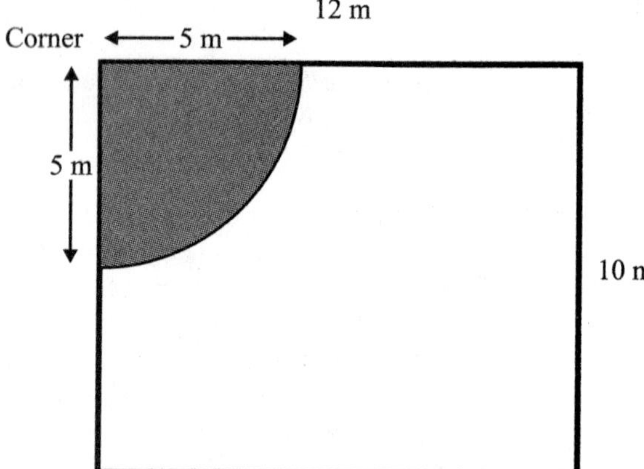

Practice Quiz 2

Answers and Solutions

1. a) $\frac{12}{10} = \frac{15}{y}$

$12y = 150$

$y = 12.5$ cm

$\frac{12}{10} = \frac{18}{x}$

$12x = 180$

$x = 15$ cm

b) $\frac{8}{6}=\frac{10}{x}$

$x=7.5$ cm

$\frac{8}{6}=\frac{9}{y}$

$y=6.75=6.8$ cm

2. The surface area of the box = 32 cm^2
The dimensions of the box = 2 cm by 2 cm by 3 cm

First, list the possible volume dimensions for 12 cm^3.
1 cm by 1 cm by 12 cm
1 cm by 2 cm by 6 cm
2 cm by 3 cm by 2 cm
1 cm by 4 cm by 3 cm

You know that for a rectangular prism, the dimensions with the smallest surface area will be those that are closest to a cube. Therefore the solution is 2 cm by 2 cm by 3 cm. From these dimensions, you can calculate surface area:

$A=2(2)(2)+2(2)(3)+2(2)(3)$

$A=32\text{ cm}^2$

3. The area covered by the sprinklers is 315.4 m^2.

There are many possible solutions to this problem. The sprinklers spray water covering the area of a circle, and it is impossible to cover the entire area of the lawn using only circles unless there is some overlap. Therefore, it is desirable to minimize the overlap in order to use the least number of sprinklers. One of the more efficient solutions follows.

The scale chosen is 1 cm : 3 m.

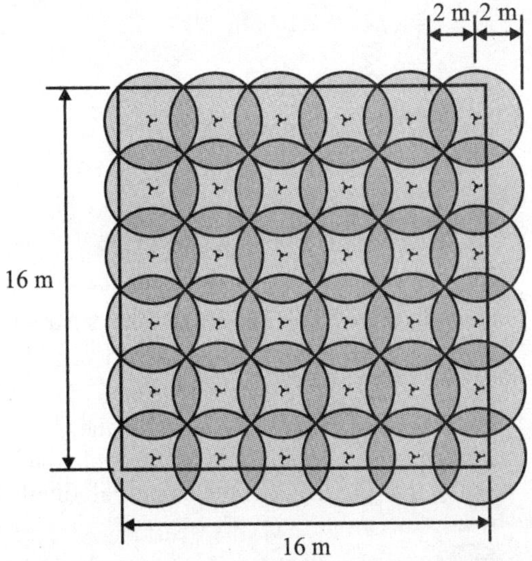

To create this pattern, start by drawing the first circle with its edge on a corner of the lawn. The circle needs to have most of its area on the lawn, so the diameter of this circle will point toward the opposite corner. The second circle needs to touch the edge of the lawn at the point where the first circle no longer intersects with the edge of the lawn. The third circle follows the second, touching the edge where the second ends.

Quickly, it becomes apparent that the sprinklers line up, and in the end they form a square, much like the shape of the lawn. It is also apparent that there is a lot of overlapping of the sprinklers and also a lot of the sprinklers will spray outside the edges of the lawn. This is unavoidable if the entire lawn is to be watered.

To find the area covered by the sprinklers, it is first important to determine the effective area covered by the sprinklers. The effective area is the useful area that the sprinklers cover. In the diagram below, you can see that if you fit a square inside the circle, that forms the effective area covered by the sprinklers.

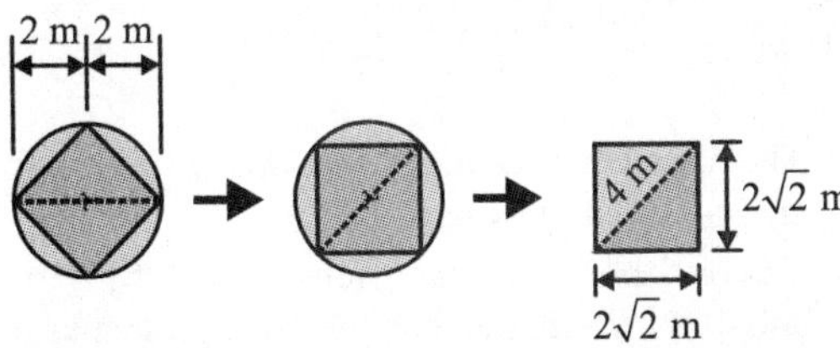

To calculate the area of the square, you need to know the length of a side. Using the Pythagorean theorem, you get:

$c^2 = a^2 + b^2$

$4^2 = x^2 + x^2$

$16 = 2x^2$

$x^2 = 8$

$x = \sqrt{8} = 2\sqrt{2}$

Thus each side of the square inside the circle has a length of $2\sqrt{2}$ m. The area of that square is $2\sqrt{2}\text{ m} \times 2\sqrt{2}\text{ m} = 8\text{ m}^2$.

The area of each overlap is equal to the difference between the area of the circles and the area of the square inside the circles, all divided by 2.

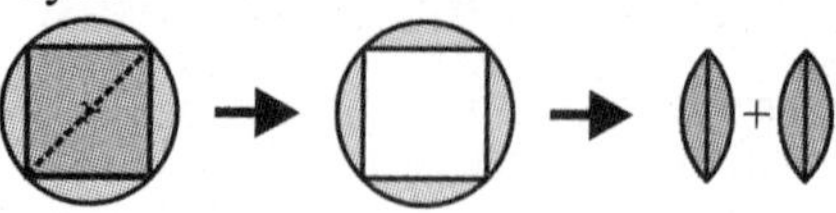

$$\begin{aligned} A &= \pi r^2 \\ &= \pi(2)^2 \\ &= 12.57\text{ m}^2 \end{aligned}$$

$$\begin{aligned} \text{overlap} &= \frac{\text{area of circle} - \text{area of square}}{2} \\ &= \frac{12.57 - 8}{2} \\ &= 2.28\text{ m}^2 \end{aligned}$$

To find out the total area the sprinklers spray, you add up the area of all the circles, and subtract the area of all the overlaps.

$$\begin{aligned} A_T &= \text{total area of circles} - \text{total area of overlaps} \\ &= (36 \times \text{area of circle}) - (60 \times \text{area of overlap}) \\ &= (36 \times 12.57) - (60 \times 2.28) \\ &= 452.39 - 136.99 \\ &= 315.40\text{ m}^2 \end{aligned}$$

4. The dimensions of the largest area Karwin can enclose are 4 m by 6 m.
The only possible dimensions are 2 m by 8 m and 4 m by 6 m, because the material comes in 2 m long units that can not be cut.
Now, $A = l \times w$

$2\text{ m} \times 8\text{ m} = 16\text{ m}^2$

$4\text{ m} \times 6\text{ m} = 24\text{ m}^2$

5. The height of the light pole is 5.3 m.
First, draw a diagram of similar triangles.

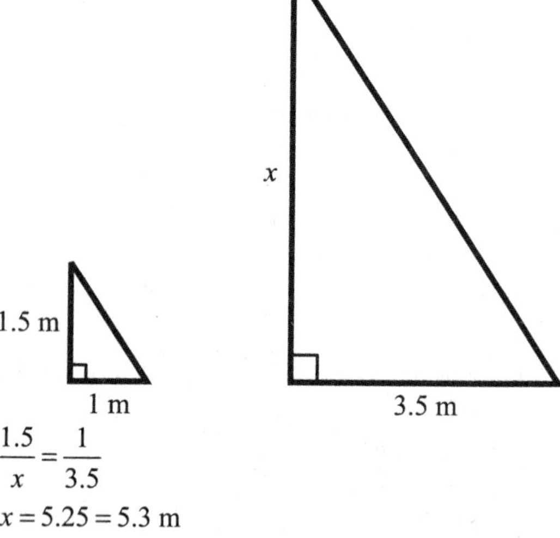

$\frac{1.5}{x} = \frac{1}{3.5}$

$x = 5.25 = 5.3\text{ m}$

6. $AC = DF$

$\angle A = \angle D$

$AB = DE$

These triangles are congruent according to condition SAS.

7.

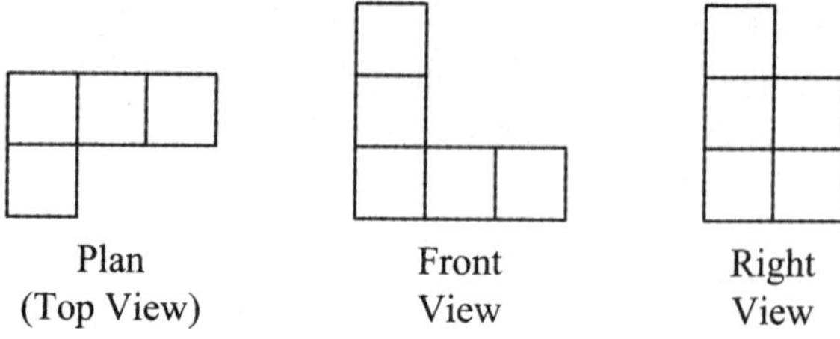

8. There are many possible solutions to this problem. However, if it is assumed that the figure is a solid single piece (there are not two or more pieces), then there are two possible solutions:

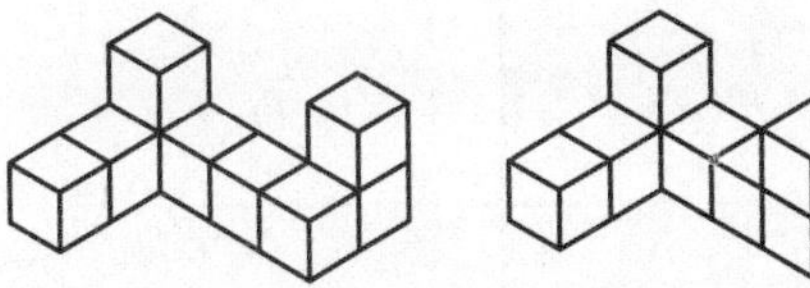

Lesson 11—Transformation of Two-Dimensional Shapes

PRACTICE EXERCISES
Answers and Solutions

1.

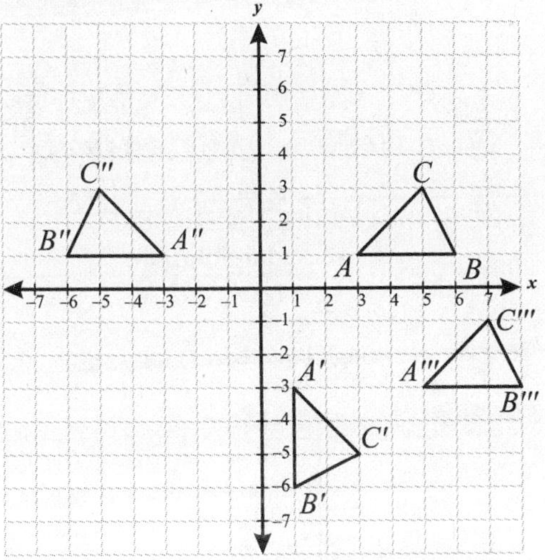

2. In the transformations performed above, the measure of the sides and angles of the image triangles remain the same as in the original triangle. Thus if all sides and angles are congruent, the triangles are also congruent.

3.

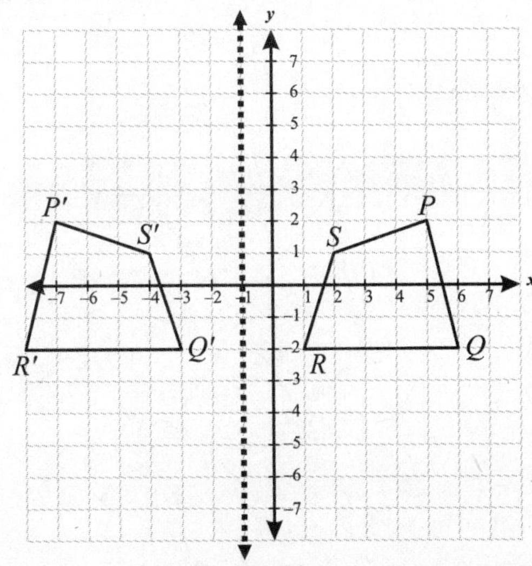

Reflection Line

4.

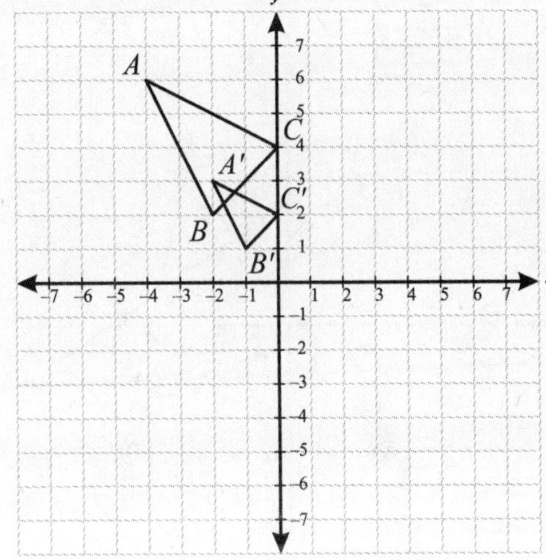

The triangles are similar because all the angles are equal and the sides are proportional.

$$\frac{AB}{A'B'} = \frac{AC}{A'C'} = \frac{BC}{B'C'} = \frac{2}{1}$$

5.

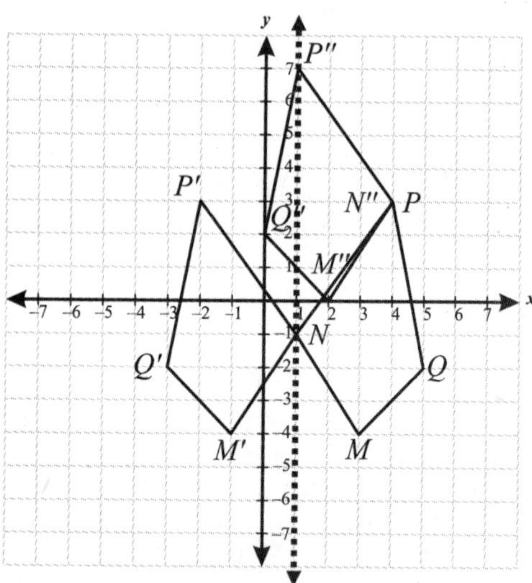

6.

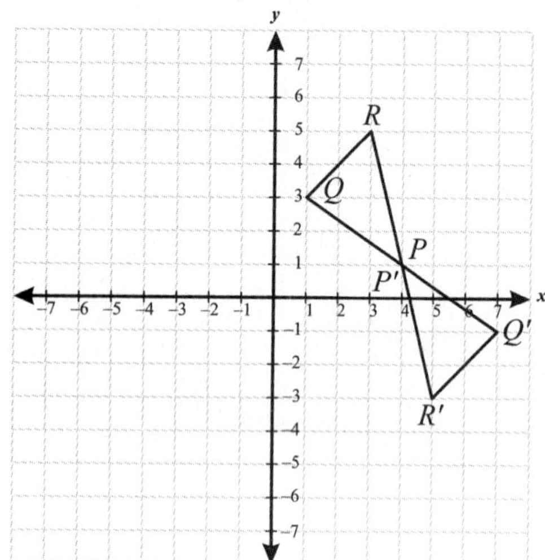

7.

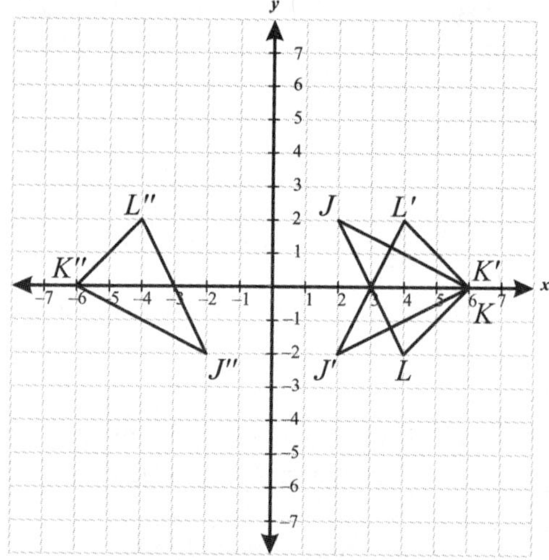

The order you perform combined reflections on a figure has no impact on the position of the final image.

Lesson 12—Finding the Original Shape Given the Transformation Image

PRACTICE EXERCISES
Answers and Solutions

1. Reflect the image back across the y-axis.

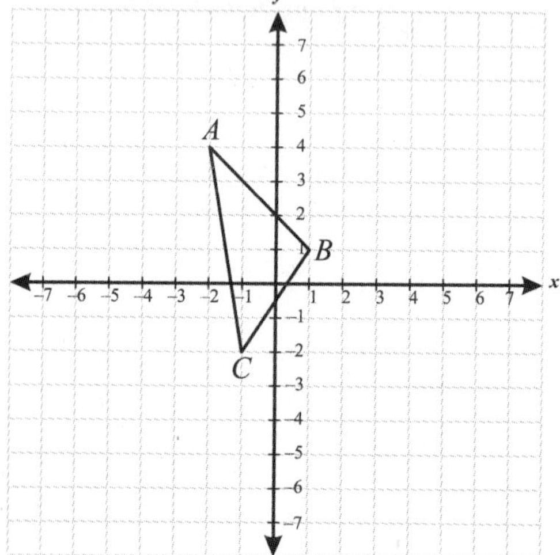

2. Rotate the image 90° clockwise.

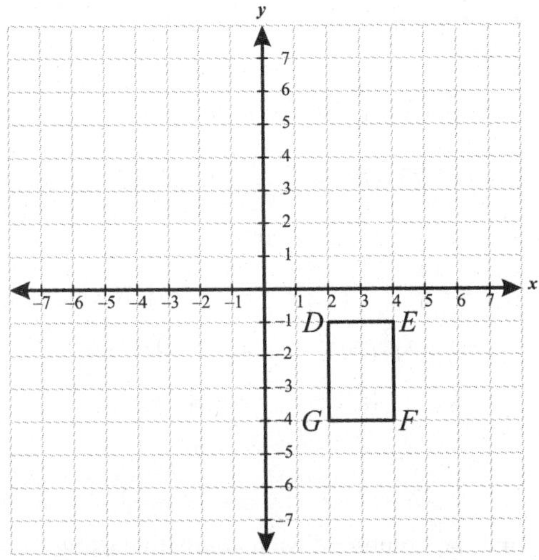

3. Translate the image 3 units left and 2 units up.

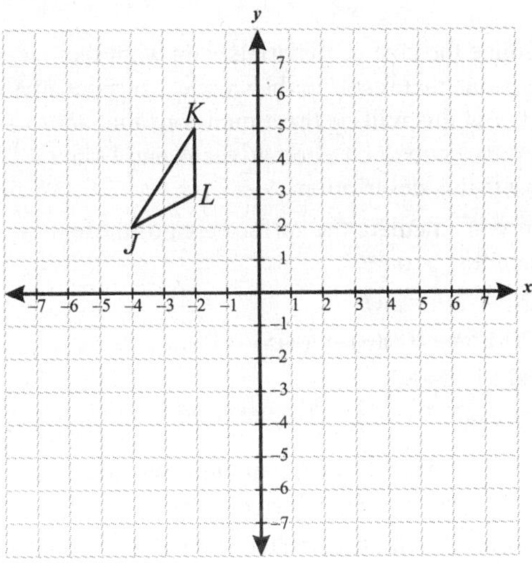

4. Find the original triangle by working backward, starting with the opposite of the last transformation performed. First, reflect the final image in the x-axis and then translate by subtracting 1 from the x-coordinates and 3 from the y-coordinates of the vertices.

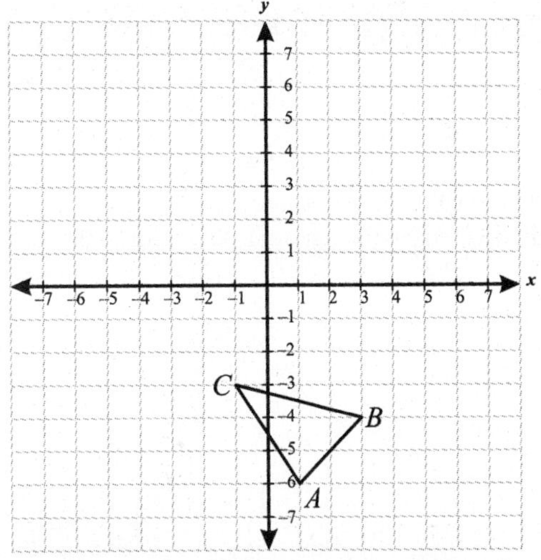

Lesson 13—Identifying the Transformation

PRACTICE EXERCISES
Answers and Solutions

1. The transformation is a reflection about a line 1 unit above the x-axis, or $y = 1$.

2. The transformation is a 90° counterclockwise rotation of triangle *GHI* about the point (0, 0), or the transformation is a 270°clockwise rotation of triangle *GHI* about the point.

3. The transformation is a translation 3 units right and 5 units up (3, 5).

Practice Test

Answers and Solutions

1. Since the value of sine is the side opposite the angle divided by the hypotenuse, the ratio is $\dfrac{\overline{CD}}{\overline{BD}}$.

2. The answer is 76°.

$\angle C = \tan^{-1}\left(\dfrac{12}{3}\right)$

$\angle C = \tan^{-1}(4)$

$\angle C = 76°$

3. The answer is 20.8 cm.

$\cos 35° = \dfrac{17}{x}$

$\dfrac{0.819}{1} = \dfrac{17}{x}$

$0.819x = 17$

$x = 20.8$

4. The vertical height of the kite is 5.8 m

$\sin 70° = \dfrac{x}{15}$

$x = 14.1\text{m}$

Add on the height above the ground that the kite string is being held, which is 1.5 m. Therefore, the total height above the ground is 15.6 m.

5. The answer is 71°.

$\cos x = \dfrac{2}{6}$

$\angle x = \cos^{-1}\left(\dfrac{2}{6}\right)$

$\angle x = 71°$

6. **a)** The answer is 184.7 cm^3.

$V = \dfrac{1}{3}\pi r^2 h$

$= \dfrac{1}{3}\pi(4.2)^2(10)$

$= 184.73\text{ cm}^3$

b) The answer is 554.2 cm^3.

$V = \pi r^2 h$	or $V = 3 \times \text{area of cone}$
$= \pi(4.2)^2(10)$	$= 3 \times 184.73\text{ cm}^3$
$= 554.18\text{ cm}^3$	$= 554.18\text{ cm}^3$

7. **D**

First, find the volume of each alternative using $V = lwh$.

In the given alternatives, only the dimensions in A and D result in a volume of 320 m^3.

To reduce the cost of materials, you want the dimensions that result in the smallest surface area. You know this will be the dimensions that are closest to a cube. Of alternatives A and D, the latter fits this description.

When you calculate the surface area of these dimensions, you get

$A = 2lw + 2lh + 2wh$

$A = 2(8)(5) + 2(8)(8) + 2(8)5$

$A = 80 + 128 + 80$

$A = 288\text{ m}^2$

Similar calculations for the dimensions given in A result in a much greater surface area.

Therefore, Ramir should choose the dimensions given in D.

8. **C**

50 m by 25 m

Since Cathy is only roping off three sides, the maximum area is not produced by a square shape but by dimensions where the length is twice the width.

9. **B**

The three conditions of congruence are SSS, ASA, and SAS. Thus, alternative B AAA is not a condition of congruence.

10. A

Triangle *GHI* is congruent to triangle *MJN*. Angle *G* is equal to angle *M*, angle *I* is equal to angle *N*, and angle *H* is equal to angle *J*. The angles must be written in this corresponding sequence.

11. The value of x is 22.7 m.

$$\frac{8}{x} = \frac{12}{44}$$

$$x = 29.3 \text{ m}$$

12. One tree is 42.5 m taller than the other.

Draw a diagram to represent the problem.

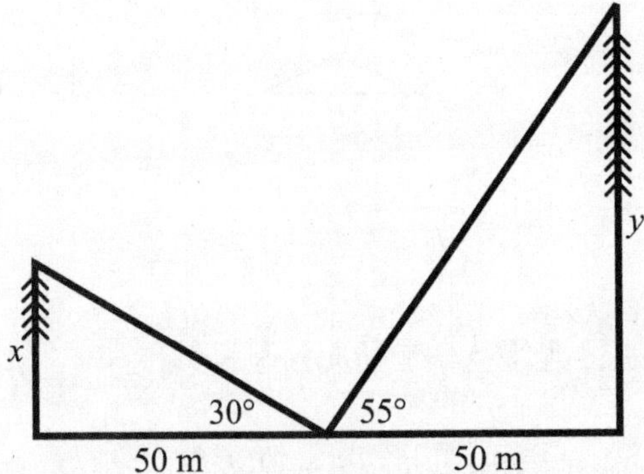

Solve for x and y, and then find their difference to determine how much taller one tree is than the other.

$$\tan 30° = \frac{x}{50}$$

$$x = 28.9 \text{ m}$$

$$\tan 55° = \frac{y}{50}$$

$$y = 71.4 \text{ m}$$

$$71.4 - 28.9 = 42.5 \text{ m}$$

13. C

Similar triangles may be congruent only when their sides are equal, not just proportional.

14.

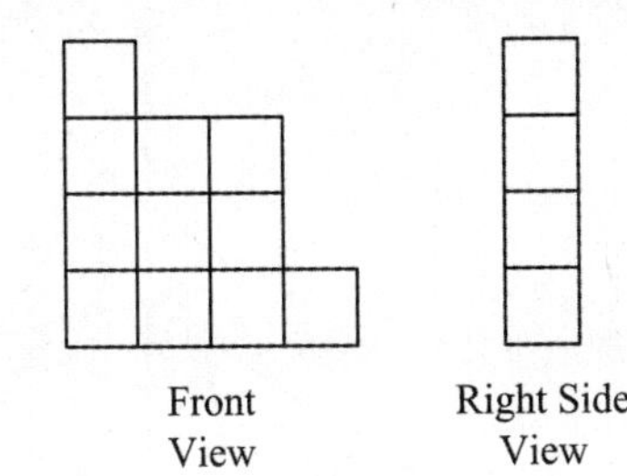

15.

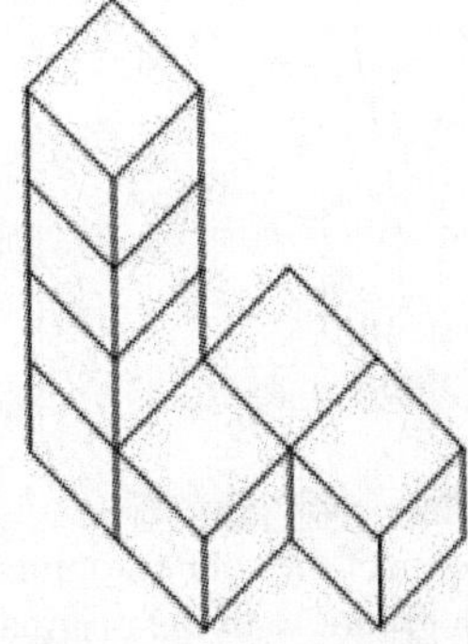

16. When doing dilatations from (0, 0), multiply the coordinates by the dilatation factor.

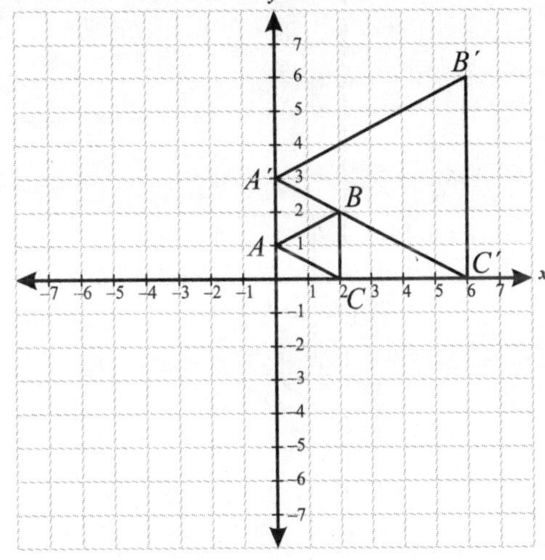

The angles in the original triangle are equal to the angles in the dilatation image. The ratio of the corresponding sides is also in the proportion of 3 to 1. Since similar triangles are defined as those with equal angles and proportional sides, the triangles in question are similar triangles.

17.

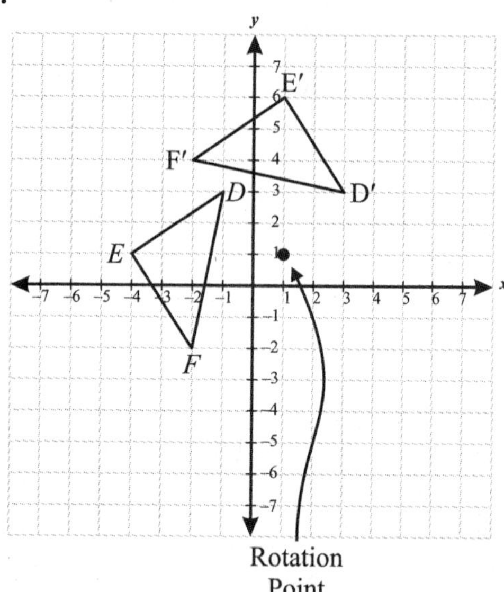

Use rotation sticks to rotate each point individually and then connect the rotated points. The rotated image is congruent with the original triangle because all the angels are equal in measure and all the sides are equal in length.

18.

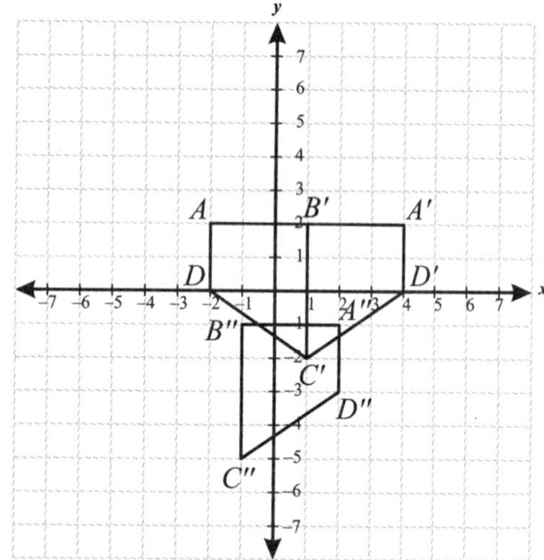

The final solution is
$A''(2, -1)$, $B''(1, -1)$, $C''(-1, -5)$ and $D''(2, -3)$

19. The transformation is a reflection about a line one unit left of the y-axis, or $y = 1$.

20. Work backward. Translate 2 units right and 3 units up, followed by a reflection about a line 2 units above the x-axis.

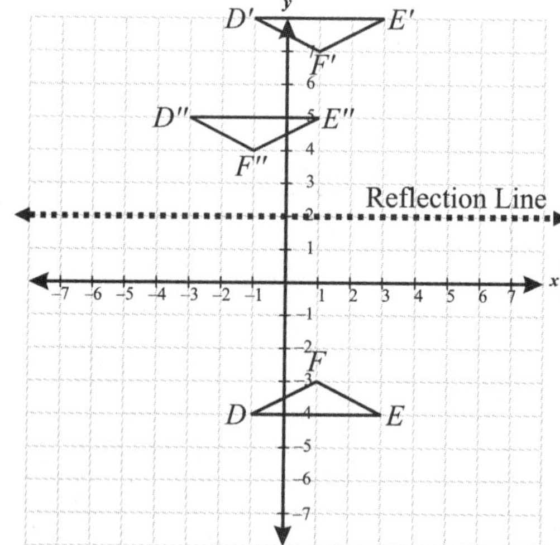

DATA ANALYSIS

Lesson 1—Investigating Relationships Between Data

PRACTICE EXERCISES
Answers and Solutions

1. **a)** As the day progresses from morning to afternoon, the temperature rises.

b) The longer the cup of hot chocolate sits, the colder it gets. Thus, as the time increases, the temperature decreases.

2. **a)** If we divide the mass by the number of loonies, you get $\frac{75}{5} = 15$, $\frac{105}{7} = 15$, and so on. Thus, the mass of each loonie is 15 g.

b) The mass of 20 loonies is $20 \times 15 = 300$ g.

3. **a)** The volume of a cube is $V = s^3$.

$V = s^3$

$V = (4)^3$

$V = 64 \text{ cm}^3$

The volume of the cube is 64 cm^3.

This answer fits with the pattern established by the data, as 64 falls between 27 and 125.

b) According to the volume formula, $216 = s^3$. You could use the "guess-and-test" method to find the solution to this question. You could also use the cube root button on your calculator.

The solution is calculated as $\sqrt[3]{216} = 6$. The length of the cube is 6 cm.

Lesson 2—Graphing Scatter Plots

PRACTICE EXERCISES
Answers and Solutions

1. **a)**

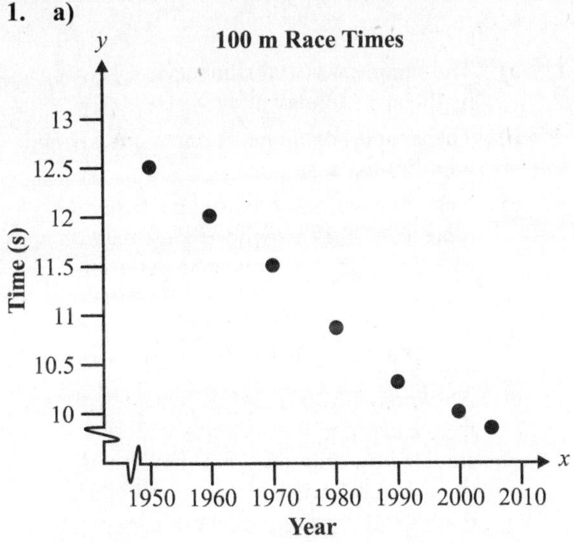

Over the years, the winning time for the 100 m race has decreased.

b)

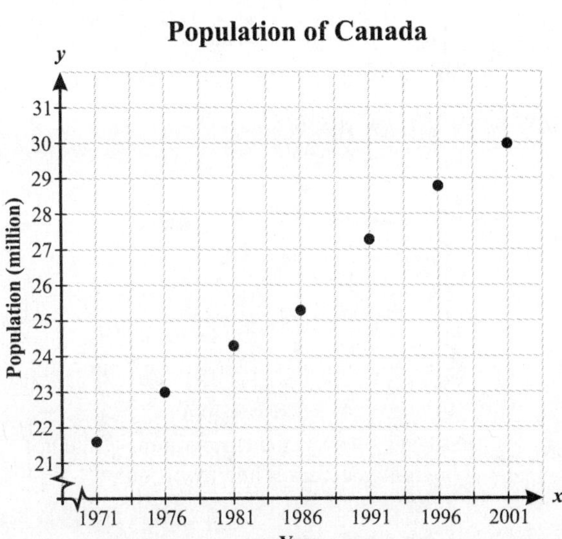

Over the years, the population in Canada has increased.

c)

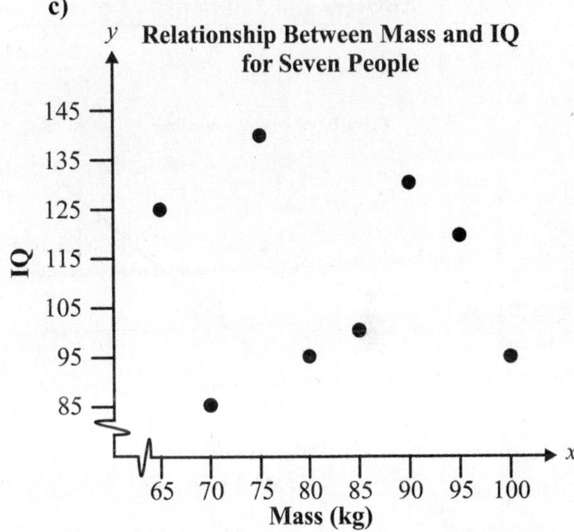

The points do not form a pattern, so there is no relationship between mass and IQ.

d)

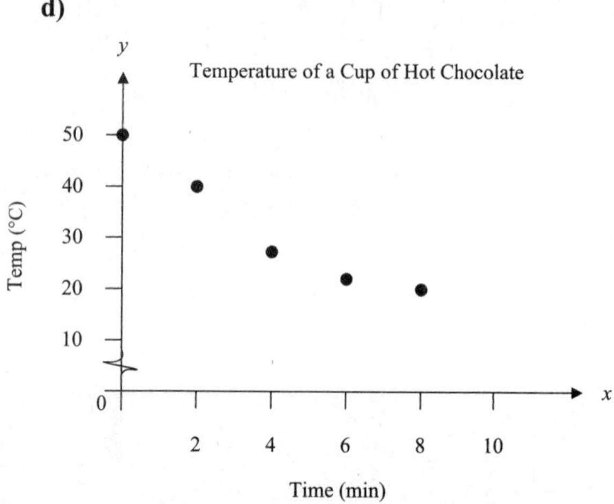

As time goes by, the temperature of the hot chocolate decreases and levels out.

Lesson 3—Line of Best Fit

PRACTICE EXERCISES
Answers and Solutions

1. a)

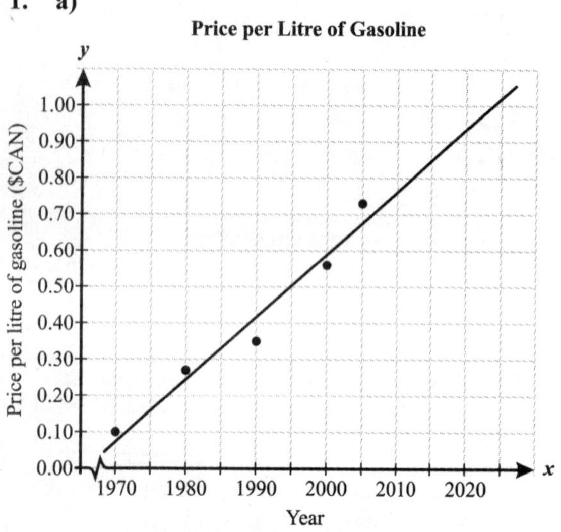

Answers may vary slightly.

b) In 2015, the price of gasoline can be expected to be \$0.85/L. This would not be reasonable if the price continued to rise at the same rate as it did from 2000 to 2005; the price would be much higher.

c) The price of a liter of gasoline in 1985 was probably about \$0.33/L.

2. a)

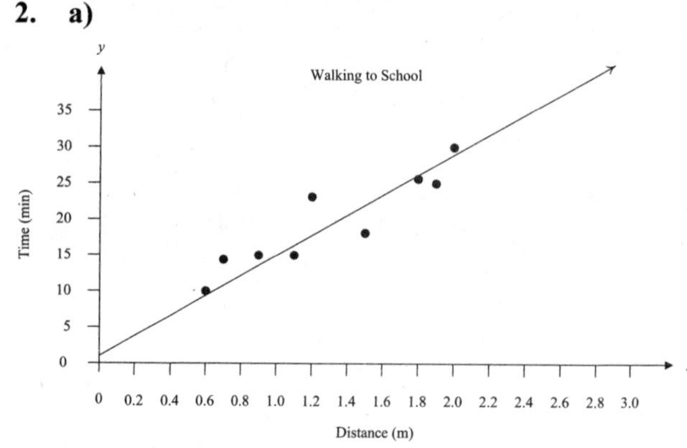

b) If a student takes 20 min to get to school, he or she lives approximately 1.4 km away from school.

c) If a student has to walk 2.4 km to school, it takes him or her approximately 34 min.

Lesson 4—Sampling Methods

PRACTICE EXERCISES
Answers and Solutions

1. a) The sample was 100 students in Calgary malls on a Monday night.

b) The samples could be gathered quickly and with limited cost.

c) Yes. The method is biased because it only represents students who are in a mall on a Monday night and only students from Calgary.

d) The method was not appropriate for the data or the issue.

e) Answers will vary. Select five students from each school in Alberta and ask each student how many hours of homework he or she does each week. This would give a more valid representation of the population.

2. a) The sample was randomly chosen from names in boxes representing one grade each.

b) It was designed to give a good representation of the high school population.

c) No. The randomness of the sampling removes the possibility of bias.

d) The method was appropriate for the data and the issue.

e) It was fine the way it was.

3. a) They sampled all the girls from one high school in each province.
   b) They probably tried to get a good representation across the country.
   c) The sample is biased toward girls because only girls are sampled.
   d) The method was not appropriate as boys needed to be included in the sample.
   e) Sample a few boys and girls from several high schools throughout all provinces. This would give a more valid representation of the population.

Practice Quiz

Answers and Solutions

1. As the time passes, or increases, the height of the snowman decreases.

2. a)

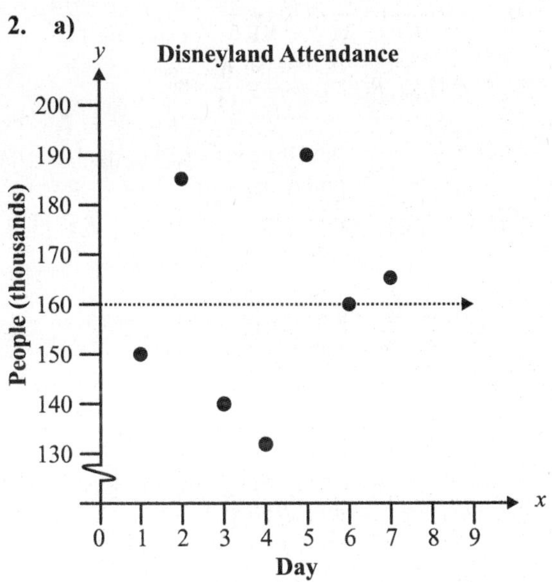

   b) There seems to be no obvious relationship between the day and the attendance.
   c) I would predict an attendance of 160 000.
   d) Very hot or very cold weather would likely cause a reduction in attendance. Rainy weather would probably also reduce attendance, since Disneyland is mostly outdoors.

3. a) The survey is intended to represent all of the families in Alberta.
   b) The sample consisted of 40 people at a veterinary clinic.
   c) The sample is not random. The sample is biased because people at a veterinary clinic probably have pets.
   d) The sample is not a good representation of the population because the sample is biased.

Lesson 5—Statistical Information and the Media

PRACTICE EXERCISES
Answers and Solutions

1. a) Many people have pets and, in most cases, they have nothing to do with starting house fires. There is a minimal relationship between the occurrence of house fires and the ownership of pets.
   b) Many people in China are dying from lung cancer and these statistics support the fact that more men are dying of lung cancer

Lesson 6—Theoretical and Experimental Probability

PRACTICE EXERCISES
Answers and Solutions

1. a) $P(t) = \frac{2}{11}$
   b) $P(c) = \frac{1}{11}$
   c) $P(\text{not an } a) = \frac{9}{11}$

2. a) $P(2) = \frac{18}{120}$

   $P(2) = \frac{3}{20}$

   b) $P(5) = \frac{25}{120}$

   $P(5) = \frac{5}{24}$

c) $P(3)=\frac{25}{120}$

$P(3)=\frac{5}{24}$

$\frac{5}{24}\times 300=62.5$

$=63$

The outcome 3 can be expected to occur 63 times.

d) $P(1)=\frac{12}{120}$

$P(1)=\frac{1}{10}$

$\frac{1}{10}\times 250=25$

The outcome 1 can be expected to occur 25 times.

3. Trevor's method will not increase his chances of winning. On each selection of numbers, all 49 numbers are equally likely to occur. Past results will have no influence on future probability.

4. A 50% chance of precipitation means that there is an equal chance of rain as of no rain. So, if the chance of precipitation is 60%, there is a slightly higher chance that it will rain rather than not rain. There is still a 40% chance that it will not rain.

5. **a)** There are 4 desired outcomes: 3, 4, 5, and 6. Since each card occurs once in each of the 4 suits of a deck, there are a total of 16 favourable outcomes.

There are 50 possible outcomes (Remember that 2 cards have been dealt).

$P(3, 4, 5, 6)=\frac{16}{50}$

$P(3, 4, 5, 6)=\frac{8}{25}$

b) The favorable outcomes are queen or jack.

$P(\text{j}, \text{q})=\frac{8}{50}$

$P(\text{j}, \text{q})=\frac{4}{25}$

c) There are no favourable outcomes. The probability is 0.

Lesson 7—Independent Events

PRACTICE EXERCISES
Answers and Solutions

1. **a)** $P(G_4)=\frac{1}{6}; P(R_6)=\frac{1}{6}$

$P(G_4, R_6)=\frac{1}{6}\times\frac{1}{6}$

$=\frac{1}{36}$

b) $P(G_{\text{even}})=\frac{3}{6}=\frac{1}{2}; P(R_3)=\frac{1}{6}$

$P(G_{\text{even}}, \text{R}_3)=\frac{1}{2}\times\frac{1}{6}=\frac{1}{2}$

c) $P(R_{5,6})=\frac{1}{3}; P(G_9)=\frac{1}{6}$

$P(R_{5,6}G_1)=\frac{1}{3}\times\frac{1}{6}=\frac{1}{18}$

d) $P(G_{2,3,5})=\frac{1}{2}; P(R_6)=\frac{0}{6}$

$P(G_{\text{prime}}R_{>6})=\frac{1}{2}\times\frac{0}{6}=\frac{0}{12}=0$

2. $\frac{1}{10}\times\frac{1}{10}\times\frac{1}{10}=\frac{1}{1000}$

3. **a)** $P(Q)=\frac{4}{52}, P(10)=\frac{4}{52}$

$P(Q,10)=\frac{4}{52}\times\frac{4}{52}=\frac{16}{2704}=\frac{1}{169}$

b) $P(D)=\frac{13}{52}=\frac{1}{4}; P(6)=\frac{4}{52}=\frac{1}{13}$

$P(D,6)=\frac{1}{4}\times\frac{1}{13}=\frac{1}{52}$

c) $P(Face)=\frac{1}{13}+\frac{1}{13}+\frac{1}{13}=\frac{3}{13}; P(Q_{\text{hearts}})=\frac{1}{52}$

$P(Face, QH)=\frac{3}{13}\times\frac{1}{52}=\frac{3}{676}$

4. $\frac{1}{2}\times\frac{1}{2}\times\frac{1}{2}\times\frac{1}{2}=\frac{1}{16}$

5. $\frac{1}{41}\times\frac{1}{41}\times\frac{1}{41}=\frac{1}{68\,921}$

Remember to count 0 as one of the possible numbers to the combination. This is how you will get the total number of outcomes, which is 41.

Practice Test

Answers and Solutions

1. D

In graph D, the points follow a pattern: as one variable increases, so does the other variable.

2. D

$\frac{1}{6}\times\frac{1}{2}=\frac{1}{12}$

3. A

A random sample is in which everyone has an equal chance of being selected.

4. C

$\frac{\text{favourable outcomes}}{\text{total possible outcomes}}=\frac{3}{100}$

5. C

The fact that Jenna's birthday is in March has no effect on the probability that Amy's birthday is in March. Thus, the probability that Amy's birthday is in March is $\frac{1}{12}$.

6. a) A

$\frac{1}{26}\times\frac{1}{10}$

Only one letter will be chosen out of 26 possibilities and one digit out of the 10 digits 0 through 9.

b) A

$\frac{1}{26}\times\frac{1}{10}=\frac{1}{260}$

7. a) A

1

$\frac{12}{50}=\frac{6}{25}$

b) C

65

$P(2)=\frac{18}{50}=\frac{9}{25}$

$\frac{9}{25}\times 180=64.8$

$\frac{9}{25}\times 180=65$

The number of times a die can be rolled can only be expressed as a whole number. Fractions and decimals are not meaningful as there is no such thing as a partial roll. Since the outcome 2 will occur more than 64 times, the probability is that it will occur 65 times.

8. B There would not be any relationship between shoe size and the number of hours spent listening to music.

9.

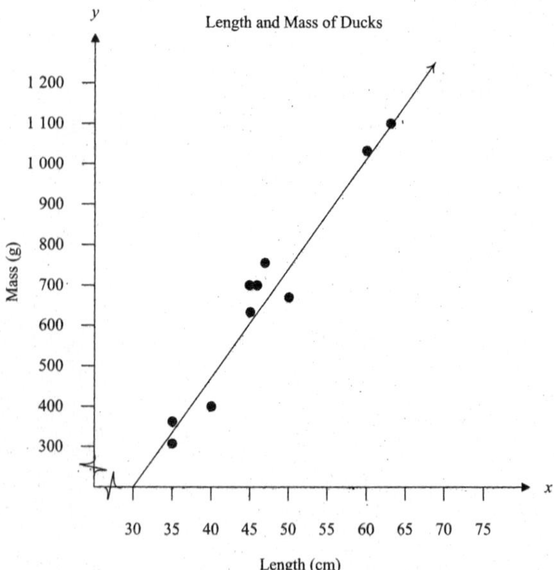

a) The longer the duck, the greater the mass of the duck.

b) A duck with a length of 55 cm would have a mass of approximately 880 g.

c) A duck with a mass of 1 200 g would have a length of approximately 67 cm.

10. a) W B

$$\frac{3}{10} \times \frac{3}{10} = \frac{6}{11} = \frac{3}{50}$$

b) O B W

$$\frac{5}{10} \times \frac{2}{10} \times \frac{3}{10} = \frac{30}{1000} = \frac{3}{100}$$

c) O

$$\frac{5}{10} \times \frac{5}{10} = \frac{25}{100} = \frac{1}{4}$$

d) W W W

$$\frac{3}{10} \times \frac{3}{10} \times \frac{3}{10} = \frac{27}{1\,000}$$

NOTES

NOTES

ORDERING INFORMATION

All School Orders

School Authorities are eligible to purchase these resources by applying the Learning Resource Credit Allocation (LRCA – 25% school discount) on their purchase through the Learning Resources Centre (LRC). Call LRC for details.

***THE KEY** Study Guides* are specifically designed to assist students in preparing for unit tests, final exams, and provincial examinations.

***KEY** Study Guides* – $29.95 each plus G.S.T.

SENIOR HIGH		JUNIOR HIGH	ELEMENTARY
Biology 30 Chemistry 30 English 30-1 English 30-2 Math 30 (Pure) Math 30 (Applied) Physics 30 Social Studies 30 Social Studies 33	Biology 20 Chemistry 20 English 20-1 Math 20 (Pure) Physics 20 Social Studies 20 English 10-1 Math 10 (Pure) Science 10 Social Studies 10	Language Arts 9 Math 9 Science 9 Social Studies 9 Math 8 Math 7	Language Arts 6 Math 6 Science 6 Social Studies 6 Math 4 Language Arts 3 Math 3

Student Notes and Problems (SNAP) Workbooks contain complete explanations of curriculum concepts, examples, and exercise questions.

SNAP Workbooks – $29.95 each plus G.S.T.

SENIOR HIGH		JUNIOR HIGH	ELEMENTARY
Chemistry 30 Math 30 Pure Math 30 Applied Math 31 Physics 30	Chemistry 20 Math 20 Pure Math 20 Applied Physics 20 Math 10 Pure Math 10 Applied Science 10	Math 9 Science 9 Math 8 Math 7	Math 6 Math 5 Math 4 Math 3

Visit our website for a "tour" of resource content and features at

www.castlerockresearch.com

#2340, 10180 – 101 Street
Edmonton, AB Canada T5J 3S4
e-mail: learn@castlerockresearch.com

Phone: 780.448.9619
Toll-free: 1.800.840.6224
Fax: 780.426.3917

2006 (3)

SCHOOL ORDER FORM

THE KEY	QUANTITY
Biology 30	
Chemistry 30	
English 30-1	
English 30-2	
Math30 (Pure)	
Math 30 (Applied)	
Physics 30	
Social Studies 30	
Social Studies 33	
Biology 20	
Chemistry 20	
English 20-1	
Math 20 (Pure)	
Physics 20	
Social Studies 20	
English 10-1	
Math 10 (Pure)	
Science 10	
Social Studies 10	
Language Arts 9	
Math 9	
Science 9	
Social Studies 9	
Math 8	
Math 7	
Language Arts 6	
Math 6	
Science 6	
Social Studies 6	
Math 4	
Math 3	
Language Arts 3	

SNAP WORKBOOKS Notes and Problems/ Student Notes and Problems	QUANTITY Workbooks	QUANTITY Solutions Manuals
Chemistry 30		
Chemistry 20		
Physics 30		
Physics 20		
Math 30 Pure		
Math 30 Applied		
Math 31		
Math 20 Pure		
Math 20 Applied		
Math 10 Pure		
Math 10 Applied		
Science 10		
Science 9		
Math 9		
Math 8		
Math 7		
Math 6		
Math 5		
Math 4		
Math 3		

TOTALS

KEYS	
WORKBOOKS	
SOLUTION MANUALS	

Learning Resources Centre

Castle Rock Research is pleased to announce an exclusive distribution arrangement with the Learning Resources Centre (LRC). Under this agreement, schools can now place all their orders with LRC for order fulfillment. As well, these resources are eligible for applying the Learning Resource Credit Allocation (LRCA), which gives schools a 25% discount off LRC's selling price. Call LRC for details.

Orders may be placed with LRC by
telephone: (780) 427-5775
fax: (780) 422-9750
internet: www.lrc.learning.gov.ab.ca
or mail: 12360 - 142 Street NW
Edmonton, AB T5L 4X9

Learning Resources Centre

PAYMENT AND SHIPPING INFORMATION

Name: ______

School Telephone: ______

SHIP TO

School: ______

Address: ______

City: ______ Postal Code: ______

PAYMENT

☐ by credit card

VISA/MC Number: ______ Expiry Date: ______

Name on Card: ______

☐ enclosed cheque

☐ invoice school P.O. number: ______

Castle Rock Research Corp

#2340, 10180 – 101 Street, Edmonton, AB T5J 3S4 Tel: 780.448.9619 Fax: 780.426.3917
email: learn@castlerockresearch.com Toll-free: 1.800.840.6224

www.castlerockresearch.com

2006 (4)